HAMPSHIRE

A GENEALOGICAL
BIBLIOGRAPHY

by

Stuart A. Raymond

Published by
Federation of Family History Societies Publications) Ltd
The Benson Room, Birmingham & Midland Institute,
Margaret Street, Birmingham, B3 3BS, England

Copies also obtainable from:
S.A. & M.J. Raymond, 6, Russet Avenue, Exeter, EX1 3QB, U.K.

First published 1995

Cataloguing in publication data:

Raymond, Stuart A., 1945-
Hampshire: a genealogical bibliography. British genealogical
bibliographies. Birmingham, England: Federation of Family History
Societies, 1995.

DDC 016.9291094227

ISBN 1-86006-002-1

ISSN: 1033-2065

Printed and bound by Oxuniprint, Walton Street, Oxford OX2 6DP

Contents

	Introduction	4
	Libraries and Record Offices	6
	Abbreviations	8
	Bibliographic Presentation	8
1.	The history of Hampshire	9
2.	Bibliography and Archives	11
3.	Journals and Newspapers	14
4.	Pedigrees, Biographical Sources, *etc.*	15
5.	Occupational Sources	17
6.	Family Histories, *etc.*	23
7.	Parish Registers and Other Records of Births, Marriages and Deaths	41
8.	Monumental Inscriptions	51
9.	Probate Records	56
10.	Official Lists of Names	59
11.	Directories and Maps, *etc.*	61
12.	Ecclesiastical Records	65
13.	Records of National and County Administration	70
14.	Records of Parochial and Borough Administration	71
15.	Estate Records	77
16.	Educational Sources	85
17.	Migration	88
	Family Name Index	89
	Place Name Index	92
	Author Index	98

Introduction

This bibliography is intended primarily for genealogists. It is, however, hoped that it will also prove useful to historians, librarians, archivists, research students, and anyone else interested in the history of Hampshire. It is intended to be used in conjunction with my *English genealogy: an introductory bibliography,* and the other volumes in the *British genealogical bibliographies* series. A full list of these volumes appears on the back cover.

Many genealogists, when they begin their research, do not realise just how much information has been published, and is readily available in printed form. Not infrequently, they head straight for the archives, rather than checking printed sources first. In so doing, they waste much time, and also impose needless wear and tear on irreplaceable archives. However, when faced with the vast array of tomes possessed by major reference libraries, it is difficult to know where to begin without guidance. This bibliography is intended to point you in the right direction. My aim has been to list everything relating to Hampshire that has been published and is likely to be of use to genealogists. In general, I have not included works which are national in scope but which have local content. Many such works may be identified in *English genealogy: an introductory bibliography,* to which reference is made at appropriate points below. I have also excluded the numerous notes and queries found in family history society and similar journals, except where the content is of importance. Where I have included such notes, replies to them are cited in the form 'see also', with no reference to the names of respondents. Local and church histories have been excluded except in a few cases. They frequently provide invaluable information for the genealogist, but are far too numerous to be listed here. This is a bibliography of published works; hence the many manuscript histories, transcripts, *etc.,* to be found in Hampshire libraries are excluded.

Be warned: just because information has been published, it does not necessarily follow that it is accurate. I have not made any judgement on the accuracy of most works listed: that is up to you. If you are able, it is always best to check printed sources against their originals, to determine how accurate the editor was.

A further warning: don't confuse the 'County of Southampton' (the old official name for Hampshire, which included the Isle of Wight), and the Borough of Southampton. A reference to Carisbrooke, Southampton, in old books and documents, actually means Carisbrooke, Isle of Wight.

Anyone who tries to compile a totally comprehensive bibliography of Hampshire genealogy is likely to fall short of his aim. The task is almost impossible, especially if the endeavour is made by one person. That does not, however, mean that the attempt should not be made. Usefulness, rather than comprehensiveness, has been my prime aim - and this book will not be useful to anyone if its publication were to be prevented by a vain attempt to ensure total comprehensiveness. I am well aware that there are likely to be omissions - although none, I hope, of books which every Hampshire genealogist should examine. My purpose has been to enable you to identify works which are mostly readily available, and which can be borrowed via the inter-library loan network irrespective of whether you live in Southampton or Melbourne. Most public libraries are able to tap into this network; your local library should be able to borrow most items I have listed, even if it has to go overseas to obtain them.

If you are an assiduous researcher, you may well come across items I have missed. If you do, please let me know, so that they can be included in the next edition.

The work of compiling this bibliography has depended heavily on the resources of the libraries I have used. These include the local studies libraries at Southampton, Winchester and Portsmouth, Hampshire Record Office, the Hartley Library at the University of Southampton, Exeter University Library, Exeter Central Library, the British Library, and the Society of Genealogists, amongst others. I am grateful to the librarians of all these institutions for their help. I am grateful too for the assistance rendered by Hampshire Genealogical Society. Brian Christmas and Richard Preston both kindly read and commented on early drafts of my manuscript, Terry Humphries typed the manuscript, and Bob Boyd saw the book through the press. I am grateful too to the officers of the Federation of Family History Societies, whose support is vital for the continuation of this series. My thanks also to my wife Marjorie and to my children, who have lived with this book for many months.

Stuart A. Raymond

Libraries and Record Offices

Isle of Wight

Isle of Wight County Record Office
26 Hillside Street
NEWPORT
Isle of Wight
PO30 1LL

Portsmouth

Local Studies Library
Portsmouth Central Library
Guildhall Square
PORTSMOUTH
PO1 2DX

Portsmouth City Records Office
3 Museum Road
PORTSMOUTH
PO1 2LE

Southampton

Local Studies Library
Southampton Central Library
Civic Centre
SOUTHAMPTON
SO9 4XP

Cope Collection
Southampton University Library
Highfield
SOUTHAMPTON
SO9 5NH

Southampton City Records Office
Civic Centre
SOUTHAMPTON
SO9 4XL

Winchester

Local Studies Library
Winchester Library
Jewry Street
WINCHESTER
SO23 8RX

Hampshire County Record Office
20 Southgate Street
WINCHESTER
SO23 9EF

In addition, most other branches of Hampshire County Library hold some local studies materials.

Abbreviations

F.H.J.S.E.H.G.S.	*Family history journal of the South-East Hampshire Genealogical Society*
G.R.	*Gosport records*
H.F.C.L.H.N.	*Hampshire Field Club local history newsletter*
H.F.H.	*Hampshire family historian*
H.N.Q.	*Hampshire notes and queries*
H.P.R.M.	*Hampshire parish registers: marriages*
H.R.S.	Hampshire record series
I.O.W.F.H.S.	*Isle of Wight Family History Society [journal]*
M.G.H.	*Miscellanea genealogica et heraldica*
P.P.H.F.C.	*Papers and proceedings of the Hampshire Field Club*
P.P.R.S.	Phillimore's parish register series
P.S.R.Soc.	Publications of the Southampton Record Society
S.R.Ser.	Southampton Record Series

Bibliographic Presentation

Authors' names are in SMALL CAPITALS. Book and journal titles are in *italics*. Articles appearing in journals, and material such as parish register transcripts, forming only part of books, are in inverted commas and textface type. Volume numbers are in **bold** and the individual number of the journal may be shown in parentheses. These are normally followed by the place of publication (except where this is London, which is omitted), the name of the publisher and the date of publication. In the case of articles, further figures indicate page numbers.

1. THE HISTORY OF HAMPSHIRE

If genealogy fascinates you, then you will want to know something about the way in which your ancestors lived, worked, ate, worshipped, slept, etc. In order to understand the world of parish registers, manorial records and probate courts, you need to read good local histories. For Hampshire, a good place to begin is:

TURNER, BARBARA CARPENTER. *A history of Hampshire.* 2nd ed. Chichester: Phillimore & Co., 1978.

The authoritative work, giving much information on manorial descents, is:

The Victoria history of the counties of England. Hampshire and the Isle of Wight. 5 vols with index. Archibald Constable and Co., 1900-1914.

Other general studies include:

CAMPION, P. *A recent history of Hampshire, Wiltshire, Dorset.* Poole: Wessex Press, [19--?]. Survey of estates and country houses.

MONKHOUSE, F.J., ed. *A survey of Southampton and its region.* Southampton: British Association for the Advancement of Science, 1964.

WEBB, JOHN, YATES, NIGEL, & PEACOCK, SARAH, eds. *Hampshire studies presented to Dorothy Dymond, C.B.E., M.A., D.Litt., on the occasion of her ninetieth birthday.* Portsmouth: Portsmouth City Records Office, 1981. Collection of essays.

MOORE, PAM. *The industrial heritage of Hampshire and the Isle of Wight.* Chichester: Phillimore, 1988.

Many works deal with particular periods and topics. The list which follows offers a small selection of books and articles which have been published, and which are widely available. It is arranged in rough chronological order.

BIDDICK, KATHLEEN, & BIJLVELD, CATRIEN C.J.H. 'Agrarian productivity on the estates of the Bishopric of Winchester in the early thirteenth century: a managerial perspective', in CAMPBELL, BRUCE M.S., & OVERTON, MARK, eds. *Land labour and livestock: historical studies in European agricultural productivity.* Manchester: Manchester University Press, 1991, 95-123.

TITOW, J.Z. *Winchester yields: a study in medieval agricultural productivity.* Cambridge: Cambridge University Press, 1972.

BERESFORD, MAURICE. 'The six new towns of the Bishops of Winchester, 1200-55', *Medieval archaeology* 3, 1960, 187-215. Based partially on deeds, accounts, etc.

LEVETT, A. ELIZABETH. *The Black Death on the estates of the See of Winchester.* Oxford studies in social and legal history 5. Oxford: Clarendon Press, 1916.

FUSSELL, G.E. 'Four centuries of farming systems in Hampshire, 1500-1900', *P.P.H.F.C.* 17, 1952, 264-87.

HOULBROOKE, R.A. *Church courts and the people during the English Reformation, 1520-1570.* Oxford: O.U.P., 1979. Based on the records of the Dioceses of Winchester and Norwich.

FRITZE, RONALD H. 'The role of family and religion in the local politics of early Elizabethan England: the case of Hampshire in the 1560s', *Historical journal* 25, 1982, 267-87.

JONES, J.D. 'The Hampshire beacon plot of 1586', *P.P.H.F.C.* 25, 1968, 105-18.

WHITE, H.T. 'A Hampshire plot', *P.P.H.F.C.* 12, 1934, 54-60. Includes a list of 'conspirators' from the Meon Valley, 1586.

GODWIN, G.N. *The Civil War in Hampshire (1642-45) and the story of Basing House.* Southampton: Henry March Gilbert and Son, 1904. Reprinted Alresford: Laurence Oxley, 1973.

STAPLETON, BARRY. 'Migration in pre-industrial England: the example of Odiham', *Southern history* 10, 1988, 47-93. 17-19th c.

COLEBY, ANDREW M. *Central government and the localities: Hampshire, 1649-1689.* Cambridge: C.U.P., 1987.

RAVENHILL, W.W. "Records of the rising in the West, A.D. 1655', *Wiltshire archaeological and natural history magazine* 13, 1872, 119-88; 14, 1874, 38-67. See also 15, 1875, 235-6.

TAYLOR, J. 'Plague in the towns of Hampshire: the epidemic of 1665-6', *Southern history* 6, 1984, 104-22.

9

FOSTER, RUSCOMBE. *The politics of county power: Wellington and the Hampshire gentlemen, 1820-52.* New York: Harvester Wheatsheaf, 1990.

VINSON, A.J. 'Poor relief, public assistance, and the maintainance of the unemployed in Southampton between the wars', *Southern history* 2, 1980, 179-225.

Older works often provide much more information of direct genealogical relevance than more recent histories. They frequently print transcripts of monumental inscriptions, wills, extracts from parish registers, *etc.*, and include pedigrees and notes on the descent of property. For Hampshire, a number of such works are available, and are listed here in order of the dates of original publication.

WARNER, RICHARD, [ed.] *Collections for the history of Hampshire and the Bishopric of Winchester, including the Isles of Wight, Jersey, Guernsey and Sark ...* 6 vols. The author, 1789-95. Parochial survey, giving much information on manorial descents, inscriptions, *etc.*. v.2. includes abstracts of *Domesday book.*

TUNNICLIFFE, WILL. *A topographical survey of the counties of Hants, Wilts, Dorset, Somerset, Devon and Cornwall.* Salisbury: B.C. Collins, 1791.

WARNER, RICHARD. *Topographical remarks, relating to the south-western parts of Hampshire ...* 2 vols. R. Blamire, 1793. Includes an appendix with many abstracts of medieval charters; also pedigree of De Redvers.

DUTHY, JOHN. *Sketches of Hampshire ...* Alresford: Laurence Oxley, 1972. Originally published Winchester: Jacob and Johnson, 1839. Parochial survey.

WOODWARD, B.B., WILKS, THEODORE C., & LOCKHART, CHARLES. *A general history of Hampshire, or the County of Southampton, including the Isle of Wight.* 3 vols. Virtue & Co., 1862-9.

Numerous histories of Hampshire parishes and towns *etc.* are available; a full listing would fill another book. The following very brief listing identifies a number of works which are particularly useful to the genealogist, together with a few which ought to be read for general background by anyone interested in the county's history.

Bosmere Hundred

BINGLEY, WILLIAM. *Topographical account of the Hundred of Bosmere in Hampshire, comprising the parishes of Havant, Warblington and Hayling.* [Southampton?]: Havant Press, 1817. Includes lists of clergy, a few monumental inscriptions, *etc.*

Colemore and Priors Dean

HERVEY, THOMAS. *A history of the united parishes of Colmer and Priors Dean.* Colmer: privately published, 1880. Includes many extracts from the parish registers, notes on families, 1522 rental, 1525 subsidy, *etc.* The second edition, published in 1891, is an abridged version.

Isle of Wight

BAMFORD, E. ed. *A Royalist's notebook: the commonplace book of Sir John Oglander, kt. of Nunwell (1585-1655).* Constable & Co., 1936. Includes extensive notes on neighbouring families of the Isle of Wight; also folded pedigree, 16-17th c.

LONG, W.H., ed. *The Oglander memoirs: extracts from the mss. of Sir J. Oglander, kt, of Nunwell, Isle of Wight, Deputy-Governor of Portsmouth and Deputy Lieutenant of the Isle of Wight, 1595-1648.* Newport: County Press, 1888. Includes much information on Isle of Wight families, *etc.*

JAMES, E. BOUCHER. *Letters archaeological and historical relating to the Isle of Wight.* 2 vols. Henry Frowde, 1896. Includes many brief essays of genealogical interest, some of which are listed elsewhere in this bibliography.

WORSLEY, SIR RICHARD. *The history of the Isle of Wight.* A. Hamilton, 1781. Reprinted in facsimile, East Ardsley: E.P. Publishing, 1975. Many documents, medieval-18th c., are edited in the appendices, which include a summary list of manorial descents throughout the Island. Also includes a folded pedigree of Redvers, medieval.

JONES, JACK, & JOHANNA. *The Isle of Wight: an illustrated history.* Wimborne: Dovecote Press, 1987.

WINTER, C.W.R. *The enchanted Isle: an island history.* [ ]: Cross Publishing, 1990. Popular history of the Isle of Wight.

HOCKEY, S.F. *Insula Victa: the Isle of Wight in the Middle Ages.* Phillimore, 1982.

Portsmouth

STAPLETON, BARRY, & THOMAS, JAMES H. *The Portsmouth region.* Gloucester: Alan Sutton, 1989. Collection of essays.

KITSON, SIR HENRY. 'The early history of Portsmouth Dockyard, 1496-1800', *Mariner's mirror* **33**, 1947, 256-65; **34**, 1948, 3-11, 87-97 & 271-9.

Selborne

WHITE, GILBERT. *The natural history and antiquities of Selborne in the county of Southampton* ... T. Bensley, 1789. Reprinted in facsimile Menston: Scolar Press, 1970. Many other editions.

Southampton

DAVIES, J. SILVESTER. *A history of Southampton, partly from the ms. of Dr. Speed, in the Southampton archives.* Southampton: Gilbert & Co., 1883. Reprinted Exeter: Wheaton, 1989. Includes lists of subscribers, mayors and bailiffs, clergy, *etc.,* with notes on various institutions. Many names.

PLATT, COLIN. *Medieval Southampton: the port and trading community, A.D. 1000-1600.* Routledge & Kegan Paul, 1973. Includes an extensive appendix of biographical notes.

PATTERSON, A. TEMPLE. *A history of Southampton, 1700-1914.* S.R.Ser., **11**, **14** & **18**. 1966-75.

MORGAN, J.B., & PEBERDY, PHILIP. *Collected essays on Southampton.* Southampton: Southampton County Borough Council, 1958.

Winchester

ATKINSON, TOM. *Elizabethan Winchester.* Faber and Faber, 1963.

ROSEN, A. 'Winchester in transition, 1580-90', in CLARK, P., ed. *Country towns in pre-industrial England.* Leicester: Leicester University Press, 1981, 143-95.

2. BIBLIOGRAPHY AND ARCHIVES

A. *Bibliography*

This book is devoted primarily to the listing of genealogical works on Hampshire. It therefore excludes most of the more general historical works on the history of the county. For these, the standard bibliography is still:

GILBERT, H.M., & GODWIN, G.N. *Bibliotheca Hantoniensis: a list of books relating to Hampshire including magazine references &c &c.* Southampton: Ye Olde Boke Shoppe, 1891. Includes list of Hampshire newspapers by F.E. Edwards.

A number of 19th century bibliographies (including the previous work), booksellers lists and library catalogues are reprinted in facsimile in:

TURLEY, RAYMOND V., ed. *Hampshire and Isle of Wight bibliographies: selected nineteenth century sources.* Winchester: Barry Shurlock, 1975.

A useful collection of printed books and unpublished transcripts of original sources is held by the Hampshire Genealogical Society. See:

HAMPSHIRE GENEALOGICAL SOCIETY. *Library Catalogue.* [ ]: the Society, 1983.

For a brief leaflet on Hampshire County Library's genealogical resources, see:

HAYWARD, K. *Trace your family history in the library.* Rev. ed. [ ]: Hampshire County Council, 1993.

See also:

HAYWARD, K. 'Hampshire County Library and the family historian', *H.F.H.* **15**(3), 1988, 153-9.

A number of bibliographical guides and brief notes on particular localities are available, and are listed here. Some of these works also include much information on archival materials.

Andover

'Andover: a local history bibliography', *Look back at Andover* **1**, 1990, 22-4. Brief.

Gosport

CLENNELL, ALISON. *Tracing your family history: hints for beginners.* Gosport: Hampshire County Council, 1988. Based on the collection at Gosport Library, and noting some useful unpublished material.

Isle of Wight

PARKER, ALAN G. *Isle of Wight local history: a guide to sources.* Newport: Isle of Wight Isle of Wight Teachers Centre, 1975. Originally a Library Association fellowship thesis. Important.

ADAMS, R.H. 'Agricultural history of the Isle of Wight: a bibliography of farming, enclosure of common lands, land drainage, reclamation of tidal lands, and bee keeping', *Isle of Wight Natural History and Archaeological Society proceedings* **5**(5), 1960, 219-23. Includes notes on manuscript sources.

HOCKEY, S.F. 'Sir John Oglander's notes on sources for a history of the Isle of Wight', *Archives* **7**, 1966, 230-31. Brief note on main sources available in the 17th c., noting present locations.

Lymington

LLOYD, ARTHUR. *Lymington index of local history, based chiefly on King's Old times revisited & bibliography.* Lymington: Buckland Trust, 1992. Includes extensive bibliography of Lymington.

New Forest

COLLINS, JOHN. *Resources for family historians in the New Forest area.* Sway: the author, 1991.

FLOWER, NICHOLAS. *The New Forest.* Bibliography series **3**. Banbury: Nature Conservancy Council, 1980. Includes list of maps of the New Forest, 1609-1875, as well as more general works.

PERKINS, W. FRANK. *A New Forest bibliography.* 2nd ed. Lymington: C.T. King; Southampton: H.M. Gilbert & Son, 1935. 1st ed. by Heywood Sumner.

POPHAM, RITA M. *A New Forest bibliography.* Bournemouth: Bournemouth Local Studies Publications, 1979.

Portsmouth

PORTSMOUTH AND SOUTH EAST HAMPSHIRE LOCAL STUDIES CENTRE. *Sources for local studies and their locations.* Portsmouth: The Centre, 1980. Covers Portsmouth area.

HOAD, MARGARET J. 'Sources for the medieval history of Portsmouth', *Portsmouth archives review* **5**, 1981, 65-70. General discussion of sources, some of which may be of genealogical value.

Southampton

FORREST, G. *A guide to genealogical sources.* Southampton: Hampshire County Council, 1989. In Southampton Central Reference Library and Local Studies Collection.

JAMES, T.B., ed. *Southampton sources, 1086-1900.* S.R.Ser. **26**, 1983. Detailed checklist of sources for the history of Southampton in various local and national record repositories. Important.

PATTERSON, A. TEMPLE. *Handlist of materials available for the study and teaching of local history.* [Southampton]: Southampton Historical Association, [1968]. Extensive listing of Southampton local history.

Southampton's history: a guide to the printed resources. 2nd ed. Southampton: Southampton District Library, 1977.

B. *Archives*

Archival sources should not be consulted until you have checked all relevant published material. When you have done that, consult:

EDWARDS, F.H., & E. *A guide to genealogical sources for Hampshire.* Portsmouth: Hampshire Genealogical Society, 1983. Mainly a summary list of holdings in Hampshire record offices and libraries. Updated in *H.F.H.* **11**(3), 1984, 177.

HAMPSHIRE ARCHIVISTS GROUP. *Archives of Hampshire and the Isle of Wight: a report.* 2nd ed. [ ]: The Group, 1966. Summary listing of the holdings of Hampshire Record Office, Isle of Wight Record Office, Portsmouth Record Office, Southampton Record Office, Southampton University Library, Winchester College, and various minor repositories.

HAMPSHIRE ARCHIVES TRUST. *Annual report.* 1986/7- . Includes brief surveys of important collections county-wide.

Newsletter of the Hampshire Archives Trust. 1986- . Includes lists of accessions to various Hampshire repositories, with other notes and news.

12

For various miscellaneous collections of source material, see:
'Photographic collections in Hampshire', *Newsletter of the Hampshire Archives Trust* Summer 1986, 20-25.
'Hampshire County Library: auction sale catalogues', *H.F.C.L.H.N.* 1(7), 1983, 158-60. List of holdings, late 18th-early 19th c. These catalogues often give names of owners and/or tenants.
HAMPSHIRE ARCHIVISTS GROUP. *Transport in Hampshire and the Isle of Wight: a guide to the records.* Publications 2. [ ]: Hampshire Archivists Group, 1973. Lists a wide variety of records from all levels of government - many of potential genealogical interest.
There are a number of archive repositories in Hampshire, and various guides to their holdings are available. See:

Hampshire Record Office
HUGHES, ELIZABETH. *Sources for Hampshire genealogy at the Hampshire Record Office.* 2nd ed. [Winchester]: Hampshire Record Office, 1992. Summary guide.
ALLEN, ADRIENNE. 'Record Office review: Hampshire Record Office', *Family tree magazine* 9(12), 1993, 45.
1974-84 Hampshire Record Office: ten year report. Winchester: Hampshire Record Office, [1984?]. Brief history of the Office.
'Hampshire Record Office accessions ...', *H.F.C.L.H.N.* 1(1-8), 1980-83, passim, and *Section newsletters ... [Hampshire Field Club]* 1- , 1984- , passim. Briefer notes are included in the predecessors of these newsletters.
For the records of the Diocese of Winchester, see below, section 12.

Isle of Wight Record Office
EARL, E.G. 'Isle of Wight Record Office: summary list of the more important documents', *Hampshire archaeology and local history newsletter* 1(2), 1965, 23-5.

Portsmouth City Records Office
YATES, W.M. *Portsmouth City Records Office: guide to the collections, part one: church records.* [Portsmouth]: Portsmouth City Records Office, 1977. Lists parish registers and a wide range of other documents, both Anglican and nonconformist. No further parts published.
RAYMOND, PAUL. 'Portsmouth City Record Office: making history come alive', *Family tree magazine* 8(5), 1992, 41.
'Records Office accessions, January-December 1976', *Portsmouth archives review* 2, 1977, 81-6.
'Records Office accessions', *Portsmouth archives review* 1-5, 1976-81, passim.
'Portsmouth Record Office: notes on some accessions ...', *H.F.C.L.H.N.* 1(3-8), 1981-3, passim.

Southampton Record Office
The Southampton Record Office. Southampton: City of Southampton, 1966. Brief guide with summary list of collections.
Southampton records, 1: guide to the records of the Corporation and absorbed authorities in the Civic Record Office. Southampton: Southampton Corporation, 1964.
Sources for family history in Southampton City Archives Office. 2nd ed. Southampton: Southampton City Archives Office, 1993.
WELCH, EDWIN. 'Southampton Record Office', *P.P.H.F.C.* 22(3), 1963, 151-4. Brief list of holdings.
Report on the work of the Civic Record Office, Southampton. Southampton: the Office, 1963-69/70. Includes notes on accessions.
'Southampton City Record Office: main accessions', *H.F.C.L.H.N.* 1(3-8), 1980-3, passim.

3. JOURNALS AND NEWSPAPERS

Every genealogist with Hampshire ancestry should join one of the local family history societies. Amongst their other activities, they regularly publish:
The Hampshire family historian. Portsmouth: Hampshire Genealogical Society, 1974- . The first 5 issues were entitled *Family history journal of the South East Hampshire Genealogical Society.*
Isle of Wight Family History Society [journal]. 1985-
Both of these journals include useful articles - many of which are listed below - together with notes and news on society activities, and, of particular value, detailed information on the families members are researching.
For the other activities of these societies, see:
EDWARDS, E.E 'The Hampshire Genealogical Society', *Family tree magazine* 3(6), 1987, 10.
'The Isle of Wight Family History Society', *Family tree magazine* 10(12), 1994, 11.
The major journal for Hampshire historians is:
Papers and proceedings of the Hampshire Field Club. 1885- . Title varies; from 1899, the Club re-named as *Hampshire Field Club and Archaeological Society.*
This is indexed in:
PEPPER, F.W.C. *Papers and proceedings of the Hampshire Field Club and Archaeological Society ... General index to volumes I-X (1885-1931).* Southampton: H.M. Gilbert and Son, 1932.
LEE, A.J. *Papers and proceedings of the Hampshire Field Club and Archaeological Society ... General index to volumes XI-XX (1932-1956).* Winchester: Warren and Son, 1964.
GREENWOOD, LYN. *Hampshire Field Club and Archaeological Society: index to volumes XXI (1959) - 40 (1984).* The Society, 1993. See also *P.P.H.F.C.* 44, 1988, 137-51.
The Field Club also issues a newsletter, primarily containing notes and news on historical activities, but also including some material of permanent value:
Hampshire archaeology and local history newsletter. Winchester: Hampshire Field Club, 1965-75. Title varies. continued by:
Newsletter. Hampshire Field Club, 1975-80. Continued by: HAMPSHIRE FIELD CLUB.

Local history newsletter. 1980-83. Continued by: HAMPSHIRE FIELD CLUB. *Section newsletters ... Local History, Historic Buildings, Archaeology, Geology.* 1984-
Many useful notes appeared in:
Hampshire notes and queries, reprinted from the Winchester Observer & County News. 10 vols. Winchester: Observer office, 1883-1900.
The publications of record societies and similar bodies are often of vital genealogical importance, and many are listed below. The main series for Hampshire are:
Hampshire record series. Winchester: Hampshire County Council, 1976- .
Portsmouth record series. City of Portsmouth, 1971- .
Southampton records series. Southampton: the University, 1951- .
Publications of the Southampton Record Society. 1905-41.
A number of local historical journals are available:

Andover
Lookback at Andover: the journal of the Andover History and Archaeology Society. 1980- . Published irregularly.

Fareham
Fareham past and present. Fareham: Fareham Local History Group, 1965- . Brief articles.

Gosport
Gosport records. 17 issues. Gosport: Gosport Historic Records and Museum Society, 1971-80.

Milford on Sea
Milford on Sea Record Society: an occasional magazine. 5 vols. 1909-55.

Petersfield
PETERSFIELD AREA HISTORICAL SOCIETY. *Bulletin.* 1974- .

Portsmouth
Portsmouth archives review. 7 issues. Portsmouth: City Record Office, 1976-84.
Portsmouth papers. Portsmouth: Portsmouth City Council, 1967- .

Southampton
*The journal of the Southampton Local
History Forum.* Hampshire County Library,
1991- .

Test Valley
Test Valley and border anthology. 14 issues.
[Andover]: Andover Local Archives
Committee, 1973-9.

NEWSPAPERS

Local newspapers publish much useful
information, particularly in the births,
marriages and deaths column. A historical
listing of Hampshire newspapers is included in:
WELLS, ROSEMARY. *Newsplan: report of the
pilot project in the South-West.* Library and
information research report, **38**. British
Library, 1986.
For newspaper holdings of Hampshire County
Library, see:
'Hampshire County Library: newspapers',
H.F.C.L.H.N. 1(6), 1982, 135-6.

4. PEDIGREES, BIOGRAPHICAL SOURCES, *etc.*

A. *Directories of Genealogists' Interests*
Amongst the most useful sources of
genealogical information are the directories of
members' interests published by family history
societies. These provide the names and
addresses of their members, together with lists
of surnames being researched; they are
regularly updated in society journals. See:
HAMPSHIRE GENEALOGICAL SOCIETY.
Catalogue of members interests. The Society,
1992. An up to date listing is about to be
published in conjunction with the Federation
of Family History Societies.
*British Isles genealogical register, 1994: Isle of
Wight.* Newport: I.O.W.F.H.S., Birmingham:
Federation of Family History Societies, 1994.
Part of what is sometimes referred to as the
'Big R'.
FEW, JOHN. *Island family directory.* Sandown:
I.O.W.F.H.S., 1992.

B. *Pedigree collections*
In the sixteenth and seventeenth centuries, the
Heralds made 'visitations' of the counties in
order to determine the rights of gentry to bear
heraldic arms. In doing so, they compiled
pedigrees of many local families. Their returns
continue to be important sources of
genealogical information, and various editions
have been printed:
RYLANDS, W.HARRY, ed. *Pedigrees from the
visitation of Hampshire made by Thomas
Benolt, Clarenceulx, A° 1530, enlarged with
the vissitation of the same county mede
by Robert Cooke, Clarenceulx, Anno 1575,
both wch are continued wth the vissitation
made by John Phillipot, Somersett [for
William Camden, Clarenceux] in A° 1622
most part then don & finished in A° 1634, as
collected by Richard Mundy in Harleian ms.
no. 1544.* Publications of the Harleian
Society, **64**. 1913.
*Visitation of Hampshire, 1575, 1622 & 1686, ex
mss. Phyllipps.* [Middle Hill]: Typis Medio-
Montanis, 1854. Incomplete.
SQUIBB, G.D., ed. *The visitation of Hampshire
and the Isle of Wight, 1686, made by Sir
Henry St. George, Knight, Clarenceux King
of Arms.* Publication of the Harleian Society,
N.S., **10**. 1991.

Many pedigrees are also printed in:
BERRY, WILLIAM. *County genealogies: pedigrees of the families in the county of Hants., collected from the heraldic visitations and other authentic manuscripts in the British Museum, and in the possession of private individuals, and from the information of the present resident families.* Sherwood, Gilbert & Piper, 1833. Includes list of sheriffs, 1154-1830.

C. Heraldry
The Heralds' prime responsibility was for the grant of arms. Those granted to families in the Isle of Wight are noted in:
COLE, HENRY D. *The heraldic bearings of the families & residents of the Isle of Wight, as borne by their ancestors.* 3 pts. Sprague & Co., [1891].
For Southampton heraldry, see:
GREENFIELD, B.W. 'The heraldry and exterior decorations of the Bargate, Southampton', *P.P.H.F.C.* 4, 1898-1903, 97-136. Includes notes on various families whose arms are displayed.
A number of individual grants of arms have been separately published:

Bee
'Confirmation of arms and grant of crest to John Bee of Basingstoke, 1573', *M.G.H.* N.S. 4, 1884, 386-7.

Hales-Lisle
'Exemplification of arms to Edward Hales-Lisle, esq.', *Genealogist* 7, 1883, 270-71. 1822; includes change of name from Edward Hales Taylor.

Henslow
'Grant of arms and crest to Thomas Henslow', *M.G.H.* 2nd 4, 1892, 350. 1591.

St. Clair
WILLIAMS, C.L. SINCLAIR. 'The arms of St. Clair', *Coat of Arms* N.S., 6(135-6), 1985/6, 201-9. Includes medieval pedigree.

D. Biographical sources
A brief list of Hampshire gentry, compiled by the map-maker, John Norden in 1594, is included in:
KITCHEN, FRANK. 'The gentry of Hampshire, 1594', *H.F.H.* 15(3), 1988, 203-4.

A number of brief biographies of prominent Hampshire men are printed in:
'Hampshire worthies', *H.N.Q.* 1, 1883, 151-69.
A number of biographical dictionaries were published in the early 20th century and are listed here by date of original publication:
PRESS, C. MANNING. *Hampshire & Isle of Wight leaders social and political.* Gaskill Jones & Co., 1903.
JACOB, W.H. *Hampshire at the opening of the twentieth century.* Pikes new century series 13. Brighton: W.T. Pike & Co., 1905. Includes W.T. Pike, ed. *Contemporary biographies.* Reprinted on microform as: *A dictionary of Edwardian biography: Hampshire.* Edinburgh: Interfich, 1987.
Hampshire and some neighbouring records: historical, biographical and pictorial. Allan North, [1909?]. Biographical dictionary.
Who's who in Hampshire. Worcester: Ebenezer Baylis & Son, 1935.
For an index to biographical information on Farnham residents, see:
MUKERJI, J.A. 'Some of Farnham's 19th century residents: people born in Hampshire living in and around Willey and Runwick, Farnham, Surrey', *H.F.H.* 11(2), 1984, 89. Index to the author's collection of biographical material.
A much more extensive index to biographical information on Southampton residents is provided by:
FORREST, G. *Men and women of Southampton: an index to sources of biographical information.* Southampton: Hampshire County Library, 1983. Indexes sources in Southampton Reference Library.
Brief biographies of Southampton people are contained in:
MANN, JOHN EDGAR. *Southampton people: eminent Sotonians and assorted characters.* Southampton: Ensign, 1989.

5. OCCUPATIONAL SOURCES

Many works offer information on persons of particular occupations. The list which follows may be supplemented by consulting my *Occupational sources for genealogists.* For clergymen, see below, section 12, for members of Parliament, section 13, and for teachers and students, section 16.

Actors
RANGER, PAUL. 'The lost theatres of Winchester, 1620-1861', *P.P.H.F.C.* **31**, 1974, 65-108. Gives information on some actors; also notes on sources.
See also Theatrical Personnel

Agisters
STAGG, DAVID. *Agisters of the New Forest.* [ ]: New Forest Association, 1983. Includes list of agisters since 1878, with biographical notes.

Airmen
BURCH, L.L.R. *The Flowerdown link: a story of telecommunications and radar throughout the Royal Flying Corps and Royal Air Force.* Lowestoft: Dewberry Printing, 1980. Flowerdown, north of Winchester, was home to the RAF's Electrical and Wireless School. Many names are mentioned.

Apprentices
WILLIS, ARTHUR J. *A calendar of Southampton apprenticeship register, 1609-1740.* ed. A.L. Merson. S.R.Ser. **12.** 1968.
LOWE, J. 'Isle of Wight apprenticeships', *I.O.W.F.H.S.* **16**, 1990, 20-21; **17**, 1990, 26-7. Extracts from Willis's *Calendar* above.
ROBERTS, C. 'Apprenticeship indentures', *H.F.H.* **5**(4), 1979, 118-23; **6**(1), 1979, 40-41; **6**(2), 1979, 87-9 & **6**(3), 1979, 123-5.
'Portsmouth apprenticeship records', *F.H.J.S.E.H.G.S.* **1**(1), 1974, 15-17. Lists apprentices and masters, late 17th-early 18th c.
See also Barber Surgeons, Painter Stainers and Woodworkers

Artists
TURLEY, RAYMOND V., ed. *A directory of Hampshire and Isle of Wight art: local* subjects featured in the principal London exhibitions during the late-18th and 19th centuries, arranged by artist and indexed topographically. Southampton: University of Southampton, 1977.
TURLEY, RAYMOND V. 'A survey of Hampshire and Isle of Wight art exhibited in London, 1760-c.1900', *P.P.H.F.C.* **34**, 1977, 65-76. Includes list of artists.

Authors
HANDLEY-TAYLOR, GEOFFREY. *Berkshire, Hampshire and Wiltshire authors today, being a checklist of authors born in these counties together with brief particulars of authors born elsewhere who are currently working or residing in these counties ...* Eddison Press, 1973.
WILKINSON, C.H. 'Hampshire writers', *P.P.H.F.C.* **18**, 1954, 223-62. Discusses over 100 authors.

Bankrupts
CHRISTIE, PETER. 'Hampshire bankrupts', *H.F.H.* **4**(3), 1977, 67-8; **4**(4), 1978, 99; **5**(2), 1978, 39; **5**(3), 1978, 79; **5**(4), 1979, 105; **6**(1), 1979, 8; **6**(2), 1979, 50-51 & **7**(3), 1980, 102. List, 1731-89.

Barber Surgeons
THOMAS, JAMES H. 'Hampshire and the company of Barber-Surgeons, 1658-1720', *H.F.H.* **10**(1), 1983, 15-18. Lists apprentices and their masters, giving fathers' names, residences and occupations.

Booktrades
BOLTON, CLAIRE. *A Winchester bookshop and bindery, 1729-1991.* Oxford: Alembic Press, 1991. Identifies booksellers.
OLDFIELD, JOHN. *Printers, booksellers and libraries in Hampshire, 1750-1800.* Hampshire papers 3. Winchester: Hampshire County Council, 1993. Includes 'checklist of printers and booksellers in Hampshire, 1750-1800'.
PERKIN, MICHAEL. 'Hampshire notices of printing presses, 1799-1867', in ISAAC, PETER, ed. *Six centuries of the provincial book trade in Britain.* Winchester: St.Pauls's Bibliographies, 1990, 151-64. Appendix lists 46 presses, with many names.

Booktrades continued

PIPER, A. CECIL. 'The early printers and booksellers of Winchester', *The Library* 4th series, 1, 1920-21, 103-10. Includes list of printers and booksellers, 17-19th c.

Brewers

BALDWIN, MARY R. *Brewers of old Ringwood.* Ringwood: Ringwood Brewery, [1990]. This booklet is full of people.

ELEY, PHILIP. *Portsmouth Breweries, 1492-1847.* Portsmouth papers 51, 1988. Includes list of breweries, 1784-1847, naming occupants.

Carriers

FREEMAN, M.J. 'The carrier system of South Hampshire, 1775-1851', *Journal of transport history* N.S., 4, 1977-8, 61-85. Includes references to sources for carriers.
See also Merchants

Clockmakers

NORGATE, MARTIN. *Directory of Hampshire clockmakers.* Winchester: Hampshire County Council Museum Service, 1993.

Convicts

CHAMBERS, JILL. *Hampshire machine breakers: the story of the 1830 riots.* Clifton, Beds: Chambers, 1990. Includes extensive listing of prisoners; also petitions from the inhabitants of Barton Stacey, Bullington and Worston, with many names; also list of special constables.

WEBB, NORMAN RICHARD, [ed.] *A calendar of the prisoners in the new prison, or county bridewell, near the City of Winchester, for the Easter sessions to be holden at the Castle of the said City on Monday, April 16, 1798.* Farnborough: the author, [1988?]. Includes many notes on prisoners; also on members of the County Bench.

WEBB, N.R. 'Calendar of prisoners, 1785-1799: Winchester new bridewell', *H.F.H.* 14(2), 1987, 124-5.

Cricketers

ALTHAM, H.S., et al. *Hampshire county cricket: the official history of the Hampshire County Cricket Club.* Phoenix Sports Books, 1957. Includes various lists of cricketers, 1895-1956.

ASHLEY-COOPER, F.S. *The Hambledon cricket chronicle, 1772-1796, including the reproduction of the minute and account books of the club.* Herbert Jenkins, 1924. Many names of cricketers.

HAYES, DEAN. *Famous cricketers of Hampshire.* Tunbridge Wells: Spellmount, 1993. Brief biographies.

ISAACS, VICTOR, & THORN, PHILIP. *Hampshire cricketers, 1800-1982.* Retford: Association of Cricket Statisticians, [1982]. List.

Criminals

ROGERS, PAT. 'The Waltham Blacks and the Black Act', *Historical journal* 17, 1974, 465-86. General discussion of a gang of criminals; also includes list of a Berkshire gang.
See also Convicts

Dockyard Workers

KNIGHT, R.J.B., ed. *Portsmouth Dockyard papers, 1774-1783: the American War: a calendar.* Portsmouth Record Series 6. City of Portsmouth, 1987. Includes many names of dockyard workers, with list of, and biographical notes on, dockyard and other office-holders.

ROSE, SUSAN, ed. *The navy of the Lancastrian Kings: accounts and inventories of William Soper, Keeper of the King's ships, 1422-1427.* Publication of the Navy Records Society 123. 1982. Gives names of many dockyard workers and mariners of Southampton.

Drovers

GREEN, I.M. 'Drovers and the movement of livestock in N.W. Hants, 1770-1840', *H.F.H.* 11(2), 1984, 108-10. Based on the accounts of Appleshaw fair; gives names of many drovers, 1810, including some from Dorset, Somerset and Berkshire.

'Drovers and the movement of livestock in N.W. Hampshire, 1770-1840', *H.F.C.L.H.N.* 1(8), 1983, 171-4. Includes list of drovers attending Appleshaw fair, 1810.

Excise Officers

HOAD, J.P.M. 'Excise officers of the I.O.W., 1750 to 1773', *I.O.W.F.H.S.* 19, 1990, 25-7; 20, 1991, 22-3.

18

Footballers

HOLLEY, DUNCAN, & CHALK, GARY. *The alphabet of the Saints: a complete who's who of Southampton F.C.* Leicester: ACL & Polar Publishing, 1992.

The statistics of Aldershot Football Club. Basildon: Association of Football Statisticians, [1982?] Includes names of players from 1926.

Freemasons

AYLING, KENNETH G. *Moose in Wessex.* Bristol: Regional Grand Lodge of Wessex, 1963. History of the Loyal Order of Moose, 1926-63, primarily in Dorset, Wiltshire and Hampshire.

HOMEWOOD, H.R. *History of the Lodge of Unity no 132: Ringwood, Hampshire.* Poole: J. Looker, 1951. Includes roll of masters, 1764-1950, list of members from 1764, and various other freemasons' name lists.

METTAM, H.A., & STRAIN, R.N.C. *Mercury Lodge no 4581, E.C. of the antient fraternity of free and accepted masons: the history of the first fifty years.* [ ], [1953?] Includes biographical notes on many personalities.

WHITTING, C.J. *History of the Lodge of Hengist, no 195: Bournemouth.* Bournemouth: W. Mate & Sons; London: George Kennings, 1897. Includes roll of members, 1770-1897.

Gunsmiths

NORGATE, MARTIN. *Directory of Hampshire gunsmiths.* Winchester: Hampshire County Council Museums Service, 1993.

Huntsmen

HOPE, J.F.R. *A history of hunting in Hampshire.* Winchester: Warren and Son, 1950. Many brief biographies of huntsmen.

Hymn Writers

SALE, D.M. *The hymn writers of Hampshire.* Winchester: Winton Publications, 1975.

Innkeepers

LOWER TEST VALLEY ARCHAEOLOGICAL STUDY GROUP. *A history of the pubs and inns of Romsey.* Southampton: L.T.V.A.S. Group, 1974. Includes list of publicans, 18-20th c.

The inns of Petersfield: its inns, hotels, taverns, alehouses and public houses through four centuries, with a selection of those in the surrounding rural parishes. Petersfield papers 3. Petersfield: Petersfield Area Local History Society, 1977. Gives a few names of innkeepers.

'Ryde licensees, 1871', *I.O.W.F.H.S.* 13, 1989, 8-9. Lists 82 persons granted licences or beer certificates.

'Where were your ancestors drinking the day the Great War broke out?' *I.O.W.F.H.S.* 8, 1988, 1. Lists publicans on the Isle of Wight, 1914. See also 9, 1988, for Newport publicans.

'A Winchester assessment in the year 1703', *H.N.Q.* 7, 1896, 34-6. Brief list of innkeepers paying land tax.

Lawyers

C[HITTY], H. 'Lawyers employed by Winchester College during the fifteenth century', *Notes and queries* 12th series 1, 1916, 361-3 & 383-5. Lists 70 names.

Machine Breakers

See Convicts

Magistrates

THURSTON, E.J. *The magistrates of England and Wales, Western Circuit: Cornwall, Devonshire, Dorsetshire, Hampshire, Somersetshire, Wiltshire.* Hereford: Jakemans, 1940. Biographical dictionary.

See also Convicts

Marines

LOWE, J.A., ed. *Records of the Portsmouth Division of Marines, 1764-1800.* Portsmouth Record Series 7. City of Portsmouth, 1990.

Medics

PINHORN, M.A. 'Isle of Wight medics', *I.O.W.F.H.S.* 16, 1990, 18-19.

WATSON, DOROTHY M. *Proud heritage: a history of the Royal South Hants Hospital, 1838-1971.* Southampton: G.F. Wilson & Co., 1979. Includes many names, including list of matrons, presidents, chairmen, *etc.*

Merchants

RUDDOCK, ALWYN A. *Italian merchants and shipping in Southampton, 1270-1600.* S.R. Ser. 1. 1951.

Merchants *continued*

PELHAM, R.A. 'The victualling of the English fleet at Hamble in 1339', *Hampshire archaeology and local history newsletter* 1(1), 1965, 19-21. Includes accounts with names of merchants providing wheat, cider and ale.

STUDER, PAUL, ed. *The port books of Southampton or (Anglo-French) accounts of Robert Florys, water-bailiff and receiver of petty customs, A.D. 1427-1430.* P.S.R.Soc. 15. 1913. Gives names of many merchants, *etc.,* as do the following:

FOSTER, BRIAN, ed. *The local port book of Southampton for 1435-36.* S.R.Ser. 7. 1963.

COBB, HENRY S., ed. *The local port book of Southampton for 1439-40.* S.R.Ser. 5. 1961.

QUINN, D.B., ed. *The port books or local customs accounts of Southampton for the reign of Edward IV.* 2 vols. P.S.R.Soc. 37-8. 1937-8.

JAMES, THOMAS BEAUMONT, ed. *The port book of Southampton, 1509-10.* S.R.Ser. 32-3. 1990.

BUNYARD, BARBARA D.M., ed. *The brokage book of Southampton from 1439-40.* P.S.R.Soc. 40, 1941. v.1. 1439-1440. Gives names of many merchants and carriers.

COLEMAN, OLIVE, ed. *The brokage book of Southampton, 1443-44.* S.R.Ser. 4 & 6. 1960-61.

STEVENS, K.F., ed. *The brokage books of Southampton for 1477-8 and 1527-8.* S.R.Ser. 28. 1985.

Millers

WOODD, ARTHUR B. 'Efford Mill', *Milford-on-Sea Record Society: an occasional magazine* 4(3), 1928, 5-19. Gives some names of millers, medieval-19th c.

Packhorse Men

JONES, B.C. 'Westmorland pack-horse men in Southampton', *Cumberland and Westmorland Antiquarian and Archaeological Society transactions* N.S. 59, 1959, 65-84. Includes extracts from Southampton Cloth Hall accounts, 1552-3, giving names.

Painter Stainers

SURRY, NIGEL. 'Hampshire apprentices to the Painter Stainers Company: their professional activities and social origins, c.1660-1795', *P.P.H.F.C.* 37, 1981, 63-71. Includes list.

Paper Makers

SHORTER, A.H. 'Paper-mills in Hampshire', *P.P.H.F.C.* 18, 1954, 1-11. Gazetteer, with some names of millers.

THOMAS, J.H. 'Warnford paper mill, Hampshire', *Industrial archaeology* 5, 1968, 393-7. Identifies paper makers, 17-18th c.

Passengers

See Sailors

Photographers

COLES, ROBERT. *Picture postcards of Lymington & the New Forest: an alphabetical list of publishers.* Lymington: A. Coles, 1985.

'Isle of Wight studio photographers', *I.O.W.F.H.S.* 29, 1993, 2-5. List, 1914-15.

Pipemakers

ARNOLD, C.J. 'The nineteenth century clay tobacco-pipe industry at Portchester, Hants', *P.P.H.F.C.* 31, 1974, 43-52. Includes list of pipemakers, mainly 19th c.

Police

CRAMER, JAMES. *A history of the police of Portsmouth.* Portsmouth papers, 2. 1967.

FOSTER, R.E. 'A cure for crime? The Hampshire rural constabulary, 1839-1856', *Southern history* 12, 1990, 48-67.

Postmen

BRAYSHAY, MARK. 'The royal post-horse routes of Hampshire in the reign of Elizabeth I', *P.P.H.F.C.* 48, 1992, 121-34. Includes list of 16-17th c. postmasters.

Printers

See Booktrades

Prisoners of War

DEACON, A.D. 'Some French prisoners of war on parole in Hampshire', *P.P.H.F.C.* 43, 1987, 197-205. General discussion, with some names; includes references to sources.

Royalists

CLUTTERBUCK, R.H. 'Excerpts from the royalist composition papers relating to Hampshire', *H.N.Q.* 4, 1889, 111-14. Lists sequestered royalists, 1655.

Sailors

CARSON, E.A. 'The customs records of Portsmouth', *Journal of the Society of Archivists* **5**, 1974-7, 429-36. Brief description of records containing much information on ships and their crews.

CLISSOLD, PETER. 'Ships and monuments in churches in the Solent area', *Mariners' mirror* **58**, 1972, 205-215. See also **67**, 1981, 367-70. Notes many memorials to seamen.

HEARN, J. RUDLAND. 'Hampshire and Isle of Wight shipping visiting the Liberty of the Water of the Thamer in 1760-61', *Hampshire archaeology and local history newsletter* **1**(4), 1966, 51-6. Names masters of vessels visiting Plymouth.

LOTON, JAMES. 'H.M.S. Contest [1846-49]', *H.F.H.* **15**(4), 1989, 289-90. Lists crew members.

WILLIAMS, LORELEI. 'Island petitioners to Trinity House', *I.O.W.F.H.S.* **3**, 1986, 2-3. Trinity House provided relief for poor seafarers and dependents; Isle of Wight petitioners for relief are listed here.

A catalogue of crew lists and ships' agreements, 1863-1913, in the Southampton City Record Office. Southampton: the Office, 1983. Cover title: *Southampton crew lists, 1863-1913: a catalogue of the records.*

'Hampshire mariners in South Australia', *H.F.H.* **19**(1), 1992, 58. Brief list, 19th c.

Report of the Committee on Commerce, United States Senate, pursuant to S.Res. 283, directing the Committee on Commerce to investigate the causes leading to the wreck of the White Star liner 'Titanic' ... 1912. Reprinted Riverside, Connecticutt: T.C's Press, 1975. Includes list of the crew (many of whom were from Southampton) and passengers.

See also Dockyard Workers and Mariners

Salt Men

LLOYD, A.T. *The Salterns.* New Milton: Lymington Historical Record Society, 1965. General account of salt pans in the Lymington area; few names, but includes references to potentially useful sources.

Soldiers and Militiamen *etc.*

Many Hampshire men served in the army or the militia, and much information on them is available in the various regimental histories *etc.* which have been published. These cannot all be listed here. The works noted below include only those publications which have lists of officers and/or men or other information of direct genealogical interest. The list is in chronological order.

JACOB, W.H. 'Hampshire royalist soldiers', *H.N.Q.* **8**, 1896, 91-2. List of maimed soldiers claiming pensions, 1662.

LITTLE, REGINALD H. 'Military history from local sources', *Amateur historian* **7**(3), 1967, 112-8. Discusses sources for the military careers of seven officers resident in Sopley, 18-19th c.

LLOYD-VERNEY, COLONEL. *Records of the Infantry Militia Battalions of the County of Southampton from A.D. 1757 to 1894.* Longmans, Green and Co., 1894. Also includes HUNT, J. MOUAT F. *Records of the Artillery Militia Regiments of the County of Southampton from A.D. 1853 to 1894.* Names many officers.

LAWES, EDWARD. 'Searching the South Hants regiments of militia, 1780-1814', *H.F.H.* **8**(1), 1981, 17-20. Includes a list of records.

WILLIAMS, J. ROBERT. 'Hampshire Volunteers of the Napoleonic period', *H.F.H.* **11**(3), 1984, 170-73; **11**(4), 1985, 225-7. List of pay-lists at the Public Record Office, with names from that for the Hayling Island Volunteer Artillery, 1808, the Company of Havant Volunteers, 1800; also list of Hampshire volunteer units.

LAWES, EDWARD. 'Militia records', *H.F.H.* **8**(4), 1982, 135-8. Lists family allowances paid to over 130 volunteers of the army reserve serving in Hampshire, 1804; names wives and children.

WILLIAMS, J. ROBERT. 'Some Hampshire veterans of the Napoleonic wars', *H.F.H.* **10**(4), 1984, 179-83; **11**(1), 1984, 30-33. Lists Chelsea out-pensioners from Hampshire, 1807-38.

'Hampshire militia men, born in the north east parishes', *H.F.H.* **14**(3), 1987, 206-7. List, 1825-31.

Soldiers and Militiamen *etc. continued*

McNULTY, P.M. 'The Blues away', *H.F.H.* **15**(3), 1988, 211. List of Hampshire men serving in the Royal Horse Guards at Clewer Cavalry Barracks, Combermere, Berkshire, from 1851 census.

HANCOCK, PHILIP. 'Hampshire men of the Light Brigade', *H.F.H.* **8**(1), 1981, 35-6. List of those serving in 1854, with brief notes.

CAVE, T. STURMY. *History of the First Volunteer Battalion Hampshire Regiment, 1859 to 1889 ...* Winchester: Warren & Son, 1905. Many names, including various 'battalion army lists'.

FAULKNER, H.C. 'Military men', *H.F.H.* **7**, 1980-81, 52-6 & 94-9. Lists Hampshire officers from the *Army list,* 1874.

ATKINSON, C.T. *The Royal Hampshire Regiment, volume one: To 1914.* Glasgow: Robert Maclehose for the Regiment, 1950. Includes roll of officers, 1881-1914.

ATKINSON, C.T. *The Royal Hampshire Regiment, volume 2: 1914-1918.* Glasgow: Robert Maclehose & Co., for the Regiment, 1952. Includes list of honours and awards, and roll of officers.

Soldiers died in the Great War, part 41: The Hampshire Regiment. H.M.S.O., 1921. Reprinted Polstead: J.B. Hayward & Son, 1989.

IMPERIAL WAR GRAVES COMMISSION. *The war dead of the Commonwealth: the register of the names of those who fell in the Great War and are buried in cemeteries and churchyards in the northern and eastern parts of the county of Hampshire and in the Isle of Wight, 1914-1918.* The Commission, 1930. Reprinted with amendments, Maidenhead: Commonwealth War Graves Commission, 1988.

LOWE, J. 'I.W. Territorial Rifles', *I.O.W.F.H.S.* **18**, 1990, 34-5; **21**, 1991, 32-3. Lists members killed, wounded, missing, and sick, in 1915.

The national roll of the Great War, 1914-1918, Section IV: [Hampshire]. National Publishing Co., [1918?].

NICHOLSON, G.H., & POWELL, H.L., eds. *History of the Hampshire Territorial Force Association and war records of units, 1914-1919.* Southampton: Hampshire Advertiser, 1921. Many names.

'Hampshire's ANZAC heroes: Hampshire heroes at Gallipoli', *H.F.H.* **18**(2), 1991, 138-9. List of Hampshire men who fell at Gallipoli, 1915.

GATES, WILLIAM G. *Portsmouth and the Great War.* Portsmouth: W.H. Barrell, [1919?]. Includes roll of honour, and 'list of special service awards'.

JESSEL, SIR H.M. *The story of Romsey Remount Depot.* Abbey Press, [1920]. Horse depot. Includes roll of officers, 1914-18.

The Distinguished Conduct Medal, 1914-20: citations: the Hampshire Regiment. London Stamp Exchange, [1985].

In memory of eighteen hundred men who from this town made the great sacrifice, 1914-1919. Southampton: [ ], 1920. Lists names from the Southampton cenotaph.

DANIELL, DAVID SCOTT. *The Royal Hampshire Regiment, volume three: 1918-1954.* Aldershot: Gale & Polden, 1955. Includes list of honours and awards.

Spoon Makers

KENT, TIMOTHY ARTHUR. *West Country spoons and their makers, 1550-1750.* J.H. Bourdon-Smith, 1992.

Theatrical Personnel

HARE, ARNOLD. *The Georgian theatre in Wessex.* Phoenix House, 1958. General history, mentioning many names.

WEBB, JOHN. 'Portsmouth theatre account book, 1771-4', *Portsmouth archives review* **4**, 1979-80, 44-60. The accounts give many names of actors, *etc.*

See also Actors

Tradesmen

ELLACOTT, PETER. *Trades people of Westbourne, 1845-1938.* Bygone Westbourne 1. [Westbourne]: Westbourne Local History Group, 1981. Lists many tradesmen whose names appear in directories.

In an age when coins of the realm were in short supply, many tradesmen issued their own tokens. Studies of these often provide useful genealogical information. See:

RAPER, ANTHONY C. 'The token coinage of Andover', *Test Valley and border anthology* **7**, 1975, 143-50 & **9**, 1976, 202-6.

WETTON, J.L. *The Hampshire seventeenth century traders' tokens.* Lymington: Kings, 1964. Incorporates the author's *The Isle of Wight seventeenth century traders' tokens,* originally published Lymington: Kings, 1962.

Verderers
PASMORE, ANTHONY. *Verderers of the New Forest: a history of the New Forest, 1877-1977.* Old Woking: Pioneer Publications, [1977].

Woodworkers
GOODMAN, W.L. 'Woodworking apprentices and their tools in Bristol, Norwich, Great Yarmouth, and Southampton, 1535-1630', *Industrial archaeology* **9**, 1972, 376-411 & 447. Gives some names.

6. FAMILY HISTORIES, *etc.*

A considerable amount of research on Hampshire family history has been published. This list includes published books and journal articles; it does not, however, include the numerous notes and queries published in journals such as the *Hampshire family historian,* except where substantial information is provided. Studies which remain unpublished are not listed. Many pedigrees of particular families are listed here; for collections of pedigrees, consult section 4.

Abraham
ABRAHAM, A.G. 'The Abrahams of Totton and Eling', *H.F.H.,* **15**(4), 1989, 251-3. Includes pedigree, 18-19th c.
ABRAHAM, A.G. 'Transportation for life', *H.F.H.* **15**(2), 1988, 107-10. Includes Abraham family pedigree, 18-19th c.
ABRAHAM, A.G. 'Chapel people', *H.F.H.* **15**(1), 1988, 18-20. Abraham family; includes pedigree, 17-20th c.

Achard
STRINGER, K.H. 'Some documents concerning a Berkshire family and Monk Sherborne Priory, Hampshire', *Berkshire archaeological journal* **63**, 1967-8, 23-37. Includes pedigree of Achard, 12-14th c., and eight deeds.

Adams
McKECHNIE, ANNE. 'The Adams family: a brief history of our Adams' since the early 19th century', *H.F.H.* **19**(1), 1992, 42-3.

Annetts
ANNETTE, F.H. 'Annetts and Annett in the Wessex region', *Wiltshire Family History Society [Journal]* **6,** 1982, 4-6. In Wiltshire, Berkshire, Hampshire and Gloucestershire, 18th c.

Arnold
SEILES, MARY. 'Island families no.3: Arnold', *H.F.H.* **6**(3), 1979, 107-8 & **6**(4), 1979, 150-51. Extracts from Isle of Wight parish registers, 16-18th c.

23

Assheton
MOLONEY, J.L. 'Ridworth's link with the Assheton family', *Lookback at Andover* **4**, [1983], 8-10. 17-19th c.

Atkinson
JOYE, GILL. 'A Naval family', *H.F.H.* **9**(3), 1982, 112-5. Atkinson family, 19th c.
TILMOUTH, JAMES E. 'The Nelson connection', *H.F.H.* **12**(4), 1986, 219-21. See also **13**(1), 1986, 38-9. Atkinson family, 18-19th c.

Baker
See Sewell

Bannister
DEVONSHIRE, K. 'Who was William Bannister's father', *I.O.W.F.H.S.* **25**, 1992, 37-9. 17-18th c.
See also Minter

Baring
BISSET-THOM, A. 'The Barings', *H.N.Q.* **1**, 1883, 135-50. 18-19th c.

Barrett
BARRETT, JACK, & BUGDEN, ERIC. 'The lost fortune: a story of the Barretts of Poole and money in Chancery', *H.F.H.* **12**(4), 1986, 266-8. Includes pedigrees, 17-20th c.

Barry
HARRISON, J.P. 'The Barrys of Fordingbridge', *H.F.H.* **12**(3), 1985, 185-6. Includes pedigree, 1642-1700.

Baskett
See Nutty

Batson
BATSON, PAT. 'The Batson brothers', *H.F.H.* **14** (1), 1987, 16-17. See also **14**(2), 1987, 101. 19-20th c.

Battelle
BATTELLE, LUCY CATHERINE. *A history of the Battelle family in England.* Columbus: Battelle Press, 1985. 13-20th c., of Suffolk, Derbyshire, Hampshire, Essex, *etc.* Includes pedigree.

Bayliffe
BAYLIFFE, B.G. 'An armigerous family: Elizabeth Bayliffe formerly Searle', *H.F.H.* **15**(2), 1988, 128. Includes pedigree, 18th c.

Beazley
BEAZLEY, F.C. *Pedigree of the family of Beazley.* Mitchell Hughes & Clarke, 1921. Of Alverstoke, Hampshire, Kenley and Wallington, Surrey, and Oxton, Cheshire; 18-20th c.
See also Byseley

Bennett
BENNETT, JUNE. 'The Bennett family: drapers of Lymington, Farnham and Basingstoke', *H.F.H.* **8**(2), 1986, 107-10. 19th c.
See also Whitaker

Bent
FELTON, E.C. 'The English ancestry of John Bent of Sudbury', *New England historical and genealogical register* **49**, 1895, 65-71. Includes extracts from Wayhill parish register, 1564-1635, and will abstracts.

Berkeley
BROWNEN, G. 'The Berkeleys of Bisterne, *etc.*, Hants: their homes and their chantries', *Proceedings of the Bournemouth Natural Science Society* **4**, 1913, 94-8. 14-15th c.

Bettesworth
See Hill

Bignell
PEARCE, JEANETTE, & TOMLINSON, JANE. 'Bignells Cottage, Itchen Abbas', *H.F.H.* **15**(2), 97-9. Bignell family, 18-19th c.

Bilson
CHALLEN, W.H. 'Thomas Bilson, Bishop of Winchester, his family, and their Hampshire, Sussex and other connections', *P.P.H.F.C.* **19**, 1955-7, 35-46 & 253-75. 16-17th c.

Bisley
See Byseley

Blaker
DAVIS, TESSA. 'The Hampshire Blakers: four generation of shipwrights', *H.F.H.* 9(2), 1982, 72-3. 18-19th c.

Blakiston
See Whitaker

Bligh
HADDON, GORDON. 'The two Bligh admirals', *H.F.H.* 17(4), 1991, 251-3. See also 17(4), 1991, 287. Bligh of Cornwall, Plymouth, Hampshire, *etc.* Includes pedigree, 15-19th c.

Blower
'Blower Close', *H.F.H.* 18(4), 1992, 267-9. Blower family of Hampshire and Essex, *etc.,* includes pedigree, 18-20th c.

Blundell
BLUNDELL, L.S. 'The Blundells', *H.F.H.* 10(4), 1984, 200-203; 11(1), 1984, 14-19; 11(2), 1984, 73-9 & 11(3), 1984, 149-56. See also 11(4), 1985, 218-9. Of Southampton, London, Guernsey, *etc.,* includes pedigrees, 14-19th c.

Bonham-Carter
THORP, JENNIFER D. *The Bonham Carters: a Hampshire family. Exhibition by the Hampshire Archives Trust ... 1987.* The Trust, 1987. Includes pedigrees, 17-20th c.

Brickwood
ELEY, PHILIP. 'A history of Brickwoods Ltd of Portsmouth', *Brewery history: the journal of the Brewery History Society* 65, 1991, 76-84. Includes useful information on the Brickwood family, 18-19th c.

Bridger
REEVES, JOHN A. 'A Bridger family of Hampshire', *H.F.H.* 2(1), 1975, 7-9. Includes pedigree, 16-19th c.

Brigstocke
ALLAN, G.K. 'The Brigstocke Bible', *I.O.W.F.H.S.* 25, 1992, 7-11. Includes pedigree, 17-20th c.

Bristow
CUST, SIR LIONEL. 'Bristow of Binstead and Micheldever, Hants', *M.G.H.* 5th series 7, 1929-31, 3-14 & 51-7. 17-18th c., includes wills, *etc.*

Brocas
BURROWS, MONTAGU. *The family of Brocas of Beaurepaire and Roche Court, hereditary masters of the royal buckhounds ...* Longmans, Green and Co., 1886. Medieval-19th c., includes folded pedigree, with abstracts of 462 deeds relating to Hampshire, Berkshire, Surrey and Yorkshire, *etc.* 'Account of the family of Brocas of Beaurepaire, in Hants', *Topographer* 4, 1790, 53-8. Medieval.

Brooke
BALCH, THOMAS WILLING. *The Brooke family of Whitchurch, Hampshire, England, together with an account of acting-governor Robert Brooke of Maryland and Colonel Ninian Beall of Maryland and some of their descendants.* Philadelphia: Allen Lane & Scott, 1899. 16-19th c.

Brune
See Prideaux

Budd
'Budd family tree', *Fareham past and present* 4(4), 1993, 26-7. 19-20th c.

Bull
PROWTHING, JUNE. 'The Bulls of Longdown', *H.F.H.* 17(1), 44-5. Includes pedigree, 18-20th c.

Bullaker
McCANN, TIMOTHY J. 'Some Hampshire relatives of a Chichester martyr', *F.H.J.S.E.H.G.S.* 1(4), 1974, 73-4. Bullaker family; includes 16th c. pedigree.

Burden
BUTLER, E.L. 'My grandparents, no.4: John James Burden, R.N.', *H.F.H.* 8(3), 1981, 114-6; 8(4), 1982, 153-5. 18-19th c.

Burfitt
BURFITT, SUE. 'The Burfitts in Twyford', *H.F.H.* 18(4), 1992, 261-2. 19-20th c.

Burleigh
See Sewell

Byseley

BEAZLEY, F.C. 'Pedigree of Byseley, Bisley or Beazley, of Newington and Warborough, Co.Oxon; Ryde and Alverstoke, Co.Southampton, and Oxton, Co.Chester', *M.G.H.* 5th series **6**, 1926-8, 390-408. 16-20th c.

Carver

'Carver bible', *H.F.H.* **11**(2), 1984, 126. Of Titchfield; 19th c. extracts.

Cassford

GRIFFITHS, JUNE. 'Cassfords ... both sides of the water', *I.O.W.F.H.S.* **5**, 1987, 2-3. 18th c.

Cave

TURNER, BARBARA CARPENTER. 'A notable family of artists: the Caves of Winchester', *P.P.H.F.C.* **22**(1), 1961, 30-34. 18th c.

Cawte

CAWTE, E.C. 'Tales my Uncle William might have told me', *H.F.H.* **18**(4), 1992, 318-9; **19**(1), 1992, 77-8; **19**(2), 1992, 152-3; **19**(4), 1993, 234-5 & **20**(1), 1993, 44-5. Cawte family, 18-19th c., includes apprenticeship indentures, extracts from manorial records, bonds, and will.

Chance

CAWSER, J.R. 'Shadow of a Chance', *H.F.H.* **19** (1), 1992, 38-9. Chance and Staples families, 19-20th c.

Chitty

CHITTY, ERIK. 'Chitty of Chiltley?', *F.H.J.S.E.H.G.S.* 1(4), 1974, 81-2. Includes pedigree of Chitty of Hampshire and Surrey, 16-17th c.

Chiverton

'A note on the Chiverton family', *Genealogical quarterly* **30**(4), 1964, 154-5. Medieval-20th c.

Christian

'The Christian family in the Isle of Wight', in JAMES, E. BOUCHER. *Letters archaeological and historical relating to the Isle of Wight.* Henry Frowde, 1896, v.2., 347-51. 18-19th c.

Clarke

See Sewell

Cole

EDWIN-COLE, JAMES. *Genealogy of the family of Cole, of the County of Devon, and of those of its branches which settled in Suffolk, Hampshire, Surrey, Lincolnshire and Ireland.* John Russell Smith, 1867. 14-19th c.

Compton

GIBSON, WILLIAM. 'Clerical dynasticism: the Compton family of Minstead and Sopley', *Hatcher review* **3**(30), 1990, 488-99.

Cooke

'Cooke: entries on fly-leaves of a Bible ...', *M.G.H.* 3rd series **4**, 1902, 48-51. Of Hampshire and Kent; 18-19th c.

Cotton

EVERITT, ALFRED T. 'Cotton family of Warbleton (Warblington), Hants', *Notes and queries* 12th series **10**, 1922, 36-7. 16-17th c.

SEILES, MARY. 'Island families no.2: Cotton', *H.F.H.* **5**(4), 1979, 116-7 & **6**(1), 1979, 13-15. Extracts from Isle of Wight parish registers, 18-19th c.

Cox

JONES, KENNETH R. 'The Cox family of Quarley manor house', *Lookback at Andover* **1**, 1980, [6-11]. 18th c.

Creeth

CREETH, LILIAN. 'The bright sparks', *H.F.H.* **12**(2), 1985, 84-7. Creeth family, 19-20th c.

Dabridgecourt

L., C.E. 'Pedigree of Dabridgecourt of Stratfield Say, Co.Hants.', *Topographer and genealogist* **1**, 1846, 197-207.

Dagwell

DAGWELL, DAVID N. 'The ubiquitous Dagwells', *H.F.H.* **15**(1), 1988, 57-8. Brief general article.

De Cosne

'Pedigree of De Cosne', *M.G.H.* N.S. **4**, 1884, 240-41. Of Southampton; 18th c.

De Estur
WHITEHEAD, JOHN L. 'Genealogical and other notes relating to the De Estur family of the Isle of Wight', *P.P.H.F.C.* **6**, 1907-10, 230-52. Medieval; includes pedigrees.

De Insula
WHITEHEAD, JOHN L. 'Genealogical and other notes relating to the De Insula, otherwise De L'Isle, De Lisle, or Lisle family', *P.P.H.F.C.* **6**, 1907-10, 111-39. Medieval; includes pedigrees.

De Lisle
See De Insula

Delmé
MINNS, G.W. 'On a portrait of Lady Betty Delmé by Sir Joshua Reynolds, formerly at Cams Hall, Fareham, with notes on the family of Delmé', *P.P.H.F.C.* **3**, 1894-7, 99-114. Includes folded pedigree, 17-19th c.
'Delmé of Cams', *Fareham past and present* **4**(4), 1993, 5-12. 18-20th c.
See also Garnier

Devenish
DEVENISH, BERTHA. *Archives of the Devenish family collected by Henry Weston Devenish.* Weymouth: J.H.C. & B. Devenish, 1933. Of Hamshpire, Sussex and Dorset; includes pedigrees (some folded), medieval-20th c., also pedigrees of Hoo and Welles families.
DEVENISH, ROBERT JONES, & McLAUGHLIN, CHARLES. H. *Historical and genealogical records of the Devenish families of England and Ireland, with an inquiry into the origin of the family name and some account of the family lines founded by them in other countries.* Chicago: Lakeside Press, 1948. Of many counties, but especially of Hampshire, Sussex and Dorset, medieval-20th c. Includes folded pedigrees, and an extensive bibliography.

Dewar
DEWAR, M.W. 'The Dewars of the Doles', *Test Valley and border anthology* **1**, 1973, 2-7. 18-20th c.

Dillington
'Dillington pedigrees', *M.G.H.* 2nd series **1**, 1886, 380-82. 17th c.

Dimes
COPE, WENDY. 'The day of the funeral', *H.F.H.* **18**(1), 1991, 2. Dimes family; includes pedigree, 18-20th c.
COPE, WENDY. 'The plight of Thomas Dimes and his family, as seen in the Overseers' records, Crondall', *H.F.H.* **19**(1), 1992, 17-18.

Ditchburn
NINEHAM, A.W. 'Merchantmen all', *H.F.H.* **9**(2), 1982, 73-4. Ditchburn family, 19th c.

Dobson
JOYCE, G. HAYWOOD. 'Dobson and Fell families', *Genealogist* **3**, 1886, 145-7. 17-18th c.

Dowling
SHERWOOD, ANTONY. 'The Dowling line', *H.F.H.* **11**(1), 1984, 58-62. See also **11**(3), 1984, 165-7. Includes pedigrees, 16-20th c.
SHERWOOD, ANTONY. 'The Dowling line: a shadow of doubt', *H.F.H.* **12**(2), 1985, 89-90. Includes pedigree, 16-17th c.

Dummer
CHESTER, JOSEPH LEMUEL. 'The family of Dummer', *New England historical and genealogical register* **35**, 1881, 254-71 & 321-32. 13-18th c.
'Pedigree of Dummer of Penne Domer, Co.Somerset, and of Dummer, Co.Hants', *Somersetshire Archaeological and Natural History Society proceedings* **17**, 1871, 114-5. 12-17th c.

Du Moulin-Browne
C., I.M. 'Du Moulin-Browne of Easebourne, and Moore of Fawley', *Genealogist* N.S. **8**, 1892, 30-33. Easebourne, Sussex. 18-19th c.

Dyer
DYER, DAVID. 'The Dyer family: builders and restorers of fine houses and churches in Hampshire', *H.F.H.* **17**(2), 1990, 115-20. 18-20th c., includes brief pedigree.
DYER, DAVID. 'The Dyers of Alton', *H.F.H.* **12**(4), 1986, 234-5. 18-20th c.

Eardley
See Garnier

Edmeade

WILLIAMS, G.H. 'Edmeades of Meopham, Strood and Winchester', *H.F.H.* **4**(3), 1977, 69-70. 16-20th c.

Edwards

HAMILTON-EDWARDS, GERALD. 'Family history material in registers of deeds', *Genealogist's magazine* **16**, 1971, 517-35. Edwards family, 18-19th c.
See also Sewell

Elliott

ELLIOTT, ANGUS G. 'Elliott family: fisherfolk of Fogo', *H.F.H.* **13**(3), 1986, 180-82. Of Christchurch, Hampshire, and Fogo, Newfoundland, 18th c.

Ellis

ELLIS, WILLIAM SMITH. *Notices of the Ellises ...* John Russell Smith, 1857. Medieval.

Elton

SEILES, KEITH. 'Elton marriages prior to 1750 on the Isle of Wight', *H.F.H.* **7**(2), 1980, 59-60.

Emery

'Emery records from the parish registers of Romsey, England', *New England historical and genealogical register* **89**, 1935, 376-7. 16-17th c.

Englefield

TRAPPES-LOMAX, T.B. 'The Englefields and their contribution to the survival of the faith in Berkshire, Wiltshire, Hampshire and Leicestershire', *Biographical studies* **1**, 1951, 131-48. Roman Catholic family.

Evelyn

'Genealogical memoranda relating to the family of Evelyn', *M.G.H.* 2nd series **1**, 1886, 82-3, 100, 152-6, 176-7, 210, 222-3, 229-34, 258-9, 296-7, 319-22, 332 & 352-6; **2**, 1888, 8-11, 24-5, 38-9, 135-8, 184-6, 229, 245, 312 & 327-8; **3**, 1890, 242-5, 267-8, 269-71 & 298-300. Of Surrey, Hampshire and Wiltshire, 16-18th c. Includes pedigrees, monumental inscriptions, parish register extracts, marriage licences, *etc.*

Fane

CAREW, JOYCE. *Dusty pages: a story of two families and their homes.* Bridport: C.J. Creed, 1971. Fane and Fortescue families, of Dorset, Devon, Somerset and Hampshire.

Fearnley

See Ingham

Fell

See Dobson

Fettiplace

SLAGLE, A.RUSSELL. 'The Fettiplace family', *New England historical and genealogical register* **123**, 1969, 241-57. See also **129**, 1975, 75-7. 13-17th c., of Hampshire, North Denchworth and East Shefford, Berkshire, and Coln St. Aldwyn, Gloucestershire.

Fitzpiers

WATSON, G.W. 'Fitz Piers and De Say', *Genealogist* N.S. **34**, 1918, 181-9. Includes pedigrees, 12-13th c., and deeds.

Fletcher

FLETCHER, JOHN S. 'A Portsea connection: the Fletchers of Sheerness and South London, and their maritime link with Portsea', *H.F.H.* **15**(4), 1989, 256-60. Includes pedigree, 19-20th c.

Fortescue

See Fane

Foster

HUNT, LEVITT W. 'The Fosters and Stubbington House', *H.F.H.* **10**(4), 1984, 162-4; **11**(1), 1984, 43-6. 19-20th c.

Fox

SMITH, J. CHALLENOR. 'The families of Fox and Tattershall', *Genealogist* N.S. **30**, 1912, 150-53. 16th c., also of Middlesex.

Fruen

LOWE, DORIS, & HOGG, MARY. 'Tracking the Fruens', *H.F.H.* **18**(3), 1991, 168-71. 19th c.

Gadd

HOOKER, R.E. 'Title deeds and genealogy', *F.H.J.S.E.H.G.S.* **1**(3), 1974, 54-5. Includes pedigree of Gadd, 19th c.

Gannaway
'Gannaway entries', *H.F.H.* **8**(3), 1981, 89-90. 18-19th c. extracts from the registers of various Southampton parishes.

Garnier
GARNIER, A.E. *The chronicles of the Garniers of Hampshire during four centuries, 1530-1900 ...* Norwich: Jarrold & Sons, 1900. Includes folded pedigrees of various related families: Delmés, Rigby, Taylor, Parry, Eardley, Hillier and Hobhouse.

Gifford
See Kingsmill

Glamorgan
'The Glamorgan family in the Isle of Wight and Clamerkins Bridge', in JAMES, E. BOUCHER. *Letters archaeological and historical relating to the Isle of Wight.* Henry Frowde, 1896, v.1, 234-6. Medieval.

Gignoux
'Pedigree of Gignoux and Vignoles', *M.G.H.* N.S. **4**, 1884, 241. Of Southampton, 18th c.

Goldwyer
BAYLEY, A.R. 'Goldwyer of Somerford Grange and Salisbury Close', *Genealogists' magazine* **7**(9), 1937, 455-9. 16-19th c.

Goodall
See Young

Goodridge
See Lisle-Taylor

Gosden
GOSDEN, HILARY. 'How I started my family tree', *I.O.W.F.H.S.* **2**, 1986, 2-3. Gosden family; includes pedigree, 17-20th c.

Gosling
SEILES, MARY. 'Island families, no.1: Gosling', *H.F.H.* **5**(3), 1978, 78-9. Isle of Wight parish register extracts, pre 1735.

Gough
'Gough ancestry', *H.F.H.* **14**(1), 1987, 39. Pedigree, 18-20th c.

Grace
FLETCHER, J.S. 'Winchester and the Thames: what they have in common', *H.F.H.* **20**(1), 1993, 12-15; **20**(2), 1993, 121-5. Grace of Winchester; Mallett of Lambeth, Surrey. Includes pedigrees, 18-19th c.

Gray
HONAN, ROBERT F. *The Gray matter: the Gray family history, 16th to 20th century: from Newbury, County Berkshire to Alton, County Hampshire, Nettlebed, County Oxfordshire, Walthamstow, County Middlesex, Newmarket, County Suffolk, London and Australia.* Adelaide: Lutheran Publishing House, 1987. Includes pedigree, with monumental inscriptions, etc.

Gudge
See Hill

Guidott
SUCKLING, F.H. 'Guidott family', *Notes and queries* 11th series **12**, 1915, 258. See also 422-3. 16-18th c.

Gunner
HODGSON, R.A. 'Gunners Bank: the Bishops Waltham and Hampshire Bank', *Portsmouth archives review* **2**, 1977, 26-53; **3**, 1978, 68-91 & **4**, 1979-80, 61-79. Includes pedigree of Gunner, with much information on the family business.

Gurdun
BAIN, JOSEPH. 'Selbourne Priory charters: Sir Adam Gurdun', *Genealogist* N.S. **11**, 1895, 10. Gurdun family, 13th c.
BAIN, JOSEPH. 'Sir Adam Gurdun of Selborne', *Genealogist* N.S. **4**, 1887, 1-4. See also 106-7 & 124. 13-14th c.

Hall
'The Hall family of Winchester', *H.F.H.* **12**(2), 1985, 81. Pedigree, 18-20th c.

Halliday
HALLIDAY, C.A.T. *Hallidays.* Whitchurch: the author, 1980. Includes folded pedigree.

Hanbury

'Which Thomas Hanbury?', *Petersfield Area Historical Society bulletin* 1(4), 1976, 9-11. Includes Hanbury pedigree, 16-17th c. *See also* Sewell

Hanmer

HANMER, CALVERT. *The Hanmers of Morton and Montford, Salop, with supplementary chapters on the Hanmers of Hanmer, the Hanmers of the Fens, Sir Thomas Hanmer the Speaker, the Calverts of Furneaux Pelham, the Staffordshire Underhills, and the Lanyon Owens of Southsea.* John Lane, 1916. Includes folded pedigrees, medieval-20th c., with extracts from parish registers and various other records.

Harfell

TURNER, BARBARA CARPENTER. 'A Royalist chapter clerk and his family', *Winchester Cathedral record* **40**, 1971, 29-33. Harfell family, 17th c.

Harris

[FOSTER, JOSEPH.] *A narrative of the descendants of Samuel Harris of Fordingbridge, Hants., together with a notice of the family of Masterman of London.* Chiswick Press, 1878. Includes pedigrees, 17-19th c.

Hattatt

ARMSTRONG, JOHN HATTATT. 'The rustler of Wallop: a sequel', *H.F.H.* 14(1), 1987, 26-8. Hattatt family, 18-19th c., includes pedigree.

Havill

ICETON, D. 'Havill family bible', *H.F.H.* 12(1), 1985, 52. Late 19th c.

Hayward

'Hayward/Legge wedding at Sholing, 1932', *H.F.H.* 19(3), 1992, 158-9. Includes Legge pedigree, 19-20th c.

Hazelgrove

WATKIN, JEFF. 'The Hazelgrove family: butchers of Hazelgrove for four generations', *H.F.H.* 12(4), 1986, 227-9. 19-20th c.

Heighes

REEVES, J.A. 'A short history of the Heighes family of Hampshire', *H.F.H.* 3(1), 1976, 26-30. Of Binstead; includes pedigree, medieval-19th c.

Henley

BLORE, G.H. 'A forgotten family: the Henleys of Grange', *P.P.H.F.C.* **20**, 1956, 34-43. 17-18th c.

SUCKLING, F.H. 'George Henley of Bradley, Hants', *Notes and queries* 10th series **9**, 1908, 140-44. 17-18th c.

Henwood

EVERSON, VALERIE. 'The Henwoods of Hampshire', *H.F.H.* 12(3), 1986, 214-5. 16-20th c.

Hill

EBSWORTH, JILL. 'The Hills of Hampshire', *H.F.H.* 16(3), 196-8. Also includes notes on Bettesworth, Gudge, Pink and other related families.

Hillier

See Garnier

Hinton

TRICKETT, FRANCES. 'Hinton family of North West Hampshire', *H.F.H.* 16(2), 1989, 91-6. Includes pedigree, 17-20th c.

Hobhouse

See Garnier

Hobson

'The Hobson or Hopson family, and Milton's *Sonnet* to the Lady Margaret, wife of Captain Hopson', in JAMES, E. BOUCHER. *Letters archaeological and historical relating to the Isle of Wight.* Henry Frowde, 1896, v.2, 171-9. 16-17th c.

Hollis

See Larcom

Holloway

HOLLOWAY, RONALD. 'Holloway: Hampshire mapmakers', *H.F.H.* 10(2), 1983, 63-4. 18-19th c.

Holloway *continued*

WEBB, N.R. 'Brushes with the law', *H.F.H.* **13**(3), 1986, 189-94. Holloway family references in calendars of prisoners and minutes of the Winchester bridewell, 1788-1841, *etc.*, also from the New South Wales census, 1828.

Hopson
See Hobson

Hoy

PINHORN, MALCOLM. 'The Hoys of Thornhill Park', *H.F.H.* **8**(2), 1981, 54-6. See also **8**(3), 1981, 119-20. 19th c.

Hulbert

NEWTON, MARION, & JACKSON, G.H.M. *The rise and fall of Stakes Hill Lodge, 1800-1973.* [ ]: Kadek Press, 1977. Hulbert family history; includes pedigree, 19-20th c.

Hunt

'The Hunts of Fareham', *Fareham past and present* **4**(5), 1993, 49. Pedigree, 19-20th c.

Huntingford

McCULLOCH, L. 'Isle of Wight Huntingfords', *I.O.W.F.H.S.* **26**, 1992, 35. Extracts from parish registers, 17-18th c.

Huxford

HUXFORD, R.C. 'The Huxfords of Arreton', *I.O.W.F.H.S.* **14**, 1989, 3-6. Includes pedigree, 18th c.

Ingham
See Whitaker

Ingpen

INGPEN, ARTHUR ROBERT. *An ancient family: a genealogical study showing the Saxon origin of the family of Ingpen.* Longmans, Green & Co., 1916. Includes pedigrees; of Hampshire and Berkshire.

Jeans
See Whitaker

Jervoise

JERVOISE, F.H.T. 'The Jervoises of Herriard and Britford', *Ancestor* **3**, 1902, 1-13. 16-17th c., includes undated inventory of Sir Richard Poulett. Britford, Wiltshire.

Kemp

HITCHIN-KEMP, FRED., et al. *A general history of the Kemp and Kempe families of Great Britain and her colonies, with arms, pedigrees ... etc.* Leadenhall Press, 1902-3. Also of Norfolk, Dorset, Staffordshire, Suffolk, Hampshire, *etc.* Includes many pedigrees.

Kent

C[HITTY], H. 'Kent family and Headbourne Worthy', *Notes and queries* 12th series **4**, 1918, 274-7. See also 12th series **5**, 1919, 52-3 & 183-5. 15-18th c.

Kingsley
See Symonds

Kingsmill

FRITZE, RONALD HAROLD. 'A rare example of Godlyness amongst gentlemen: the role of the Kingsmill and Gifford families in promoting the reformation in Hampshire', in LAKE, PETER., ed. *Protestantism and the national church in sixteenth-century England.* Croom Helm, 1987, 144-61.

Kingston
See Lisle

Kittoe
See Sewell

Kneller

VIRGOE, J.M. 'The Knellers of King's Somborne', *H.F.H.* **13**(2), 1986, 93-5. General.

Knollys

GREENFIELD, B.W. 'Notes respecting Grove Place, Nursling, and the manor of Southwells', *P.P.H.F.C.* **3**, 1894-7, 115-26. Includes folded pedigrees of Knollys, 16-19th c., and Pagett, Mill, Pawlet, *etc.*, 16-17th c.

SUCKLING, F.H. 'Knollys family', *Notes and queries* 11th series **12**, 1915, 141. See also 205 & 242-3. 15-17th c.

Larcom

BURROWS, MONTAGU. *History of the families of Larcom, Hollis, and McKinley.* Oxford: E. Pickard Hall and J.H. Stacy, 1883. 19th c., includes folded pedigree of Larcom, 18-19th c.

Lavington
NOWELL, FREDERICK. 'The Lavingtons', *H.F.H.* 15(2), 1988, 100-102. See also 15(3), 1988, 166-7. 18th c.

Legay
BROWNBILL, J. 'Legay of Southampton and London', *Notes and queries* 12th series **8**, 1921, 341-2, 362-4 & 385-6. See also 451-2. 16-18th c.

Legg
'Medicine Hat', *H.F.H.* **18**(4), 1992, 303. Extracts from the Legg family bible, 19th c.

Legge
See Hayward

Leigh
HOCKEY, S.F. 'Who was the wife of Sir John Leigh: Agnes, Mary or Anne?', *Proceedings of the Isle of Wight Natural History and Archaeological Society* **5**(10), 1965, 483. 15-16th c.

Lindeseie
LINZEE, JOHN WILLIAM. *The Lindeseie and Limesi families of Great Britain, including the probates at Somerset House, London, England, of all spellings of the name Lindeseie from 1300-1800.* 2 vols. Boston, Mass.: Fort Hill Press, 1917. Of various counties, but especially Scotland and Hampshire; includes pedigrees and extensive extracts from various sources.

Linnington
See Nutty

Linter
LINTER, GRAHAM. 'In search of the Linter family', *H.F.H.* **12**(4), 1986, 244-6. Includes pedigree, 19-20th c.

Linzee
EVANS, D.M.H. 'The Linzees of Portsmouth & the Royal Navy', *H.F.H.* **9**(2), 1982, 49. 18-19th c.

Lisle
ROGERS, W.H. HAMILTON. 'Lisle-Kingston-Lisle of Wodeton, Isle of Wight, Thruxton, Hants, and of Wilts and Dorset', in his *Archaeological papers relating to the counties of Somerset, Wilts., Hants and Devon.* [ ]: the author, 1902. *See also* De Insula

Lisle-Taylor
PULMAN, J., & WADE, EDWARD FRY. 'Pedigree of Lisle-Taylor and Goodridge', *Genealogist* **7**, 1883, 267-9. 16-19th c.

Long
'Pedigree of the Longs of Semington: Rood Ashton and Preshaw branches', *M.G.H.* N.S. **2**, 1880, 46(f). Folded pedigree, 16-19th c. Semington and Rood Ashton are in Wiltshire.

Lovibond
'All references to the name Lovibond in the Isle of Wight County Record Office ...', *I.O.W.F.H.S.* **29**, 1993, 35-43. Mainly notes from deeds, *etc.*, 16-19th c.

Lymerston
BAIGENT, FRANCIS JOSEPH. 'On the family of De Lymerston and its heiress, the founder of the Tichborne dole', *Journal of the British Archaeological Association* **11**, 1855, 277-302. Lymerston and Tichborne families, medieval.

McKinley
See Larcom

Mackrell
BURROWES, L.R. 'Mackrell's last journey', *H.F.H.* **14**(1), 1987, 18-20. Includes pedigree, 18-20th c.

Main
HURST, N.H.G. 'The Main line', *H.F.H.* **7**(4), 1981, 135-6. 19th c.
HURST, N.H.G. 'The Main line (2)', *H.F.H.* **8**(1), 1981, 25-6. 18-19th c.
HURST, N.H.G. 'The Main line, 3', *H.F.H.* **8**(2), 1981, 69-70. 19th c.

Main *continued*

HURST, N.H.G. 'The Main line, 4', *H.F.H.* **8**(3), 1981, 117. List of pilot licences granted to members of the Main family by Trinity House, 19th c.

MAIN, MARGARET. 'Branches of the Main line', *H.F.H.* **17**(3), 1990, 176-8; **17**(4), 1991, 315-7 & **18**(1), 1991, 28-32. 17-20th c.

Mallet

See Grace

Manser

BOWDITCH, JULIA. *A hundred years in Sherfield-upon-Loddon: a history of J.A. Manser & Son Ltd., and the village of its origin.* Sherfield: J.A. Manser & Son, 1987. Manser family company. 19-20th c.

Mason

SANBORN, V.C. 'Sir John Mason and the Masons of Hampshire', *Genealogist* N.S. **34**, 1917, 34-40. 16-17th c., includes *inquisition post mortem* of Anthony Weekes, 1607.

Maudit

ROUND, J. HORACE. 'Maudit of Hartley Maudit', *Ancestor* **5**, 1903, 207-10. 12th c.

May

RAY, F. *The Mays of Basingstoke, with special reference to Lieut.-Colonel John May.* Simpkin & Co., 1904. 18-19th c.

Mayo

CHORLEY, JENNIFER. 'The Mayo family in Winchester (1811-1939)', *Winchester Cathedral record* **59**, 1990, 17-22. Includes pedigree.

Meux

SLADE, J.J. 'Meux family in the Isle of Wight', *Wiltshire archaeological and natural history magazine* **50**(177), 1942, 103-4. 16-17th c.

Mew

BEAZLEY, F.C. 'The Mew family of Freshwater, I.W., yeomen, circa 1650-1831', *H.N.Q.* **3**, 1887, 24-6. Includes pedigree.

'The Mewes family', in JAMES, E. BOUCHER. *Letters archaeological and historical relating to the Isle of Wight.* Henry Frowde, 1896, v.1, 455-7. 17-18th c.

GREEN, S. 'Mews or Mewys family', *Notes and queries* 12th series **2**, 1916, 26. See also 93-4, 331-3, 419 & 432-4; **3**, 1917, 16-17, 52-3, 113, 195, 236, 421-2 & 454; **5**, 1919, 163. 16-18th c.

Mildmay

SAGE, EDWARD J. 'Mildmay of Marks, Shawford and Hazel Grove', *M.G.H.* **2**, 1876, 263-7. Pedigree, 17-18th c. Marks, Essex; Hazel Grove, Somerset.

Mill

See Knollys

Millington

See Symonds

Minter

CLARKE, M.K. 'Minter, Prain & Bannister: roots on the Island', *I.O.W.F.H.S.* **3**, 1986, 4-5. Includes summary pedigree of Bannister, 16-19th c.

Mitchell

CLASBY, VALERIE FRANCES. 'Who was Great-Grandmother?', *H.F.H.* **16**(4), 1990, 270-72. Mitchell family of Hampshire and London, 19-20th c.

Moore

See Du Moulin-Browne

Morris

BROOM, C., 'The Morris family', *I.O.W.F.H.S.* **16**, 1990, 12-14. Includes pedigree, 18-20th c.

Nedham

See Sewell

Nenge

SLOGGETT, BRIAN. 'Before 1538?', *H.F.H.* **8**(3), 1981, 103-5. General study, using pedigrees of Nenge of East Meon and Wylkyns of Wonston as case studies.

Newbolt

JACOB, WILLIAM HENRY. 'An old Winchester family: the Newbolts', *H.N.Q.* **4**, 1889, 69-70. 16-17th c.

Nicholls
NAISH, SANDRA. 'Nicholls family bible', *H.F.H.*
11(2), 1984, 72. 19th c.

Norton
HALL, DEREK, & BARBER, NORMAN. 'The
Nortons of Southwick: the genealogy of a
seventeenth century Hampshire family',
H.F.H. 10(4), 1984, 189-94 & 11(1), 1984, 63-7.
Includes pedigree.
LONG, W.H. 'The Nortons of Rotherfield
and Southwick', *H.N.Q.* 5, 1890, 64-5.
16-18th c.
'Norton of Rotherfield and Southwick', *H.N.Q.*
2, 1884, 108-12.
PINK, W.D. 'The Nortons of Rotherfield
baronetcy', *H.N.Q.* 5, 1892, 124-7. 17th c.

Noyes
'The Noyes family: from the town clerks'
correspondence file (5/CR/1)', *Test Valley
and border anthology* 11, 1977, 253-5. 17th c.

Nutty
MOORE, C.A. 'The Isle of Wight connection',
I.O.W.F.H.S. 14, 1989, 12-14. Nutty, Baskett,
Linnington, *etc.,* 18-19th c.

Oglander
ASPINALL-OGLANDER, CECIL. *Nunwell
symphony.* Hogarth Press, 1945. Oglander
family, 15-20th c.

Ogle
MOORE, PAM. 'The Ogles at Worthy Park',
Hatcher review 4(32), 1991, 19-30.

Oke
TEMPLETON, JOHN. 'The 19th century Oke
family of Southampton', *H.F.H.* 12(1), 1985,
15-16.

Owen
See Sewell

Pagett
See Knollys

Paice
MACKARILL, DIANA R. 'Lettice in limbo',
H.F.H. 17(2), 1990, 89-92. Paice family,
17-18th c.

MACKARILL, DIANA R. 'An ordinary family:
the Paices of Basingstoke', *H.F.H.* 17(1), 1990,
26-9. See also 17(2), 1990, 104. 18-20th c.

Parry
See Garnier

Pawlet
See Knollys

Payne
PAYNE, S.K. 'London born and bred', *H.F.H.*
18(3), 1991, 179-81. Payne family of
Hampshire, Berkshire and London; includes
pedigree, 18-20th c.

Pecover
See Pither

Penton
WOOD, ELIZABETH. 'The Pentons of
Winchester', *Section newsletters [Hampshire
Field Club]* 15, 1991, 25-9. Includes pedigree,
17-19th c.

Pert
'Ernest Pert, Royal Navy gunner', *H.F.H.* 14(2),
1987, 95-7. Of Berkshire, Hampshire and
Sussex. Includes Pert family pedigree,
19-20th c.

Phillimore
BARTON, MARILYN. 'The first Phillimores at
Shedfield', *Newsletter of the Hampshire
Archives Trust* Spring 1989, 27-37. 19th c.

Philpot
WILLIAMS, G.H. 'The first Hampshire printers',
G.R. 10, 1975, 9-13. Philpot family, 17-18th c.

Pidgley
PEDGLEY, DAVID E. 'The mobile Pidgleys',
H.F.H. 14(2), 1987, 93-4. Of Hampshire and
Sussex; includes pedigree, 18-19th c.

Pierce
'Pierce family tree', *H.F.H.* 19(2), 1992, 101.
Pedigree, 17-20th c.

Pink
ALBERY, E.M. 'The Pink family', *H.F.H.* 11(4),
1985, 258-9. 19th c.

Pink *continued*

PINK, W. DUNCOMBE. 'Pincke of Bighton, Co.Southampton', *M.G.H.* 3rd series **2**, 1896, 185. See also 192. 17th c.

PINK, W. DUNCOMBE. 'Pincke (or Pinke) of Brown Candover, Alton, etc., Co. Southampton', *M.G.H.* 3rd series **2**, 1898, 251-5. 17-19th c.

PINK, W. DUNCOMBE. 'Pincke (Pinke or Pink) of Kempshott in the parish of Winslade, Co.Southampton', *M.G.H.* 3rd series **2**, 1898, 105-12. 16-19th c.

PINK, W. DUNCOMBE. 'Pinke of North Waltham, Co.Southampton', *M.G.H.* 3rd series **2**, 1898, 187-8. 17-19th c.

PINK, W. DUNCOMBE. 'Pincke of West Stratton in the parish of Micheldever, Co. Southampton', *M.G.H.* 3rd series **2**, 1896, 186. 17th c.

'Pinke of Bradley, Newton Valence, *etc.*, Co.Southampton, and of Aston Thorold (otherwise Turrold), Co.Berks', *M.G.H.* 3rd series **2**, 1989, 256-8.

See also Hill

Pinnell
See Pither

Pither

PITHER, JOHN S. 'The three P's', *H.F.H.* **18**(2), 1991, 110-11. Pither, Pecover and Pinnell families; includes pedigree, 18-20th c.

Pitman

PITMAN, H.A. 'Pitman of Quarley and North Tidworth', *M.G.H.* 5th series **6**, 1926-8, 72-8. 17-18th c., also of Wiltshire.

Poore

DENTON, COLIN, & BRICKELL, GEORGE. 'The Poore family: a preliminary survey', *Test Valley and border anthology* **3**, 1974, 54-6. 19th c.

Popham

POPHAM, FREDERICK W. *A West Country family: the Pophams from 1150.* Sevenoaks: the author, 1976. Of Somerset, Devon and Hampshire.

ROUND, J. HORACE. 'The rise of the Pophams', *Ancestor* **7**, 1903, 59-66. Medieval.

Port

GUNNER, W.H. 'An account of the alien priory of Andwell, or Enedewell, in Hampshire, a cell of the Abbey of Tyrone, with some remarks on the family of De Port of Basing its founders', *Archaeological journal* **9**, 1852, 246-61. Includes pedigree of Port, 12-13th c.

ROUND, J.H. 'The Ports of Basing', *Genealogist* N.S. **18**, 1902, 137-9. 12-13th c.

Portal

PORTAL, SIR WILLIAM WYNDHAM. *Abraham Portal - born 1726, died 1809 - and his descendants.* Winchester: Warren & Son, 1925. 18-20th c., includes folded pedigree.

PORTAL, SIR WILLIAM WYNDHAM. *The story of Portals of Laverstoke: a brief account of 200 years successful making of good papers.* Cross-Courtenay, 1925. 18-19th c. family.

Poulett
See Jervoise

Prain
See Minter

Prideaux

MACLEAN, SIR JOHN. *A brief memoir of the families of Prideaux of Devon and Cornwall, and of Brune of Hants and Dorset.* Exeter: William Pollard, 1874. Reprinted from *The History of Trigg-Minor.* Includes pedigree, medieval-19th c.

Priscott

DEAN, JUDY. 'Priscott pride', *H.F.H.* **12**(3), 1985, 145-7. 19th c.

Proctor

P[ROCTOR], F.J. *Records of the Proctor family during the following reigns: 1509 Henry VIII ... 1910 George V; also, an account of the family's association with the naval life of Old Point, Portsmouth, since they settled there after leaving Scotland over 400 years ago.* [Portsmouth]: [privately printed], [1928]. Includes pedigrees of the Hertford and London branches.

Puleston

COPE, MRS. 'Some Hampshire rectors', *P.P.H.F.C.* **8**(1), 1917, 109-12. Puleston family, 16-18th c.

Purkis

WILCOX, L.G.M. 'King William and the charcoal burner', *H.F.H.* **17**(3), 1990, 163-6. Purkis family; includes pedigree, 17th c.

Puttenham

GRAHAM, NORMAN H. 'The Puttenham family of Puttenham and Long Marston, Co.Herts., and of Sherfield, Co.Hants., Puttnam (and Putnam) of Penn, *etc.,* Co.Bucks, 1086-1956', *Notes and queries* **202**, 1957, 185-9 & 424-31; **204**, 1959, 50-56.

Ransom

ETHERIDGE, J.D.R. 'Grandmother's room', *H.F.H.* **12**(3), 1985, 211-13. Ransom family; includes pedigree, 18-19th c.

Ratsey

See Symonds

Rigby

See Garnier

Roberts

ROBERTS, H. BRICE. 'Pedigree of Roberts', *M.G.H.* 4th series **4**, 1911, 214-8. 17-20th c.

Rogers

REEKS, LINDSAY S. 'Pursuing the parentage and life of John Rogers', *H.F.H.* **8**(2), 1981, 59-65. 19th c.

ROGERS, JULIAN C. *A history of our family (Rogers of Westmeon), 1451-1902.* Phipps & Connor, 1902. Includes monumental inscriptions.

Rolf

STARK, SUSAN. 'Death on the line', *H.F.H.* **18**(1), 1991, 19-20. Rolf family; includes pedigree, 17-20th c.

FRENCH, ELIZABETH. 'Genealogical research in England', *New England historical and genealogical register* **66**, 1912, 244-52. Rolfe family of Downton, Wiltshire and Andover, Hampshire, 16-17th c. Includes pedigrees, wills and extracts from parish registers.

Rooke

ROOKE, H.W. 'Descendants of Giles Rooke, of Romsey, and Houghton, Co.Hants.', *Genealogist* N.S. **37**, 1921, 132-46. 17-19th c.

Ruffell

RUFFELL, L.E. 'Rotherfield and the Ruffells', *Newsletter of the Hampshire Archives Trust* Summer 1987, 35-7. Brief note, 19-20th c.

Rushworth

SMITH, CECIL EVAN. 'The family of Rushworth', *M.G.H.* 4th series **4**, 1911, 36-43. See also 94. Extracts from family bible, 18-19th c.

Russell

HOLLINGSBEE, KATHLEEN. 'The Russells of Russell Island, 1819-1950', *H.F.H.* **12**(3), 1985, 173-5.

St.John

WILLIAMS, META E. 'Pedigrees of the families of St.John of Basing and Lageham emended', *Notes and queries* **163**, 1932, 182-8, 298 & 352; **165**, 1933, 12-13 & **166**, 1934, 119-21. See also **166**, 1934, 230 & 285; **167**, 1933, 284 & **167**, 1934, 16. 11-15th c.

Samborne

SANBORN, V.C. *Genealogy of the family of Samborne or Sanborn in England and America, 1194-1898.* 2 pts. Concord: privately printed, 1899. Of Wiltshire, Berkshire, Hampshire, Somerset and America; includes pedigrees.

SANBORN, V.C. *The English ancestry of the American Sanborns: a supplement to the Samborne-Sanborn genealogy.* Kenilworth, Illinois: privately printed, 1916. Of Somerset and Hampshire, *etc.,* includes wills and *inquisitions post mortem*, 16-17th c.

Sanderson

See Whitaker

Sandys

SUCKLING, F.H. 'Genealogy in a Breeches bible', *Genealogist* N.S. **31**, 1915, 213-22. Sandys family, 14-17th c., includes will of Sir John Mill, 1646.

Searle

TICKNER, VINCENT. *The Searles of Froxfield in the nineteenth century.* Family history series 3. Brighton: Gamco Publications, 1990. Includes pedigree, 18-19th c., useful bibliography, and an 'index of Searles before 1900', listing entries in parish registers, *etc.*

Searle *continued*

TICKNER, VINCENT. 'Who are the correct parents of John Searle?', *H.F.H.* **19**(1), 1992, 11-13. 18-19th c.
See also Bayliffe

Sewell

OWEN, MOUNTAGUE CHARLES. *The Sewells of the Isle of Wight, with an account of some of the families connected with them by marriage.* Manchester: Manchester Courier, 1906. 16-19th c. Includes monumental inscriptions, wills, *etc.,* also notes on Burleigh, Clarke, Edwards, Nedham, Kittoe, Vaughan, Seymour, Owen, Hanbury and Baker.

Seymour
See Sewell

Shaddick

O'NEILL, S. 'The Shaddick family', *H.F.H.* **11**(4), 1985, 209. Pedigree, 19th c.

Shayer

STEWART, BRIAN, & CUTTEN, MERVYN. *The Shayer family of painters.* F. Lewis, 1981. Includes 'abridged' pedigree, 18-19th c.

Shrimpton

SHRIMPTON, VALDA. 'Let's hear it for the Hampshire indexers', *H.F.H.* **20**(3), 1993, 163-6. Shrimpton family; includes pedigree, 19-20th c.

Sinclair

WILLIAMS, C.L. SINCLAIR. 'The Sinclair family of England', *H.F.H.* **9**(4), 1983, 125-9; **10**(1), 1983, 6-10; **10**(2), 1983, 83-8 & **10**(3), 1983, 129-32. Of various counties, especially Somerset and Hampshire; medieval-20th c.

Smallbones

GEORGE, BRIAN. 'More Smallbones discovered', *Wiltshire Family History Society [journal]* **35**, 1989, 27-8. Of Berkshire, Hampshire and Wiltshire, 17-19th c.

Smith

'Pedigree of Smith', *M.G.H.* N.S. **4**, 1884, 242. Of Southampton, 18-19th c.

South

H., J.J. 'Thomas South of Bossington Hall, Hants', *Wiltshire notes and queries* **6**, 1908-10, 381-4. See also 326. 16th c.

Speed

GREENFIELD, B.W. 'Pedigree of Speed of Southampton', *M.G.H.* 3rd series **2**, 1898, 18-25. 17-18th c., includes parish register extracts and monumental inscriptions.

Sprake

RILEY, D.F. 'Origins of Sprake's Brewery, Chale Green', *I.O.W.F.H.S.* **28**, 1993, 28-31. Sprake family, 18-19th c.

Stanes

DODDERIDGE, SIDNEY E. 'Stanes of Portsea, Lymington and Southsea, Co.Hants', *M.G.H.* 5th series **1**, 1916, 176. Pedigree, 19th c.

Stanwix

'The Stanwix family and their connexion with the Isle of Wight', in JAMES, E. BOUCHER. *Letters archaeological and historical relating to the Isle of Wight.* Henry Frowde, 1896. v.2, 459-64. 18th c.

Staples
See Chance

Steele

STEELE-SMITH, H.F. 'The Steeles of Broughton: some notes', *Section newsletters [Hampshire Field Club]* **12**, 1989, 5-6. Brief note, 17-19th c.

Stephens

'The Stephens family in the Isle of Wight', in JAMES, E. BOUCHER. *Letters archaeological and historical relating to the Isle of Wight.* Henry Frowde, 1896, v.1, 649-65. 16-18th c.

Stiff

PHILLIMORE, W.P.W. 'The Stiffs of Silchester', *M.G.H.* 2nd series **4**, 1892, 233-4. Pedigrees, 16-18th c. Also of Suffolk.

Symonds

WALLIN, P. OLOF E. *Ancestors and descendants of John Symonds and Martha Florinda Ratsey of West Cowes, Isle of Wight.* Stockholm: Civiltryck, 1954. 16-20th c., includes folded pedigrees, with notes on Millington, Wright and Kingsley. Also of various other counties.

Tattershall
See Fox

Taylor
See Garnier

Thistlethwayte

SLIGHT, HENRY. *Thomas Thistlethwayte, his ancestors, and others, each lord of the manor of the Priory of Southwick from 1539 to 1850.* Portsmouth: Godfrey, 1850. Not seen; presumably a family history.

Tichborne

B[ARRON], OSWALD. 'Our oldest families, II: Tichborne', *Ancestor* **2**, 1902, 114-9. 12th c.
'An old family', *All the Year Round: a weekly journal* **6**, 1871, 583-7. Tichborne family, medieval-19th c.
A number of works deal with the Tichborne case, which involved disputed pedigrees, and attracted much attention in the late 19th c. See:
GILBERT, MICHAEL. *The claimant.* Constable, 1957.
MAUGHAM, LORD. *The Tichborne case.* Hodder and Stoughton, 1936.
WOODRUFF, JOHN DOUGLAS. *The Tichborne claimant: a Victorian mystery.* Hollis & Carter, 1957. Includes notes on printed sources, and pedigree, 18-20th c.
Charge of the Lord Chief Justice of England in the case of the Queen against Thomas Castro, otherwise Arthur Orton, otherwise Sir Roger Tichborne. 2 vols. Henry Sweet, 1874.
See also Lymerston

Tickner

HUGHES, GILLIAN. 'Charles Tickner's black book', *H.F.H.* **11**(4), 1985, 213-7. Tickner family, 18-19th c.

Tinling

WILLIAMS, G.H. 'The Tinling family;, *H.F.H.* **12**(2), 1985, 67-9; **12**(3), 1985, 176-8; **12**(4), 1986, 232-4; **13**(1), 1986, 6-8; **13**(2), 1986, 102-6; **13**(3), 1986, 158-63; **13**(4), 1987, 254-61; **14**(1), 1987, 11-14; **14**(2), 1987, 84-7; **14**(3), 1987, 151-3; **15**(2), 1988, 89-91; **15**(3), 1988, 197-9; **15**(4), 1989, 284-8. Pt.1. The family in Minorca. Pt.2. John Tinling. Pt.3. Rear-Admiral Edward Burnaby Tinling. Pt.4. Isaac Pattison Tinling. Pt.5. Charles Ashley Stubbs Tinling. Pt.6. William Tinling. Pt.7. Arthur Henry Williams. Pt.8. Johanna Greene. Pt.9. Sir David Tinling-Widdrington. Pt.10. Serendipity. Pt.11. The Thesiger-Tinling marriage. Pt.12. The first Lord and Lady Chelmsford.
WILLIAMS, G.H. 'The Tinlings of Minorca', *Fareham past and present* **10**, 1969, 8-11 & **11**, 1970, 3-6. 18th c. Fareham family.

Trattle

L., A.S. 'Trattle of Newport, Isle of Wight', *M.G.H.* 4th series **3**, 1910, 297. Pedigree, 17th c.

Turton

CHINNECK, ANTONY. 'Turton trails', *H.F.H.* **13**(2), 1986, 121-4 & **13**(3), 1986, 176-9. 19th c.

Tyrrell

TYRRELL, JOSEPH HENRY. *A genealogical history of the Tyrrells ...* Phillimore, 1980. Originally privately printed, 1909. Includes pedigrees, medieval-19th c., of Essex, Hampshire and Ireland.

Urry

URRY, R.R. 'The Urry family', *I.O.W.F.H.S.* **20**, 1991, 28-9; **21**, 1991, 34-5; **22**, 1991, 22-3; **23**, 1991, 33. 17-19th c., of the Isle of Wight.

Uvedale

GOWER, GRANVILLE LEVESON. *Notices of the family of Uvedale of Titsey, Surrey, and Wickham, Hants.* Cox & Wyman, 1865. Reprinted from *Surrey Archaeological Collections,* **3**, 1865, 63-192. Includes pedigree, 14-17th c.

Vaughan
See Sewell

Vignolles
See Gignoux

Vincent
See Wyeth

Vining
EVANS, CHARLES. 'The Vining family of Newport and Portsmouth', *F.H.J.S.E.H.G.S.* 1(5), 1975, 91-3. 17-18th c.

Wadham
'All Wadham burials from the commencement of registers to 1858, extracted from the Isle of Wight burial index ... ', *H.F.H.* 7(4), 1981, 130-31.

Waight
WAIGHT, STAN. 'The poor little Waights of Eling', *H.F.H.* 19(3), 1992, 172-4. Waight family, 17-18th c.

Wake
WILLIAMS, C.L. SINCLAIR. 'The eponymous tenants of The Wakes, Selborne', *Section newsletters ... [Hampshire Field Club]* 4, 1985, 3-4. Wake family, 13-18th c.

WILLIAMS, C.L. SINCLAIR. 'The Wake family of Selborne and the Solent', *H.F.H.* 9(2), 1982, 50-53. Medieval-18th c.

Wakefield
See Whitaker

Walcot
WALCOT, N.J. 'The Walcots of South East Hampshire', *F.H.J.S.E.H.G.S.* 1(1), 1974, 11-13. Includes pedigree, 18th c.

Wallop
WATNEY, VERNON JAMES. *The Wallop family and their ancestry.* 4 vols. Oxford: John Johnson, 1928. Includes no less than 1,063 pedigrees, medieval-20th c.

Warneford
WARNEFORD, FRANCIS E., & McDOUGALL, ELISABETH. *An English family through eight centuries: the Warnefords.* Henfield, Sussex: the author, 1991. 12-19th c., includes deed abstracts.

Wassell
'The Wassell family', *Fareham past and present* 4(1), 1992, 37-9; 4(2), 1992, 14-16; 4(3), 1992, 27-8 & 4(4), 1993, 29-30. 19-20th c.

Watts
BULL, WILLIAM. 'Material for a history of the Watts family of Southampton', *Notes and queries* 12th series 11, 1916, 101, 161-3 & 224-6. See also 277. 17-18th c.

Wavell
PINE, L.G. 'The house of Wavell', *Genealogical quarterly* 19(4), 1953, 177-82; 20, 1953, 38-41, 83-9 & 127-34.

Webster
WEBSTER, MARTYN. 'Webster family's island links span 300 years', *H.F.H.* 15(4), 198, 261-4. Isle of Wight; 17-20th c.

WEBSTER, M.C. 'The Webster family of Yarmouth', *I.O.W.F.H.S.* 10, 1988, 1-3. 18-19th c.

Weekes
See Mason

Whitaker
WHITAKER, ROBERT SANDERSON. *Whitaker of Hesley Hall, Grayshott Hall, Pylewell Park and Palermo, being some family records ...* Mitchell Hughes and Clarke, 1907. Hesley Hall, Yorkshire; Grayshott Hall and Pylewell Park, Hampshire, and Palermo, Italy. Includes pedigrees, medievel-19th c., with wills, monumental inscriptions, parish register extracts, *etc.,* concerning the Whitaker, Ingham, Fearnley, Sanderson, Blakiston, Jeans, Wakefield and Bennett families, medieval-19th c.

White
CLUTTERBUCK, R.H. 'The Whites of Selborne, Fyfield and Abbott's Ann', *H.N.Q.* 7, 1893, 74-106. 18th c.

GARDINER, LINDA. 'Gilbert White of Selborne', *P.P.H.F.C.* 4, 1898-1903, 205-17. Includes pedigree of White, 17-18th c.

'White or Whyte family, County Hants', *H.N.Q.* 2, 1884, 126-9. Mainly 16th c.

See also Whyte

Whitlock

ALLEN, MURIEL D. 'Ingredients for success', *H.F.H.* **10**(2), 1983, 65-70. Whitlock family; includes pedigree, 19-20th c.

Whyte

CURTIS, HENRY J. *Pedigrees of Whyte or White, of Farnham, Co.Surrey; Aldershot, South Warnborough, and Basingstoke, Co.Hants., and Hutton, Co.Essex, and a note on the Yateley cup.* The author, 1936. Reprinted from *Notes and queries* **171**, 1936, 110-16, 128-31, 146-51, 164-8 & 182-7. See also 395. 15-19th c.
See also White

Williams

WILLIAMS, G.H. 'A Williams family in Indian military service and later', *H.F.H.* **3**(4), 1977, 66-7. 18-20th c.

Willoughby

GREENWOOD, ISAAC J. 'Willoughby of London, Hampshire, and of Charlestown, New England', *M.G.H.* 2nd series **3**, 1890, 393-4. 16-17th c.

Windebank

VARILONE, BERYL. 'Digging up the Windebanks', *H.F.H.* **12**(3), 1985, 138-40. See also **12**(4), 1986, 293. Includes pedigree, 18-19th c.
WINDEBANK, RUTH. 'Twigs of the Windebank tree', *H.F.H.* **12**(1), 1985, 210-21. General.

Wither

BIGG-WITHER, REGINALD F. *Materials for a history of the Wither family.* Winchester: Warren & Son, 1907. 12-19th c., of Lancashire, Hampshire, *etc.* Includes wills, parish register extracts, pedigrees, *etc.*

Woodford

'Isle of Wight marriage card index: Woodford references', *H.F.H.* **7**, 1980-81, 21-2 & 107. 16-18th c.

Worsley

'The Worsleys of the Isle of Wight', in JAMES, E. BOUCHER. *Letters archaeological and historical relating to the Isle of Wight.* Henry Frowde, 1896, v.1, 481-90. 16-18th c.

Wright

See Symonds

Wyeth

'Wyeth and Vincent family bible', *M.G.H.* 5th series **8**, 1932-4, 331-2. Of Hampshire and Devon; 18th c. Also includes entries for Cragg.

Wylkyns

See Nenge

Wyndham

'Memoranda relating to the family of Wyndham of Norrington, of Salisbury, and of Dinton, Co.Wilts., of Hawkchurch, Co.Dorset, and of Eversley, Co.Hants., *etc.,* 1609-1753', *M.G.H.* 2nd series **4**, 1892, 36-8, 54-6 & 77-80. From a diary.

Yelf

FAISH, A.N. *Printer's pride: the house of Yelf at Newport, Isle of Wight, 1816-1966.* Newport: Yelf Brothers, 1967. Yelf family.

Young

YOUNG, SIDNEY. *A history of the families of Young and Goodall (Isle of Wight).* Geo. Barber, 1913. Includes folded pedigrees, 16-19th c.

Zimmerman

HARDING, J. COOPER. 'Zimmerman: a fine old German name', *H.F.H.* **13**(3), 1986, 168-71. 19th c.

7. PARISH REGISTERS AND OTHER RECORDS OF BIRTHS, MARRIAGES AND DEATHS

A. *General*

Registers of births, marriages and deaths are normally one of the first sources to be consulted by genealogists. A wide variety of guides to them are available, and many are listed in my *English genealogy: an introductory bibliography,* section 9, which should be used in conjunction with the list which follows. Church of England registers in Hampshire are listed in:

McGOWAN, ALAN. *Parish registers of Hampshire and the Isle of Wight.* Winchester: Hampshire Record Office, 1991.

See also:

FEARON, WILLIAM ANDREW E., & WILLIAMS, JOHN FOSTER., ed. *The parish registers and parochial documents in the Archdeaconry of Winchester.* Winchester: Warren, 1909. General discussion, with an extensive list; also includes list of non-parochial registers.

The guide to *Southampton records* listed above, section 2, includes a list of parish registers held at Southampton Record Office.

For the registers of nonconformist denominations, reference must still be made to the otherwise superseded:

HAMPSHIRE ARCHIVISTS GROUP. *Parish and nonconformist registers of Hampshire and the Isle of Wight.* [ ]: the Group, 1984.

Hampshire non-parochial registers are also listed in:

KIDD, R.A. 'Non-parochial registers deposited at the Public Record Office (Class RG4)', *H.F.H.* 3(3), 1976, 68-70.

SLOGGETT, BRIAN L. 'Non-parochial registers in Hampshire before 1837', *H.F.H.* 8(3), 1981, 98-101. Lists those at both the Public Record Office, and elsewhere.

For the Isle of Wight, see:

FEW, J. 'Transcripts', *I.O.W.F.H.S.* 15, 1989, 15-16. Lists parish register transcripts for the Isle of Wight.

Hampshire's marriage registers have been indexed by computer; a brief discussion of this index is in:

KNOTT, DEREK. 'Mission accomplished: H.G.S. computerised marriage index (1538-1837)', *H.F.H.* 19(4), 1993, 241-2.

Allegations for marriage licences formerly in the Winchester Diocesan Registry are listed in a number of works:

WILLIS, ARTHUR J. *Hampshire marriage licences, 1607-1640, from records in the Diocesan Registry, Winchester.* Folkestone: the author; Research Publishing, 1960.

WILLIS, ARTHUR J. *Hampshire marriage licences 1669-1680, from records in the Diocesan registry, Winchester.* Folkestone: A.J. Willis, 1963.

MOENS, WILLIAM J.C., ed. *Hampshire allegations for marriage licences granted by the Bishop of Winchester, 1689 to 1837.* 2 vols. Publications of the Harleian Society 35-6. 1893. Re-issued on microfiche. Winchester: Hampshire Record Office, 1992.

WILLIS, ARTHUR J., ed. *Hampshire marriage allegations, 1689-1837: supplement to the Harleian Society's volumes 35 and 36.* Society of Genealogists, 1962. Reprinted from *Genealogist's magazine* 14, 1962-4, 48-55 & 73-82. Lists 275 additional allegations.

A fair number of Hampshire licences were also granted in the Diocese of Salisbury. See:

NEVILL, EDMUND. 'Marriage licences of Salisbury', *Genealogist* N.S. 24-37, 1908-21, *passim.*

For some early marriages, see:

'Some early Hampshire marriages', *Genealogical quarterly* 8, 1939-40, 3-32 & 176-81.

The personal advertisements in old newspapers can provide much useful information. For an example, see:

SMITH, VALERIE. 'One day in 1888', *H.F.H.* 20(2), 1993, 97-9. Births, marriages and deaths from the *Hampshire Independent,* for 22nd December 1888.

For war casualties, see:

LOWE, J. 'Island war casualties, 1916', *I.O.W.F.H.S.* 23, 1991, 34-6. Extracts from the *Isle of Wight Times.*

Stray entries from parish registers in Essex, London, Surrey and Berkshire are noted in:

'Hampshire strays in Essex', *H.F.H.* 11(2), 1984, 80-82. Brief list from parish registers.

McGOWAN, ALAN. 'Fleet marriages, 1699-1754', *H.F.H.* 12(2), 77. Hampshire marriages in London.

McGOWAN, ALAN. 'Hampshire strays in Surrey', *H.F.H.* 12(1), 1985, 42-44; 12(3), 1985, 149-51.

SMALLBONE, K. 'Hampshire entries in the Thatcham marriage registers, 1561-1840', *H.F.H.* **5**(2), 1978, 47-8 & 63-5. Thatcham is in Berkshire.

The *Hampshire family historian* carries many similar lists of 'strays'.

For an interesting, but brief, study of the interval between birth and baptism in Hampshire nonconformist registers, see: SLOGGETT, BRIAN. 'Birth or baptism? Nonconformists', *H.F.H.* **8**(2), 1981, 38-40.

B. *Church of England Registers*

Aldershot
STOOKS, C.D. 'Marriages at Aldershot, 1590 to 1812', in PHILLIMORE, W.P.W., & ANDREWS, S., eds. *H.P.R.M.* **2**. *P.P.R.S.* **20**. Phillimore & Co., 1900, 109-24.

Alverstoke
See section 8B

Amport
GRUGGEN, G.S., ed. 'Marriages at Amport, 1665 to 1812', in PHILLIMORE, W.P.W., & ANDREWS, S., eds. *H.P.R.M.* **2**. *P.P.R.S.* **20**. Phillimore & Co., 1900, 129-44.

Andover
BENNETT, ARTHUR C. 'The parish registers of Andover', *Test Valley and border anthology* **10**, 1976, 225-31. Lists numerous volumes, 1588 to date.

Ashe
THOYTS, F.W. *A history of Esse or Ashe, Hampshire.* William Clowes and Sons, 1888. Includes an edition of the parish register, 1606-1887.

Basing
ANDREWS, S. 'Marriages at Basing, 1655 to 1812', in PHILLIMORE, W.P.W., & STOOKS, C.D., eds. *H.P.R.M.* **3**. *P.P.R.S.* **32**. Phillimore & Co., 1902, 89-103.

Basingstoke
'Marriages at Basingstoke, 1638 to 1812', in PHILLIMORE, W.P.W., & ANDREWS, S., eds. *H.P.R.M.* **5**. *P.P.R.S.* **38**. Phillimore, 1903, 73-136.

Baughurst
ANDREWS, S., ed. 'Marriages at Baughurst, 1678 to 1812', in PHILLIMORE, W.P.W., & ANDREWS, S., eds. *H.P.R.M.* **5**. *P.P.R.S.* **38**. Phillimore, 1903, 137-47.

SMALLBONE, KEN. 'Baptisms recorded at Baughurst, Hants., 1813-1837', *H.F.H.* **9**(2), 1982, 69-71.

Bentley
ANDREWS, S., ed. 'Marriages at Bentley, 1541 to 1812', in PHILLIMORE, W.P.W., ANDREWS, S. & WILLIAMS, J.F., eds. *H.P.R.M.* **9**. *P.P.R.S.* **68**. Phillimore, 1907, 115-37.

Bentworth
CAZALET, W.G., ed. 'Marriages at Bentworth, 1603 to 1837', in PHILLIMORE, W.P.W., ed. *H.P.R.M.* **11**. *P.P.R.S.* **81**. Phillimore, 1909, 81-94.

Bitterne
HOLT, JOAN M. 'Bitterne strays', *H.F.H.* **18**(2), 1991, 144-5. List, 1853-80.

Boldre
WILLIAMS, J.F., ed. 'Marriages at Boldre, 1596 to 1813', in PHILLIMORE, W.P.W., ed. *H.P.R.M.* **11**. *P.P.R.S.* **81**. Phillimore & Co., 1909, 95-176.

Botley
COOPER, MICHAEL KENNETH. 'Hampshire parishes no.3: Botley', *H.F.H.* **3**(1), 1975, 10-12. Includes list of parish registers with some brief extracts.

Brading
OGLANDER, J.H., ed. 'Marriages at Brading, I.W., 1547 to 1812', in PHILLIMORE, W.P.W., OGLANDER, J.H., & ANDREWS, S., eds. *Hampshire parish registers: Isle of Wight marriages* **12**. *P.P.R.S.* **144**. Phillimore & Co., 1910, 1-65.

Bramley
ANDREWS, S., ed. 'Marriages at Bramley, 1580 to 1812', in PHILLIMORE, W.P.W., ed. *H.P.R.M.* **1**. *P.P.R.S.* **8**. Phillimore, 1899, 85-97.

Brightstone
See Newchurch

Bullington

COURTNEY, S.T., ed. 'Marriages at Bullington, 1755 to 1812', in PHILLIMORE, W.P.W., ed. *H.P.R.M.* 1. *P.P.R.S.* 8. Phillimore, 1899, 81-2.

MADGE, F.T., ed. 'Marriages at Bullington and Tufton, 1754 to 1812', in PHILLIMORE, W.P.W., ANDREWS, S., & WILLIAMS, J.F., eds. *H.P.R.M.* 8. *P.P.R.S.* 67. Phillimore & Co., 1906, 101. Additional entries to those recorded in *H.P.R.M.* 1.

Burghclere

WILLIAMS, J.F., ed. 'Marriages at Burghclere, 1559 to 1812', in PHILLIMORE, W.P.W., ANDREWS, S., & WILLIAMS, J.F., eds. *H.P.R.M.* 8. *P.P.R.S.* 67. Phillimore & Co., 1906, 13-35.

Calbourne

ANDREWS, S. ed. 'Marriages at Calbourne, I.W., 1559 to 1812', in PHILLIMORE, W.P.W., OGLANDER, J.H., & ANDREWS, S., eds. *Hampshire parish registers: Isle of Wight marriages* 12. *P.P.R.S.* 144. Phillimore, 1910, 67-92.

Carisbrooke

'Registers of the parish church of Carisbrook in the Isle of Wight', in HISTORICAL MANUSCRIPTS COMMISSION. *Sixth report ...* C.1745. H.M.S.O., 1877, 499-500. General description.
See also Newchurch

Christchurch

CLASBY, VALERIE. 'Burials at the Priory Church of Christchurch', *H.F.H.* 14(1), 1987, 9-10. 'Stray' burials, mainly 1795-1804.
VICK, DOUGLAS. 'Christchurch marriages', *H.F.H.* 13(1), 1986, 35-6. Discussion.

Church Oakley

ANDREWS, S., ed. 'Marriages at Church Oakley, 1565 to 1812', in PHILLIMORE, W.P.W., & STOOKS, C.D., eds. *H.P.R.M.* 3. *P.P.R.S.* 32. Phillimore & Co., 1902, 51-8.

Cliddesden

ANDREWS, S., ed. 'Marriages at Cliddesden, 1636 to 1812', in PHILLIMORE, W.P.W. *H.P.R.M.* 1. *P.P.R.S.* 8. Phillimore, 1899, 143-54.

Colemore

HERVEY, THOMAS, ed. *The parish registers of Priors Dean and Colmer, to the end of the year of Our Lord, 1812.* Colmer: the editor, 1886, Covers 1538-1812.
HERVEY, THOMAS. *Index to the parish registers of Colmer and Priors Dean, in the County of Hants., A.D. 1813-1892.* Colmer: privately printed, 1893.

Combe

PHILLIMORE, W.P.W., ed. 'Marriages at Coombe, 1560 to 1812', in PHILLIMORE, W.P.W., & ANDREWS, S., eds. *H.P.R.M.* 2. *P.P.R.S.* 20. Phillimore, 1900, 19-26.

Crawley

PLEDGE, F.W., ed. 'Marriages at Crawley, 1675 to 1812', in PHILLIMORE, W.P.W., ed. *H.P.R.M.* 11. *P.P.R.S.* 81. Phillimore & Co., 1909, 43-50.

Crondall

STOOKS, C.D., ed. 'Marriages at Crondall, 1576 to 1812', in PHILLIMORE, W.P.W., & CHITTY, HERBERT, eds. *H.P.R.M.* 4. *P.P.R.S.* 34. Phillimore & Co., 1902, 115-56.

Deane

LANG, W.D.F., ed. 'Marriages at Deane, 1679 to 1812', in PHILLIMORE, W.P.W., ed. *H.P.R.M.* 1. *P.P.R.S.* 8. Phillimore, 1899, 117-23.

Dogmersfield

KNIGHT, F.H.G., ed. 'Marriages at Dogmersfield, 1695 to 1812', in PHILLIMORE, W.P.W., & STOOKS, C.D., eds. *H.P.R.M.* 3. *P.P.R.S.* 32. Phillimore & Co., 1902, 105-12.

Dummer

ANDREWS, S. 'Marriages at Dummer, 1541 to 1812', in PHILLIMORE, W.P.W., ed. *H.P.R.M.* 1. *P.P.R.S.* 8. Phillimore & Co., 1899, 99-110.

East Meon

GARD, JEAN. '19th century record of deaths in East Meon', *Petersfield Area Historical Society bulletin* 4(5), 1993, 17-18. Description of a private list of deaths, 1832-62.

Eastrop

ANDREWS, S., ed 'Marriages at Eastrop, 1759 to 1807', in PHILLIMORE, W.P.W., & ANDREWS, S., eds. *H.P.R.M.* **5**. *P.P.R.S.* **38**. Phillimore, 1903, 149-50.

East Wellow

EPSOM, CHARLES W. *Index to the registers of baptisms, marriages, & burials of the parish of Wellow, in the counties of Southampton and Wiltshire, with an appendix containing an index to briefs collected at Wellow, lists of vicars and churchwardens, and other matter.* Eyre & Spottiswoode, 1889.

East Woodhay

WILLIAMS, J.F., ed. 'Marriages at East Woodhay, 1618 to 1812', in PHILLIMORE, W.P.W., ANDREWS, S., & WILLIAMS, J.F., eds. *H.P.R.M.* **9**. *P.P.R.S.* **68**. Phillimore & Co., 1907, 21-48.

East Worldham

FERGUSON, V. *Registers of East Worldham, West Worldham and Hartley Mauditt.* Farnham: E.W. Langham, 1942. 17-19th c.

Elvetham

GILL, W., ed. 'Marriages at Elvetham, 1639 to 1812', in PHILLIMORE, W.P.W., & STOOKS, C.D., eds. *H.P.R.M.* **3**. *P.P.R.S.* **32**. Phillimore & Co., 1902, 71-87.

FORD, MICHAEL. '[Elvetham parish register, 1654-7]', *H.F.H.* **13**(1), 1986, 63-5. Transcript of marriage entries.

FORD, MICHAEL. '[Extracts from Elvetham parish register, 1713-14]', *H.F.H.* **14**(4), 1988, 272-3. Births, marriages, and burials, including some from Hartley Wintney.

Eversley

STOOKS, C.D., ed. 'Marriages at Eversley, 1559 to 1812', in PHILLIMORE, W.P.W., & STOOKS, C.D., eds. *H.P.R.M.* **3**. *P.P.R.S.* **32**. Phillimore & Co., 1902, 19-41.

Ewhurst

ANDREWS, S., ed. 'Marriages at Ewhurst, 1682 to 1823', in PHILLIMORE, W.P.W., ANDREWS, S., & WILLIAMS, J.F., eds. *H.P.R.M.* **8**. *P.P.R.S.* **67**. Phillimore & Co., 1906, 37-8.

Faccombe

PHILLIMORE, W.P.W., & HARDING. F.H., eds. 'Marriages at Faccombe, 1586 to 1812', in PHILLIMORE, W.P.W., & ANDREWS, S., eds. *H.P.R.M.* **2**. *P.P.R.S.* **20**. Phillimore & Co., 1900, 1-11.

Farnborough

STOOKS, C.D., ed. 'Marriages at Farnborough, 1584 to 1812 in PHILLIMORE, W.P.W., & STOOKS, C.D., eds. *H.P.R.M.* **3**. *P.P.R.S.* **32**. Phillimore & Co., 1902, 113-27.

Freshwater

ROBERTSON, A.J., ed. 'Marriages at Freshwater, I.W., 1559 to 1812', in PHILLIMORE, W.P.W., OGLANDER, J.H., & ANDREWS, S., eds. *Hampshire parish registers: Isle of Wight marriages* **12**. *P.P.R.S.* **144**. Phillimore & Co., 1910, 93-123.

MOENS, W.J.C. 'Freshwater registers', *M.G.H.* 3rd series **3**, 1900, 66-71 & 109-18. 16-19th c. extracts; also includes will of Mr. Culm, 1764, and list of rectors, 1648-1791.

Gosport

BUGDEN, ERIC. 'Three fascinating registers: Holy Trinity, Gosport, registers in the early 1700's', *H.F.H.* **19**(1), 1992, 30-31. Brief discussion.

Hannington

WILLIAMS, J.F., ed. 'Marriages at Hannington, 1768 to 1837', in PHILLIMORE, W.P.W., ed. *H.P.R.M.* **11**. *P.P.R.S.* **81**. Phillimore & Co., 1909, 39-42.

Hartley Mauditt

See East Worldham

Hartley Wespall

ANDREWS, S., ed. 'Marriages at Hartley Wespall, 1558 to 1812', in PHILLIMORE, W.P.W., ANDREWS, S., & WILLIAMS, J.F., eds. *H.P.R.M.* **9**. *P.P.R.S.* **68**. Phillimore & Co., 1907, 67-78.

Hartley Wintney

STOOKS, C.D. 'Marriages at Hartley Wintney, 1658 to 1812', in PHILLIMORE, W.P.W., & STOOKS, C.D., eds. *H.P.R.M.* **3**. *P.P.R.S.* **32**. Phillimore & Co., 1902, 129-43.

See also Elvetham

44

Heckfield

ANDREWS, S., ed. 'Marriages at Heckfield, 1538 to 1812', in PHILLIMORE, W.P.W., & ANDREWS, S., eds. *H.P.R.M.* **6.** *P.P.R.S.* **40.** Phillimore & Co., 1904, 101-37.

Herriard

ANDREWS, S., ed. 'Marriages at Herriard, 1701 to 1812', in PHILLIMORE, W.P.W., ANDREWS, S., & WILLIAMS, J.F., eds. *H.P.R.M.* **8.** *P.P.R.S.* **67.** Phillimore & Co., 1906, 93-9.

Highclere

WILLIAMS, J.F., ed. 'Marriages at Highclere, 1656 to 1813', in PHILLIMORE, W.P.W., ANDREWS, S., & WILLIAMS, J.F., eds. *H.P.R.M.* **8.** *P.P.R.S.* **67.** Phillimore & Co., 1906, 1-12.

Houghton

BOYCE, EDWARD JACOB. *A history of parochial registers, with copious notes, and with illustrations from those of Houghton, Hants., explanatory documents containing information of both special and general interest.* Winchester: Warren and Son; London: Simpkin & Co., 1895.

Hunton

MADGE, F.F., ed. 'Marriages at Hunton, 1575 to 1812', in PHILLIMORE, W.P.W., ANDREWS, S., & WILLIAMS, J.F., eds. *H.P.R.M.* **9.** *P.P.R.S.* **68.** Phillimore & Co., 1907, 15-20.

Hurstbourne Priors

ANDREWS, S., ed. 'Marriages at Hurstbourne Priors, 1604 to 1812', in PHILLIMORE, W.P.W., ed. *H.P.R.M.* **1.** *P.P.R.S.* **8.** Phillimore, 1899, 69-80.

Hurstbourne Tarrant

PHILLIMORE, W.P.W., ed. 'Marriages at Hurstbourne Tarrant, 1546 to 1812', in PHILLIMORE, W.P.W., ed. *H.P.R.M.* **1.** *P.P.R.S.* **8.** Phillimore & Co., 1899, 19-48.

Isle of Wight

SEILES, MARY. 'Strays found in Isle of Wight parish registers', *H.F.H.* **2**(4), 1975, 66; **3**(1), 1976, 23-4 & 40-41; **3**(3), 1976, 84; **4**(3), 1977, 73-4; **4**(4), 1978, 100-102; **5**(2), 1978, 52; **6**(1), 1979, 12-13.
See also under names of particular parishes

Kings Somborne

TURNBULL, BARBARA. 'The Kings Somborne parish registers', *Section newsletters [Hampshire Field Club]* **16,** 1991, 17-19. General discussion.

Kings Worthy

MADGE, F.T., & MARSHALL, R.T., eds. 'Marriages at Kingsworthy, 1538 to 1812', in PHILLIMORE, W.P.W., ed. *H.P.R.M.* **11.** *P.P.R.S.* **81.** Phillimore & Co., 1909, 51-63.

Knights Enham

CLUTTERBUCK, R.H., & COLES, E.T., eds. 'Marriages at Knights Elmham, 1683 to 1812', in PHILLIMORE, W.P.W., ed. *H.P.R.M.* **1.** *P.P.R.S.* **8.** Phillimore, 1899, 9-12.

Laverstoke

WILLIAMS, S., ed. 'Marriages at Laverstoke, 1657 to 1811', in PHILLIMORE, W.P.W., ANDREWS, S., & WILLIAMS, J.F., eds. *H.P.R.M.* **9.** *P.P.R.S.* **68.** Phillimore & Co., 1907, 85-9.

Linkenholt

PHILLIMORE, W.P.W., & WILLIAMS, S., eds. 'Marriages at Linkenholt, 1579 to 1812', in PHILLIMORE, W.P.W., ANDREWS, S., & WILLIAMS, J.F., eds. *H.P.R.M.* **9.** *P.P.R.S.* **68.** Phillimore & Co., 1907, 79-83.

Litchfield

WILLIAMS, J.F., ed. 'Marriages at Litchfield, 1627 to 1812', in PHILLIMORE, W.P.W., ANDREWS, S., & WILLIAMS, J.F., eds. *H.P.R.M.* **8.** *P.P.R.S.* **67.** Phillimore & Co., 1906, 81-6.

Long Sutton

'Marriages at Long Sutton, 1561 to 1812', in PHILLIMORE, W.P.W., & ANDREWS, S., eds. *H.P.R.M.* **5.** *P.P.R.S.* **38.** Phillimore, 1903, 1-10.

Maplederwell

ANDREWS, S., ed. 'Marriages at Mapledurwell, 1629 to 1812', in PHILLIMORE, W.P.W., ANDREWS, S., & WILLIAMS, J.F., eds. *H.P.R.M.* **9.** *P.P.R.S.* **68.** Phillimore & Co., 1907, 9-13.

Michelmersh

G., G.N. 'Michelmersh parish register', *H.N.Q.* **9,** 1898, 172-5. Discussion.

Milford

BROWN, A.W.W. 'Burial records, 1594-1691; memorials inside Milford church; Baptist Chapel graves', *Milford-on-Sea Record Society: an occasional magazine* 3(3), 1925, 3-58. Transcript of the parish register, with memorial inscriptions, *etc.*

SEARS, F.W. 'The transcription of the first two volumes of the Milford registers', *Milford-on-Sea Record Society: an occasional magazine* 5(6), 1955, 38-62. General description; *not* a transcript.

Monxton

CLUTTERBUCK, R.H., & HOPKINS, E.L., eds. 'Marriages at Monxton, 1716 to 1812', in PHILLIMORE, W.P.W., ed. *H.P.R.M.* **1.** *P.P.R.S.* **8.** Phillimore, 1899, 13-18.

Nately Scures

ANDREWS, S., ed. 'Marriages at Nately Scures, 1684 to 1812', in PHILLIMORE, W.P.W., ed. *H.P.R.M.* **11.** *P.P.R.S.* **81.** Phillimore & Co., 1909, 65-9.

New Alresford

MUNDY, MURIEL. 'Grave remarks', *H.F.H.* 14(1), 1987, 30-33. Notes on transcribing the New Alresford parish register, with brief extracts.

Newchurch

'The parish registers of Newchurch, Carisbrook, Niton and Brixton', in JAMES, E. BOUCHER. *Letters archaeological and historical relating to the Isle of Wight.* Henry Frowde, 1896, v.1, 508-15. General discussion. 'Brixton' is actually Brightstone.

Newnham

ANDREWS, S., ed. 'Marriages at Newnham, 1754 to 1812', in PHILLIMORE, W.P.W., ANDREWS, S., & WILLIAMS, J.F., eds. *H.P.R.M.* **8.** *P.P.R.S.* **67.** Phillimore & Co., 1906, 87-91.

Newport

PHILLIMORE, W.P.W., & ANDREWS, S., eds. *Hampshire parish registers: Isle of Wight marriages (second part): vol.XIV.* P.P.R.S. **176.** Phillimore & Co., 1912. Marriages at Newport, 1541 to 1837.

ANDREWS, S. 'Note on the parish register of Newport, Isle of Wight', *Journal of the British Archaeological Association* N.S. **22,** 1916, 81-4. General description of the registers.

Newtown

WILLIAMS, J.F., ed. 'Marriages at Newtown, 1679 to 1812', in PHILLIMORE, W.P.W., ANDREWS, S., & WILLIAMS, J.F., eds. *H.P.R.M.* **8.** *P.P.R.S.* **67.** Phillimore & Co., 1906, 73-80.

Niton

LOCK, CAMPBELL, ed. 'Marriages at Niton, Isle of Wight, 1561 to 1812', in PHILLIMORE, W.P.W., OGLANDER, J.H., & ANDREWS, S., eds. *Hampshire parish registers: Isle of Wight marriages* **12.** *P.P.R.S.* **144.** Phillimore & Co., 1910, 125-36.
See also Newchurch

Northington

See section 14E under Swarraton

North Waltham

ANDREWS, S., ed. 'Marriages at North Waltham, 1654 to 1812', in PHILLIMORE, W.P.W., & STOOKS, C.D., eds. *H.P.R.M.* **3.** *P.P.R.S.* **32.** Phillimore & Co., 1902, 43-50.

Odiham

WINDLE, W.H., ed. 'Marriages at Odiham, 1538 to 1812', in PHILLIMORE, W.P.W., & ANDREWS, S., eds. *H.P.R.M.* **6.** *P.P.R.S.* **40.** Phillimore & Co., 1904, 1-75.

Overton

ANDREWS, SAMUEL, ed. 'Marriages at Overton, 1640 to 1812', in PHILLIMORE, W.P.W., & ANDREWS, S., eds. *H.P.R.M.* **2.** *P.P.R.S.* **20.** Phillimore & Co., 1900, 73-93. See also 145-50.

Penton Mewsey

CLUTTERBUCK, R.H., & DICKINSON, CHARLES R. 'Marriages at Penton Mewsey, 1649 to 1812', in PHILLIMORE, W.P.W., ed. *H.P.R.M.* **1.** *P.P.R.S.* **8.** Phillimore, 1899, 1-8.

Petersfield

WALKER, JILL. 'Civil marriage in Petersfield', *Peterfield Area Historical Society bulletin* 4(2), 1991, 10-14. Brief note; 19-20th c.

Popham

ANDREWS, S., ed 'Marriages at Popham, 1628 to 1812', in PHILLIMORE, W.P.W., ANDREWS, S., & WILLIAMS, J.F., eds. *H.P.R.M.* **9.** *P.P.R.S.* **68.** Phillimore & Co., 1907, 151-2.

Portsea

BUGDEN, E.V. 'Transcribing Portsea parish registers: progress report', *H.F.H.* **12**(1), 1985, 13-15. Discussion.

CLARKE, MIDGE. 'Indexing ... with sidelines', *H.F.H.* **13**(1), 1986, 22-4. Discussion of Portsea register, with some extracts, 1764-72.

BUGDEN, E.V. 'Portsea, St.Mary's: forces baptisms', *H.F.H.* **12**(4), 1986, 257; **13**(1), 1986, 4; **13**(2), 1986, 120; **13**(3), 1986, 166; **13**(4), 1987, 15; **14**(1), 1987, 82-3; **15**(2), 1988, 146. Baptisms, 1813-14, of children whose fathers were in the services.

BUGDEN, E.V. 'Baptisms of children of H.M. forces: St.Mary's, Portsea, 1841-1843 (including St.Paul's Chapel)', *H.F.H.* **15**(2), 1988, 146; **15**(3), 1988, 192; **15**(4), 1989, 264; **16**(1), 1989, 21; **16**(3), 1989, 199; **16**(4), 1990, 256-7.

BUGDEN, ERIC. 'Revealing registers: unusual entries in the baptismal registers of Portsea St.Mary's in the mid-1800's', *H.F.H.* **18**(1), 1991, 43-4. Brief discussion.

Portsmouth

PINHORN, MALCOLM 'The parish registers of Portsmouth, Hampshire, prior to 1837, with a note on the records of cemeteries and burial grounds', *H.F.H.* **3**(1), 1976, 7-9. List.

PHILLIMORE, W.P.W., & EVERITT, A.T., eds. *Hampshire parish registers: marriages, vol.X: St.Thomas a Beckett, Portsmouth, 1653-1700.* P.P.R.S. **80.** Phillimore & Co., 1907.

ANDREWS, S., ed. *Hampshire parish registers: marriages, vol.XV.* P.P.R.S. **199.** Phillimore & Co., 1913. Marriages at St.Thomas à Becket, Portsmouth, 1701-1775.

COLTART, A.H., ed. *Registers of St.Thomas à Becket, Portsmouth: marriages, 1776-1812.* Portsmouth: W.H. Barrell, [1934].

WALCOT, MICHAEL. 'Stray marriages from the registers of St.Thomas à Beckett, Portsmouth, 1776-1812', *H.F.H.* **2**(3), 1975, 40-41; **2**(4), 1975, 57-8; **3**(2), 1976, 42-3; **4**(2), 1977, 39-41.

Preston Candover

ANDREWS, S., ed. 'Marriages at Preston Candover, 1584 to 1812', in PHILLIMORE, W.P.W., ANDREWS, S., & WILLIAMS, J.F., eds. *H.P.R.M.* **9.** *P.P.R.S.* **68.** Phillimore & Co., 1907, 139-49.

Priors Dean

See Colemore

Romsey

LUCE, SIR RICHARD. 'Romsey Abbey registers', *P.P.H.F.C.* **16,** 1947, 8-18. General description; includes a few extracts.

Rotherwick

ANDREWS, S., ed 'Marriages at Rotherwick, 1560 to 1812', in PHILLIMORE, W.P.W., ed. *H.P.R.M.* **11.** *P.P.R.S.* **81.** Phillimore & Co., 1909, 71-80.

Rowner

BRUNE, E.S. PRIDEAUX, ed. 'Marriages at Rowner, 1590 to 1812', in PHILLIMORE, W.P.W., ANDREWS, S., & WILLIAMS, J.F., eds. *H.P.R.M.* **8.** *P.P.R.S.* **67.** Phillimore & Co., 1906, 47-72.

St.Mary Bourne

'Marriages at St.Mary Bourne, 1663 to 1812', in PHILLIMORE, W.P.W., ed. *H.P.R.M.* **1.** *P.P.R.S.* **8.** Phillimore, 1899, 49-68.

Sherborne St.John

CHUTE, D.W., ed. 'Marriages at Sherborne St.John, 1653 to 1812', in PHILLIMORE, W.P.W., & STOOKS, C.D., eds. *H.P.R.M.* **3.** *P.P.R.S.* **32.** Phillimore & Co., 1902, 1-17.

Sherfield upon Loddon

ANDREWS, S., ed. 'Marriages at Sherfield-upon-Loddon, 1574 to 1812', in PHILLIMORE, W.P.W., ANDREWS, S., & WILLIAMS, J.F., eds. *H.P.R.M.* **9.** *P.P.R.S.* **68.** Phillimore & Co., 1907, 49-66.

South Stoneham

LE MAY, K.D. 'Hampshire parishes no.17: South Stoneham', *H.F.H.* **6**(4), 1980, 127-9. Includes lists of common surnames in the parish register.

South Warnborough

STOOKS, C.D., ed. 'Marriages at South Warnborough, 1539 to 1812', in PHILLIMORE, W.P.W., & ANDREWS, S., eds. *H.P.R.M.* **6.** *P.P.R.S.* **40.** Phillimore & Co., 1904, 77-90.

Steventon

ANDREWS, S. 'Marriages at Steventon, 1604 to 1812', in PHILLIMORE, W.P.W., ed. *H.P.R.M.* **1.** *P.P.R.S.* **8.** Phillimore, 1899, 111-16.

Stoke Charity

MADGE, F.T., ed. 'Marriages at Stoke Charity, 1542 to 1812', in PHILLIMORE, W.P.W., ANDREWS, S., & WILLIAMS, J.F., eds. *H.P.R.M.* **9.** *P.P.R.S.* **68.** Phillimore & Co., 1907, 1-8.

Stratfieldsaye

MONRO, H.G., ed. 'Stratfieldsaye marriages, 1539 to 1812', in PHILLIMORE, W.P.W., & ANDREWS, S., eds. *H.P.R.M.* **5.** *P.P.R.S.* **38.** Phillimore & Co., 1903, 11-34.

Stratfield Turgis

ANDREWS, S., ed. 'Marriages at Stratfield Turgis, 1672 to 1812', in PHILLIMORE, W.P.W., & ANDREWS, S., eds. *H.P.R.M.* **6.** *P.P.R.S.* **40.** Phillimore & Co., 1904, 139-44.

Tadley

ANDREWS, S., ed. 'Marriages at Tadley, 1691 to 1812', in PHILLIMORE, W.P.W., & ANDREWS, S., eds. *H.P.R.M.* **6.** *P.P.R.S.* **40.** Phillimore & Co., 1904, 91-100.

Tangley

PHILLIMORE, W.P.W., ed. 'Marriages at Tangley, 1703 to 1812', in PHILLIMORE, W.P.W., & ANDREWS, S., eds. *H.P.R.M.* **2.** *P.P.R.S.* **20.** Phillimore & Co., 1900, 13-18.

Tufton

COURTNEY, S.T., ed. 'Marriages at Tufton, 1754 to 1812', in PHILLIMORE, W.P.W., ed. *H.P.R.M.* **1.** *P.P.R.S.* **8.** Phillimore, 1899, 83-4.
See also Bullington

Twyford

BROOKS, E.M. 'Notes on the first parish register of Twyford', *Section newsletters [Hampshire Field Club]* 1, 1984, 3-4. Brief discussion.

Up Nately

ANDREWS, S. 'Marriages at Up-Nately, 1695 to 1750', in PHILLIMORE, W.P.W., & ANDREWS, S., eds. *H.P.R.M.* **2.** *P.P.R.S.* **20.** Phillimore & Co., 1900, 125-7.

Vernhams Dean

PHILLIMORE, W.P.W., ed. 'Marriages at Vernham, 1607 to 1812', in PHILLIMORE, W.P.W., & ANDREWS, S., eds. *H.P.R.M.* **2.** *P.P.R.S.* **20.** Phillimore & Co., 1900, 27-35.

West Worldham

See East Worldham

Weyhill

ANDREWS, S., ed. 'Marriages at Weyhill, 1564 to 1812', in PHILLIMORE, W.P.W., ed. *H.P.R.M.* **11.** *P.P.R.S.* **81.** Phillimore & Co., 1909, 19-38.

Whitchurch

WILLIAMS, J.F., ed. 'Marriages at Whitchurch, 1605 to 1812', in PHILLIMORE, W.P.W., ANDREWS, S., & WILLIAMS, J.F., eds. *H.P.R.M.* **8.** *P.P.R.S.* **67.** Phillimore & Co., 1906, 103-49.

Whitwell

LOCK, CAMPBELL, ed. 'Marriages at Whitwell, 1699 to 1837', in PHILLIMORE, W.P.W., OGLANDER, J.H., & ANDREWS, S., eds. *Hampshire parish registers: Isle of Wight marriages* 12. *P.P.R.S.* **144.** Phillimore & Co., 1910, 137-44.

Winchester

B[EAZLEY], F.C. 'Lancashire and Cheshire names in Hampshire', *Cheshire sheaf* 3rd series **6,** 1907, 63. Strays from Winchester Cathedral registers, 17-19th c.

Cathedral

'Winchester Cathedral register, 1599 to 1813', in PHILLIMORE, W.P.W., & CHITTY, HERBERT, ed. *H.P.R.M.* **4.** *P.P.R.S.* **34.** Phillimore & Co., 1902, 1-84.

St.Bartholomew

'Marriages at St.Bartholomew, Hyde, Winchester, 1563 to 1837', in COLCHESTER, W.E., ed. *H.P.R.M.* **16.** *P.P.R.S.* **213.** Phillimore & Co., 1914, 135-62.

St.Cross

See Winchester. St.Faith

St.Faith

'Marriages at St.Faith with St.Cross, Winchester, 1674 to 1837', in COLCHESTER, W.E., ed. *H.P.R.M.* **16.** *P.P.R.S.* **213.** Phillimore & Co., 1914, 119-33.

St.Lawrence

CLARK, MISS, ed. 'Marriages at St.Lawrence, Winchester, 1754 to 1812', in PHILLIMORE, W.P.W., & ANDREWS, S., eds. *H.P.R.M.* **5.** *P.P.R.S.* **38.** Phillimore & Co., 1903, 65-71.

St.Maurice

PHILLIMORE, W.P.W., & COLCHESTER, W.E., eds. *Hampshire parish registers: Marriages, vol.XIII.* P.P.R.S. **169.** Phillimore & Co., 1912. Marriages at St.Maurice, Winchester, 1538 to 1837.

St.Michael

CHITTY, MR., & MOBERLY, A.C., eds. 'Marriages at St.Michael in the Soke, Winchester, 1632 to 1812', in PHILLIMORE, W.P.W., & ANDREWS, S., eds. *H.P.R.M.* **5.** *P.P.R.S.* **38.** Phillimore & Co., 1903, 35-64.

St.Peter Cheesehill

'Marriages at St.Peter, Cheesehill, Winchester, 1597 to 1837', in COLCHESTER, W.E., ed. *H.P.R.M.* **16.** *P.P.R.S.* **213.** Phillimore & Co., 1914, 95-117.

St.Swithin

MADGE, F.T., ed. 'St.Swithun-upon-Kingsgate, Winchester: christenings and burials, 1562-1695; marriages 1564-1812', in PHILLIMORE, W.P.W., & CHITTY, HERBERT, eds. *H.P.R.M.* **4.** *P.P.R.S.* **34.** Phillimore & Co., 1902, 85-114.

St.Thomas

'Marriages at St.Thomas with St.Clement, Winchester, 1685 to 1837', in COLCHESTER, W.E., ed. *H.P.R.M.* **16.** *P.P.R.S.* **213.** Phillimore & Co., 1914, 1-93.

LAWES, WIN. 'Military marriages, St.Thomas, Winchester', *H.F.H.* 12(3), 1985, 141; 12(4), 1986, 248; 13(1), 1986, 13; 13(2), 1986, 145; 13(3), 1986, 171. Extracted from the Phillimore volume, 1759-1835.

Winchester College

CHITTY, H., ed. 'Register of the Saint Mary College of Winchester, near Winchester, otherwise called Winchester College', in PHILLIMORE, W.P.W., ed *H.P.R.M.* **11.** *P.P.R.S.* **81.** Phillimore & Co., 1909, 1-17. Includes burials, 1678-1864; baptisms, 1726-1861, and marriages, 1699-1745.

Winchfield

STOOKS, C.D. 'Marriages at Winchfield, 1660-1812', in PHILLIMORE, W.P.W., & STOOKS, C.D., eds. *H.P.R.M.* **3.** *P.P.R.S.* **32.** Phillimore & Co., 1902, 59-70.

Winslade

ANDREWS, S. 'Marriages at Winslade, 1723 to 1812', in PHILLIMORE, W.P.W., & ANDREWS, S., eds. *H.P.R.M.* **2.** *P.P.R.S.* **20.** Phillimore & Co., 1900, 95-107.

Wolverton

ANDREWS, S., ed. 'Marriages at Wolverton, 1717 to 1812', in PHILLIMORE, W.P.W., & WILLIAMS, J.F., eds. *H.P.R.M.* **8.** *P.P.R.S.* **67.** Phillimore & Co., 1906, 39-45.

Wonston

EDWARDS, F. 'The registers of Holy Trinity, Wonston', *H.F.H.* 4(2), 1977, 36-8. Brief description.

WILLIAMS, J.F., ed. 'Marriages at Wonston, 1570 to 1812', in PHILLIMORE, W.P.W., ANDREWS, S., & WILLIAMS, J.F., eds. *H.P.R.M.* **9.** *P.P.R.S.* **68.** Phillimore & Co., 1907, 91-113.

Woodmancott

ANDREWS, S. ed. 'Marriages at Woodmancote, 1772 to 1812', in PHILLIMORE, W.P.W., ANDREWS, S., & WILLIAMS, J.F., eds. *H.P.R.M.* **9.** *P.P.R.S.* **68.** Phillimore & Co., 1907, 153-4.

Wootton St.Lawrence

PHILLIMORE, W.P.W., & WARD, C.S., eds. 'Marriages at Wootton Saint Lawrence, 1560 to 1812', in PHILLIMORE, W.P.W., ed. *H.P.R.M.* **1.** *P.P.R.S.* **8.** Phillimore, 1899, 125-42.

Worting

ANDREWS, S., ed. 'Marriages at Worting, 1604 to 1812', in PHILLIMORE, W.P.W., & ANDREWS, S., eds. *H.P.R.M.* **5.** *P.P.R.S.* **38.** Phillimore & Co., 1903, 151-4.

Yateley

LE MESURIER, J., & STOOKS, C.D., eds. 'Marriages at Yateley, 1636 to 1804', in PHILLIMORE, W.P.W., & ANDREWS, S., eds. *H.P.R.M.* **2.** *P.P.R.S.* **20.** Phillimore & Co., 1900, 37-71. Includes list of other documents in the parish chest.

Yaverland

ANDREWS, S., ed 'Marriages at Yaverland, 1632 to 1812', in PHILLIMORE, W.P.W., OGLANDER, J.H., & ANDREWS, S., eds. *Hampshire parish registers: Isle of Wight marriages* **12**. *P.P.R.S.* **144**. Phillimore & Co., 1910, 145-51.

C. Nonconformist registers

Huguenot

DE GRAVE, J.W. 'Notes on the register of the Walloon church of Southampton, and on the churches of the Channel Islands', *Proceedings of the Huguenot Society of London* **5**, 1894-6, 125-78. Includes some extracts, 16-18th c., but mainly discussion.

GODFRAY, HUMPHREY MARETT, ed. *Registre des baptesmses, mariages et mortz, et jeusnes, de léglise wallonne et des isles de Jersey, Guernesey, Serq, Origny, etc., établie a Southampton par patente du roy Edouard sixe et de la reine Elizabeth.* Publications of the Huguenot Society of London **4**. 1890.

Quaker

DAVIDSON, FLORENCE A.G. 'The Quaker burial grounds at Baughurst', *P.P.H.F.C.* **7**(2), 1915, 40-46. Includes notes on the registers.

Roman Catholic

Diocese of Portsmouth parish registers. Portsmouth: Diocesan Information Office, 1989. List of Roman Catholic registers for Hampshire, Berkshire, and the Channel Islands.

Brambridge

BAIGENT, RICHARD COVENTRY., ed. 'The catholic registers of the Brambridge (afterwards Highbridge) mission in Hampshire, 1766-1869', *Publications of the Catholic Record Society* **27**, 1927, 1-52.

Brockhampton

SCANTLEBURY, ROBERT E., ed. *Hampshire registers, III: the registers and records of Brockhampton (Havant).* Publications of the Catholic Record Society **44**. 1949.

Cowes

See Newport

Gosport

SCANTLEBURY, ROBERT E., ed. *The registers of Gosport and Portsea.* Publications of the

Catholic Record Society **49**. 1955. Gosport, 1759-1834; Portsea, 1794-1847.

Lymington

HANSOM, JOSEPH S., ed. 'The catholic registers of Pylewell House, Lymington, Hampshire, 1805-1840, and Rook Cliff, Milford on Sea, Hampshire, 1813-15', *Publications of the Catholic Record Society* **14**, 1914, 295-312.

Milford

See Lymington

Newport

SCANTLEBURY, R.E., ed. *Isle of Wight registers: Newport, 1792-1887; Cowes, 1796-1856.* Catholic Record Society publications (record series) **59**. 1968. Includes pedigrees of Urry of Sheat, 17-18th c., Browne of Brenchley, Kent, 17-18th c., and Heneage of Hainton, 17-18th c., also much information on the Heneage family.

Portsea

See Gosport

Sopley

KING, JOHN HENRY, & SCANTLEBURY, R.E., eds. 'The registers of Sopley, Hampshire', *Publications of the Catholic Record Society* **43**, 1949, 87-121. Includes monumental inscriptions.

Tichborne

KING, JOHN HENRY. 'Tichborne register and mss. (1785-1837)', *Publications of the Catholic Record Society* **43**, 1949, 168-90. See also index, 191-213.

Winchester

PALMER, RAYMUND, ed. 'The registers of the Catholic mission of Winchester, 1721-1826', *Publications of the Catholic Record Society* **1**, 1905, 148-243.

SCANTLEBURY, ROBERT E., ed. *Hampshire registers, I: the registers and records of Winchester.* Publications of the Catholic Record Society **42**. 1948. This volume includes a continuation of the registers, 1826-55, together with a wide range of other documents, 18-19th c., including monumental inscriptions.

8. MONUMENTAL INSCRIPTIONS

A. *General*

Monumental inscriptions are an important source of genealogical information. Many have been transcribed and published; for an important Hampshire collection, see:

GIBSON, J.S.W. *Monumental inscriptions in sixty Hampshire churches.* Hannington: the author, 1958.

A few Hampshire inscriptions are also included in:

G[UBBINS], E. *Ancient inscriptions in Winchester Cathedral and other places.* Winchester: Warren & Co., 1884. Despite its title, however, this volume is not primarily concerned with Winchester, or, indeed, Hampshire inscriptions, but is rather more general.

Members of the Hampshire Genealogical Society have transcribed inscriptions in numerous graveyards. The Society's collection of transcriptions is listed by parish in:
'Monumental inscription holdings', *H.F.H.* 18(3), 1991, 205-6.

For an article based on this collection, see:
COLPUS, A.C. 'Monumental inscriptions', *H.F.H.* 10(3), 1983, 106-13. Includes a list of common Hampshire surnames recorded in monumental inscriptions, indicating parishes.

Transcripts of monumental inscriptions held in a variety of other repositories are listed in:
COLLINS, F.B. 'The survey of gravestones in Hampshire churchyards', *Hampshire archaeology and local history newsletter* 2(2), 1971, 50-52.

Inscriptions published in a variety of works prior to 1897 are indexed by personal name in:
'An index to some printed monumental inscriptions in Hampshire', *H.N.Q.* 3, 1887, 98-111.

For a guide to the burial places of prominent people, see:
GREENWOOD, DOUGLAS. *Wessex has their bones: who's buried where in Dorset, Hampshire, Wiltshire and the Isle of Wight.* Wimborne: Roy Gascon Associates, 1985.

For indents and hatchments, see respectively:
SADLER, A.G. *The indents of lost memorial brasses in Dorset and Hampshire.* Worthing: the author, 1975. See also appendix, 1979.

SUMMERS, PETER, ed. *Hatchments of Britain, v.7: Cornwall, Devon, Dorset, Gloucestershire, Hampshire, Isle of Wight and Somerset.* Phillimore, 1988.

A brief list of Hampshire inscriptions on Ontario gravestones is given in:
'Hampshire gravestones in Canada', *H.F.H.* 19(4), 1993, 257.

B. *By place*

Abbots Ann
See Wonston

Alverstoke
PARKER, GEORGE. *Alverstoke church inscriptions and parish registers.* Oxford: Reid & Co., 1885.

WILLIAMS, G.H. 'Alverstoke burial grounds', *G.R.* 2, 1972, 22-6. General discussion.

WILLIAMS, G.H. 'Hatchments formerly in Alverstoke church', *G.R.* 8, 1974, 4-9. See also 28.

WILLIAMS, G.H. 'Tombstones in Alverstoke churchyard', *G.R.* 1, 1971, 16-19.

Ashe
'History of Ash and Deane, Hants', *Topographer* 4, 1791, 317-28. Includes inscriptions.

Basing
See Bedhampton and Bentley

Basingstoke
ATTWOOD, J.S. 'Monumental inscriptions at Basingstoke', *H.N.Q.* 2, 1884, 130-48. Extensive list.

Bedhampton
CLARKE, MIDGE. 'Hampshire parishes, no.26: Bedhampton', *H.F.H.* 9(2), 1982, 46-7. Includes notes on inscriptions in the church.

'Monumental inscriptions', *H.F.H.* 6(4), 1980, 132-3. Indexes those at St.Thomas's, Bedhampton, 1704-1976, Bullington, 1702-96, East Dean, 1689-1945, St.Mary's, Old Basing, 1716-1954, North Hayling, 1703-1976, Plaitford, 1772-1974 (Wilts), Tunworth, 1717-1976 and Winslade, 1625-1977.

Bentley

CLARKE, MIDGE. 'Hampshire parishes, no.28: Bentley', *H.F.H.* 9(4), 1983, 130-31. Includes notes on inscriptions.

L., C.E. 'Church notes for Hampshire', *Collectanea topographica et genealogica* 8, 1843, 43-66, 132-9, 210-36 & 369-40. Includes monumental inscriptions from Bentley, Binstead, Dogmersfield, Elvetham, Eversley, South Warnborough, Froyle, Winchfield, Odiham, Basing, Cliddesden, Farley, Wallop, and Sherborne St.John.

Binstead

See Bentley

Bishops Waltham

TREMLETT, M.R. 'Index to monumental inscriptions at Bishops Waltham, list no.9, 1705-1895, with a very few in the 20th c.', *H.F.H.* 6(1), 1979, 5.

Bonchurch

GORDON, JOAN. *Here lyeth: a record of the memorials at the old church of St.Boniface in Bonchurch.* Ventnor & District Local History Society, 1989.

Brading

WHITEHEAD, DR. 'Notes on the church of St.Mary, Brading', *Journal of the British Archaeological Association* N.S. 21, 1915, 321-32. Includes notes on memorials.

Bullington

See Bedhampton

Burghclere

See Highclere

Catherington

COLPUS, A.C. 'Index to surnames from monumental inscriptions ... : Catherington', *H.F.H.* 5(4), 1979, 106-8.

Chalton

See Southsea

Cheriton

COLPUS, A.C. 'Index of surnames recorded from M.I's at Cheriton, Hants', *H.F.H.* 4(4), 1978, 106-7.

Cliddesden

See Bentley

Crondall Hundred

L., C.E. 'Church notes in the Hundred of Crondall, Hampshire', *Collectanea topographica et genealogica* 7, 1842, 211-42. Includes monumental inscriptions.

Deane

See Ashe

Dogmersfield

See Bentley

East Dean

See Bedhampton

Elmfield

'The Great War memorial, St.John's church, Elmfield, Ryde', *I.O.W.F.H.S.* 15, 1989, 17. Lists those commemorated.

Elvetham

See Bentley

Eversley

See Bentley

Farley

See Bentley

Fleet

See Southsea

Froyle

See Bentley

Fyfield

L., C.E. 'Church notes of Hampshire', *Topographer and genealogist* 2, 1853, 306-11. Notes on monumental inscriptions at Fyfield and Thruxton.

Gosport

TALBOT, M., & TALBOT, M.J. 'Plot C, Clayhall Cemetery, Gosport', *H.F.H.* 5(3), 1978, 95-6. Index of monumental inscriptions.

WHITE, D.H. LESLIE. 'Gravestones in St.John's churchyard', *G.R.* 9, 1974, 14-17. General discussion.

Havant

DURDEN, MRS., *et al.* 'M.I's in Havant cemetery', *H.F.H.* 5(2), 1978, 54; 5(3), 1978, 95; 6(1), 1979, 6; 6(2), 1979, 96.

Highclere

L., C.E. 'Church notes of Highclere and Burghclere, Co.Hants;, *Topographer and genealogist* 3, 1858, 400-11. Includes monumental inscriptions, parish register extracts, *etc.*

Hordle

LITTLEDALE, WILLOUGHBY A. ' ... monumental inscriptions in Hordle old church, *Milford-on-Sea Record Society: an occasional magazine* 3(6), 1927, 25-32.

LITTLEDALE, WILLOUGHBY A. 'Monumental inscriptions in Hordle old churchyard, Hants', *M.G.H.* 4th series 1, 1906, 269-74.

Hunton

See Wonston

Hurstbourne Tarrant

PHILLIMORE, W.P.W. 'Monumental inscriptions in Hurstbourne Tarrant church, Hampshire', *M.G.H.* 4th series 1, 1906, 33-4.

Isle of Wight

LEWIS, R.W.M. 'Complete list of the brasses of the Isle of Wight', *Transactions of the Cambridge University Association of Brass Collectors* 2(1), 1892, 2-6.

Lymington

BOSTOCK, CHARLES, & HAPGOOD, EDWARD. *Notes on the parish church, Lymington, and the daughter church of All Saints, and other matters ecclesiastical.* Lymington: Chas. T. King, 1912. Includes monumental inscriptions, list of clergy, churchwardens, *etc.*

Medstead

REEVES, JOHN A. 'Medstead church, Hants: names from headstones dug up in 1966 for use as paving stones', *H.F.H.* 8(4), 1982, 152.

Milford

'Milford church, Hants', *M.G.H.* 2nd series 1, 1886, 115-6. Monumental inscriptions.

Monxton

See Wonston

Newport

'Quaker burial ground', *I.O.W.F.H.S.* 12, 1989, 4. List of names from the Quaker burial ground, Hunnyhill, Newport.

North Baddesley

JEWERS, ARTHUR J. 'Monuments at North Baddesley, Co.Hants', *M.G.H.* 4th series 3, 1910, 64-9. Includes will of Robert Thorne, 1690.

North Hayling

See Bedhampton

Odiham

'Odiham church and brasses', *H.N.Q.* 8, 1896, 6-8.

See also Bentley

Privett

COLPUS, A.C. 'Monumental inscriptions: parish no.10: Privett, 1739-1977', *H.F.H.* 6(2), 1979, 96.

Quarley

See Wonston

Ramsdell

KENT, D., & M. 'Christchurch, Ramsdale (Ramsdell) from 1871', *H.F.H.* 5(4), 1979, 108. Index to monumental inscriptions.

Romsey

SPENCE, C. *An essay descriptive of the Abbey church of Romsey in Hampshire ...* Romsey: J. Lordan, 1841. Includes monumental inscriptions.

WALKER, JUDY. *Romsey Abbey through the centuries.* Pennington: Pendragon Press, 1993. Includes monumental inscriptions, list of abbesses and vicars, *etc.*

Sandown

'Memorial inscriptions, Christchurch, Sandown', *I.O.W.F.H.S.* 24, 1992, 31.

Sherborne St.John

See Bentley

Southampton

DOUCH, ROBERT. *Monuments and memorials in Southampton*. Southampton papers **6**. Southampton: City of Southampton, 1968. Lists statues, monuments, memorials and plaques, with biographical notes.

South Hayling

COLPUS, A.C. 'Index of surnames from M.I's recorded at South Hayling, Hants', *H.F.H.* **4**(3), 1977, 76-8.

Southsea

COLPUS, A.C. 'Index to surnames from M.I's', *H.F.H.* **5**(1), 1978, 14-15. Covers part of Highland Road Cemetery, Southsea, Chalton, 1693-1894, and part of Fleet.
'Index to monumental inscriptions in Highland Road Cemetery, Southsea, part II - from 1854', *H.F.H.* **6**(2), 1979, 58-61.

South Warnborough
See Bentley

Stockbridge

LEWANDOWSKA, LEAH. 'Some notes on the gravestones of old St.Peter's church in Stockbridge', *Test Valley and border anthology* **12**, 1978, 277-84. Only a few inscriptions given.

Stoke Charity
See Wonston

Thruxton
See Fyfield

Tunworth
See Bedhampton

Twyford

HUGHES, MARK H. 'Great energy in a country churchyard', *Hampshire local history and archaeology newsletter* **2**(7-8), 1974, 65-7. Discussion of recording sessions at Twyford, with some inscriptions.

Wallop
See Bentley

Warnford

'Warnford church', *H.N.Q.* **2**, 1884, 17-23. Includes inscriptions in the church.

West Meon

L., C. 'Monuments in Westmeon church and churchyard', *H.N.Q.* **3**, 1887, 10.

Weyhill
See Wonston

Winchester

LONGBOTTOM, F.W. 'Armorial glass in the Great Hall of Winchester', *Coat of arms* N.S., **7**(139), 1988, 44-52.

Cathedral

BLORE, G.H. *Notes on the monuments of Winchester Cathedral ...* Winchester: Friends of Winchester Cathedral, 1935.
CLARENDON, EARL OF, & GALE, SAMUEL. *The history and antiquities of the Cathedral church of Winchester, containing all the inscriptions upon the tombs and monuments, with an account of the bishops, priors, deans, and prebendaries; also the history of Hyde Abbey.* E. Curll, 1725.
MILNER, JOHN. *Milner's historical account of Winchester Cathedral, with supplements ...* 12th ed. Winchester: Robbins & Wheeler, 1840. Includes notes on some inscriptions.
VAUGHAM, JOHN. *Winchester Cathedral: its monuments and memorials.* Selwyn & Blount, 1919.
An historical and critical account of Winchester Cathedral ... extracted from the Rev. Mr. Milner's History and antiquities of Winchester. To which is added a review of its modern monuments. Winchester: Ja. Robbins, 1801. Includes some inscriptions.

St.Maurice

LANGDON, PERCY G. 'The brasses, past and present, of St.Maurice's church, Winchester', *H.N.Q.* **8**, 1896, 96-7.

Winchester College

Inscriptiones Wiccamicae. Oxford: Slatter and Rose, 1885. Epitaphs in the cloisters at Winchester College.

Winchfield
See Bentley

Winslade
See Bedhampton

Wonston

COLPUS, A.C. 'A list of the surnames encountered during recording of M.I's at Wonston, Hants', *H.F.H.* 4(2), 1977, 57-8.

W., H. 'Church notes from Wonston, Stoke Charity, &c., &c.', *Topographer* 5(1), 1821, 1-8. Monumental inscriptions; also from Hunton, Weyhill, Abbots Ann, Monxton and Quarley.

C. *By Family Name*

Barlow

A., M. 'Agatha Barlow', *H.N.Q.* 1, 1883, 43-4. Epitaph, 1595, at Easton.

Bligh

WILLIAMS, G.H. 'The Bligh tomb at Alverstoke', *G.R.* 7, 1973, 19-22. 18-19th c.

Brooke

'Brooke family memorials at Whitchurch', *H.N.Q.* 2, 1884, 42-3. 17th c.

Cheese

See Helyar

Clerk

DICKINSON, NANCY. 'The Clerk and Cole monuments', *Winchester Cathedral record* 37, 1968, 21-5.

Cole

C., H.D. 'The Cole monument in Winchester Cathedral', *H.N.Q.* 3, 1887, 22-3. See also 34. 17th c.
See also Clerk

Complyn

See Prophete

Cromwell

R., J.S. 'Memorial tablets at Hursley', *H.N.Q.* 3, 1887, 31. Cromwell family memorials, 17-18th c.

Curwen

ROSSER, W.H. 'Notes on an incised slab in Brading church, Isle of Wight', in *Transactions of the British Archaeological Association at its second annual congress, held at Winchester, August 1845 ...* Henry G. Bohn, 1846, 315-6. John Curwen, 15th c.

Dillington

'Dillington monumental inscriptions, Newchurch, Isle of Wight', *M.G.H.* 2nd series 1, 1886, 365-7.

Gaveston

W., W.S. 'Remarks on an effigy of a knight in Winchester Cathedral', *Archaeological journal* 15, 1858, 125-36. Probably of Sir Arnold de Gaveston; includes genealogical notes.

Hampton

GREENFIELD, B.W. 'Old Stoke charity: the monumental brasses and heraldry of the allied families of Hampton and Waller in the parish church, with illustrations, pedigrees and descent of the manor', *P.P.H.F.C.* 3, 1894-7, 1-27. Medieval-17th c.

Helyar

R. 'Somerset inscriptions in Hants', *Notes & queries for Somerset & Dorset* 6, 1899, 275-6. Relating to Helyar, Wyndham, Cheese and Pendilton families.

Herbert

SLADE, J.J. 'Monument of a Wiltshire woman in Godshill church', *Wiltshire archaeological magazine* 51, 1945, 174-8. Herbert family; 17th c.

Lisle

WALLER, J.G. 'On the brass of Sir John de Lisle', *Journal of the British Archaeological Association* 3, 1848, 240-42. At Thruxton; 1407.
See also Prophete

Mildmay

'The Mildmay family', *H.N.Q.* 2, 1884, 76-84. Inscriptions, *etc.,* 18-19th c., at Twyford and other places.

Paisy

See Portal

Paulet

CAYLEY, REGINALD A. *An architectural memoir of Old Basing church, Hants ...* Basingstoke: Charles J. Jacob, 1891. Includes 'The armorials and monuments of the Paulet family, Dukes of Bolton and Marquesses of Winchester', by S. James A. Salter.

Pendilton

See Helyar

Portal

NEWMAN, NICHOLAS F. 'Some monuments of
Huguenot interest in Hampshire churches',
*Proceedings of the Huguenot Society of
London* **22**(2), 1972, 173-5. Inscriptions
relating to the Portal family, 18th c., at
Freefolk and the Paisy family, 17-18th c., at
Winchester.

Prophete

BEAUMONT, E. 'Three interesting Hampshire
brasses', *P.P.H.F.C.* **7**(1), 1914, 75-80. Includes
brasses of John Prophete at Ringwood, 1416,
William and Anne Complyn, 1498, at Weeke,
and Sir John Lisle, 1407, at Thruxton.

Wadham

SLADE, J.J. 'Tomb of a Wiltshire woman in
Carisbrooke church', *Wiltshire archaeological
magazine* **51**, 1945, 14-17. Tomb of Lady
Margaret Wadham, 16th c.

'Sir Nicholas Wadham and the tomb of his
widow Margaret in Carisbrooke church', in
JAMES, E. BOUCHER. *Letters archaeological
and historical relating to the Isle of Wight.*
Henry Frowde, 1896, v.1, 437-44. See also
445-8. 16th c.

Waller

See Hampton

White

LANGDON, PERCY G. 'On a palimpsest brass of
Bishop White, at Winchester College, and
brasses of the White family at Southwick',
P.P.H.F.C. **3**, 1894-7, 79-87. 15-17th c.

PAGE-PHILLIPS, J.C. 'A palimpsest inscription at
Aldershot, Hampshire', *Transactions of the
Monumental Brass Society* **10**, 1963, 23-4.
Mary White, 1583.

Wriothesley

GREENFIELD, BENJ. W. 'The Wriothesley tomb
in Titchfield church: its effigial statues and
heraldry', *P.P.H.F.C.* **1**(3), 1889, 65-82.
Includes folded pedigrees, 14-17th c.

Wyndham

See Helyar

9. PROBATE RECORDS

Probate records - wills, inventories,
administration bonds, accounts, *etc.* - are
invaluable sources of genealogical information.
Wills in particular usually list all surviving
children. Most Hampshire wills were proved in
either the Consistory Court of the Diocese of
Winchester, or in the court of the
Archdeaconry of Winchester. A brief guide to
them is provided by:

DUNHILL, R.C. *Wills in the Hampshire Record
Office.* 2nd ed. Winchester: the Office, 1990.

These wills are indexed in:

*Will index (names, occupations, places) 1571-
1858.* Many microfiche. Winchester:
Hampshire Record Office, 1994.

Stray wills left in the Diocesan Registry when
the separate Probate Registry was established
are listed in:

WILLIS, A.J. *Wills, administrations and
inventories with the Winchester Diocesan
records.* Folkestone: the author, 1968. The
'stray' records indexed are mainly Consistory
Court wills, 1617-1640, and Archdeaconry of
Winchester wills, 1617-26.

A list of Hampshire probate inventories held at
the Public Record Office is printed in:

SMITH, V.F. 'Hampshire inventories at the
Public Record Office, London', *Section
newsletters ... [Hampshire Field Club]* **2**,
1984, 2-3.

Associated with the grant of probate was the
appointment of guardians for minors. These
are listed in:

WILLIS, ARTHUR J. *Winchester guardianships
after 1700, from Diocesan records.*
Folkestone: A.J. Willis, 1967. Reprinted, with
an index, from *Genealogist's magazine* **14**,
1962-4, 202-14, 258-66, 283-95, 328-32, 373-82
& 420-25; **15**, 1965-8, 19-26.

Abstracts and studies

A number of collections of probate records for
particular places have been subjected to
detailed study; some have been published in
full. See:

Crondall

HARRIES, JOAN. *Crondall in the time of
Elizabeth I: a study based mainly on the
probate inventories.* Farnham: Farnham
Museum, 1986. General study: few abstracts.

Long Sutton

COLDICOTT, DIANA K. *A Long Sutton miscellany, including a study of the wills (1502-1856) and probate inventories (1558-1709) from the parish of Long Sutton and Well, Hampshire.* The author, 1979. Includes a calendar of the wills, administrations and inventories, 1502-1856.

Newchurch

WILLIAMS, I.L. 'An Isle of Wight community in the 17th century: the evidence of probate inventories', *Hatcher review* 4(33), 1992, 10-29. Detailed study of Newchurch.

Rockbourne

WINSER, ANDREW. *Rockbourne wills of the 17th century.* Rockbourne: A. Winser, 1978. Transcripts of wills and inventories.

Southampton

ROBERTS, EDWARD, & PARKER, KAREN, eds. *Southampton probate inventories, 1447-1575.* 2 vols. S.R.Ser. **34-5.** 1992.

Test Valley

SPAUL, JOHN E.H. 'Early wills and inventories', *Test Valley and border anthology* **11**, 1977, 238-46; **12**, 1978, 259-68; **13**, 1979, 288-98. Will abstracts, 1497-1558.

SPAUL, J.E.H. 'Early wills and inventories 4: wives and widows, 1558', *Test Valley and border anthology* **14**, 1979, 313-24.

Winchester

CITIZEN. 'Winchester benefactions', *H.N.Q.* **1**, 1883, 97-110. Includes many extracts from wills and deeds.

Yateley

Yateley, 1558-1602: transcriptions of wills, admons., and inventories of Yateley. Yateley History Project, 1984.

Probate records for particular individuals have also been published separately. See:

Aslett

ASLETT, BILL. 'The last will and testament of husbandman Aslett', *H.F.H.* **13**(4), 1987, 241-6. Of Selborne, 1638.

Bassett

GALE, MAUREEN. 'A seventeenth-century brickmaker's inventory', *Section newsletters [Hampshire Field Club]* **4**, 1985, 23-4. Probate inventory of Richard Bassett of Laborne, 1636.

Batchelder

BATCHELDER, CHARLES E. 'Batchelder wills', *New England historical and genealogical register* **47**, 1893, 356-7. Wills of Henry Batcheler, 1612, and Elizabeth Bacheler, 1612/13. both of Wymering; also of John Bachler of Beckley, Sussex, 1602.

Brown

SMITH, V.F. 'Shopkeepers, Quakers and Normandy Street, Alton', *Newsletter of the Hampshire Archives Trust,* Winter 1986/7, 29-33. Notes on the probate inventory of Samuel Brown, 1742.

Dennet

See Lane

Dick

See Newman

Dillington

'Dillington wills', *M.G.H.* 2nd series **2**, 1888, 123-5. Of the Isle of Wight.

Drake

'Early wills', *H.N.Q.* **8**, 1896, 118-9. Will of William Drake of Andover, 1524.

Fromond

GUNNER, W.H. 'The will of John Fromond, benefactor to Winchester College', *Archaeological journal* **16**, 1859, 166-73. Of Sparsholt, 1420.

Grove

ASHER, RON. 'Using a will to establish family relationships', *H.F.H.* **3**(2), 1976, 38. Includes will of Henry Grove of Fordingbridge, 1819.

Hamme

REID, J.D. 'Nicholas Hamme of Old Alresford, a Tudor blacksmith', *Section newsletters [Hampshire Field Club]* **4**, 1985, 5-6. Probate inventory, 1557.

Hammond

THOMAS, J.H. 'The contents of a late seventeenth century Hampshire inn', *Hampshire archaeology and local history newsletter* **2**(3), 1972, 1-3. Probate inventory of Henry Hammond of Warnford, 1694.

Jacob

'A sixteenth century will', *H.N.Q.* **4**, 1889, 19-20. Will of Harry Jacob of Breamore, 1573.

Lake

'Will of Sir Richard Lake, chaplain', *Notes and queries for Somerset and Dorset* **8**, 1903, 196-7. 1474; he was chaplain of Breredyng, Isle of Wight.

Lane

HAWKER, ANNE. 'Two Basingstoke wills', *Newsletter [Hampshire Field Club]* **11**, 1979, 39. Discusses wills of Thomas Lane, 1532, and Anne Dennet, 1557.

Ledelmre

GOUGH, H. 'The Tichborne family', *M.G.H.* N.S. **1**, 1874, 287-8. Draft will of Oliver Ledelmre, chantry priest, of Tichborne, 1513.

Littlefield

FRENCH, ELIZABETH. 'Genealogical research in England: Littlefield', *New England historical and genealogical register*, **67**, 1913, 343-8. Wills of the Littlefield family of Titchfield, 17th c., also includes parish register extracts.

Maitland

BODDINGTON, REGINALD STEWART. 'Abstracts of wills', *M.G.H.* 4th series **2**, 1908, 316-7. Includes will of Thomas Maitland of Lymington, 1795.

Martin

MAYO, C.H. 'Last prioress of Wyntney, Hants', *Notes and queries for Somerset and Dorset* **3**, 1893, 55-6. Includes will of Elizabeth Martin of Hartley Wintney.

Montagu

SHIRLEY, EVELYN PHILIP. 'The will, inventory and funeral expenses of James Montagu, Bishop of Winchester, anno 1618', *Archaeologia* **44**, 1871, 393-421.

Newman

ROBERTS, C. 'More from those six sacks', *Fareham past and present* **2**(2), 1973, 16-17. Wills of Ann Newman, 1836; Mary Dick, 1850, and Nicholas Nicholls, 1794.

Nicholls

See Newman

Roby

'An Alderman's household stuff in 1545', *H.N.Q.* **8**, 1896, 101-2. Probate inventory of Arthur Roby of Winchester, 1545.

Sabin

CHRISTIE, PETER. 'The probate inventory', *H.F.H.* **3**(2), 1976, 35-7. Includes will and inventory of Robert Sabin of Portsmouth, 1677.

Shotter

SHOTTER, GEORGE. 'The will of Thomas Shotter, 1858', *H.F.H.* **11**(4), 1985, 207-8.
SHOTTER, GEORGE. 'The will of Thomas Shotter', *H.F.H.* **11**(1), 1984, 9-10. See also **11**(3), 1984, 137-8. Of Romsey, 1467.

Waight

'An old inventory', *H.N.Q.* **5**, 1890, 13-14. Inventory of John Waight of Kings' Worthy, 1636.

Worsley

'Worsley of Appuldercombe, Isle of Wight', *H.N.Q.* **3**, 1887, 85-95. Wills, 16-18th c.

Youngs

DRUITT, SYLVIA. 'The will of Jane Youngs of Burley in the County of Southampton', *Costume* **11**, 1977, 113-7. 1756.

10. OFFICIAL LISTS OF NAMES

Governments are keen on listing their subjects - a trait for which genealogists have cause to be thankful. Official lists of names have been compiled for a wide variety of purposes-taxation, defence, voting, landownership, *etc.* - but all help us to locate our ancestors in time and place. The earliest 'official list' identifies manorial lords throughout the country; for Hampshire, see:

MUNBY, JULIAN, ed. *Domesday booke, 4: Hampshire.* Chichester: Phillimore, 1982.

Taxation Lists

The records of taxation are voluminous, and provide us with many lists of taxpayers. For Hampshire, the earliest such list to be published is unusual; it records the names of persons liable to purveyance, that is, required to contribute to the maintainance of the Queen's household - the Queen, in this instance, being Elizabeth I. In doing so, it provides a full list of landowners and occupiers in 1576 for the places covered:

MONEY, WALTER, ed. *A perfect booke of all the landes as well arable as pasture, meadowes, wastes and waste groundes, with the goodness of the same, as well, as in whose handes and occupacion the same is, within the Hundreds of Evenger, Chutlye, Kingsclere, Pastroe, and Overton, vewed, seene, and numbered by estimacion in the year of Our Lord 1575 by certaine innhabitants there at the commandement of the Justices of the Peace of our soveraigne Lady the Queene Elizabeth, within Her Graces County of Southampton, and furthermore; how mutch and upon whome the whole summe and rate of wheate, sturtes, lambes and poultrye may best be levied for provision of the Queene's Majesties most honourable householde at sutch time as the same shalbe requested.* Newbury: W.J. Blacket, 1901.

Despite its defeat, the cost of the Armada to Queen Elizabeth was heavy, and many Hampshire gentry contributed to a fund to help meet this expense. Their names are listed in two articles:

ATTWOOD, J.S. 'The Armada fund', *H.N.Q.* **2**, 1884, 40-41.

'The names of those persons who subscribed towards the defence of this country at the time of the Spanish Armada, 1588, and the amounts each contributed', *H.F.H.* **12**(4), 1986, 242.

The Crown's major source of revenue in the late medieval and early modern period was the lay subsidy, which was exacted from anyone capable of paying. Surviving returns are voluminous; for Hampshire, most of the Elizabethan returns are in print:

VICK, DOUGLAS F. *Central Hampshire lay subsidy assessments, 1558-1603 (Fawley Division, Southampton, Isle of Wight and Winchester).* Farnham: D.F. Vick, 1987.

VICK, DOUGLAS F., ed. *East Hampshire lay subsidy assessments, 1558-1603 (Alton, Basingstoke and Portsdown Divisions).* Farnham: the author, 1988.

VICK, DOUGLAS F. *West Hampshire lay subsidy assessments, 1558-1603 (Andover, Kingsclere and New Forest Divisions).* Farnham: D.F. Vick, 1987.

DAVEY, C.R., ed. *The Hampshire lay subsidy rolls, 1586, with the city of Winchester assessment of a fifteenth and a tenth, 1585.* H.R.S. **4**. 1981.

YATES, E.M. *Petersfield in Tudor times.* Petersfield papers 5. Petersfield Area Historical Society, 1979. Includes subsidy lists and probate inventories.

Ship money was one of the subjects in dispute at the time of the Civil War. For an article on its collection, see:

CLIFFORD, C.A. 'Ship money in Hampshire: collection and collapse', *Southern history* **4**, 1982, 91-106.

After the Restoration, the hearth tax became the mainstay of the government's finances. Everyone who had a hearth was liable, and the returns for Hampshire in 1665 are printed in:

HUGHES, ELIZABETH, & WHITE, PHILLIPPA. *The Hampshire hearth tax assessment, 1665, with the Southampton assessments for 1662 and 1670.* H.R.S. **11**. [1991].

For the Isle of Wight, see:

RUSSELL, P.D.D., ed. *Hearth tax returns for the Isle of Wight, 1664 to 1674.* Isle of Wight record series 1. [Newport]: Isle of Wight Record Office, 1981.

Other published returns include:

OLIVER, J., & COLLINS, F.B. 'Colemore and Prior's Dean', *P.P.H.F.C.* **32**, 1975, 83-92. Primarily landscape history, but includes a transcript of the hearth tax return, 1665.

BARSTOW, H.G., ed. *The hearth tax returns of 1665 (relating to this area).* Special paper **7**. [Eastleigh]: Eastleigh & District Local History Society, 1986.

WILLIAMS, C.L. SINCLAIR. *The hearth tax return for the Hundred of Titchfield, 1664-65.* [Titchfield]: Titchfield History Society, 1985.

Muster Rolls

Muster rolls offer another potential source of information. All adult males were liable to bear arms in defence of the realm, and to appear at musters, where their names could be entered on a roll. One such roll for Hampshire is in print:

BARSTOW, H.G., & BARBER, N.D., ed. *The muster rolls.* [Eastleigh]: Eastleigh and District Local History Society, 1987. 1626 muster roll for Eastleigh.

Loyalty Oaths

From time to time, men have been required to swear allegiance to the powers that be. One such oath was known as the 'solemn league and covenant'; the list of those taking this oath in Long Sutton, 1643, is in:

ELVIN, CH.R. 'Some notes on the Solemn League and Covenant in England, with special reference to the parish of Long Sutton in Hampshire', *P.P.H.F.C.* **8**(3), 1919, 271-6.

Voters' Lists

Many lists of voters in eighteenth and nineteenth-century elections survive. A brief guide to these is in:

WHITE, PHILIPPA. *Sources for elections and census returns in the Hampshire Record Office.* [Winchester]: the Office, 1989.
See also:

SURRY, NIGEL. 'The Hampshire election of 1734', *P.P.H.F.C.* **35**, 1978, 217-25. Includes list of Hampshire freeholders living in London, and a list of 'proposed agents for the New Forest Division'.

For a Petersfield poll book of 1715, see Surry's book listed below, section 13.

The Census

Much the most useful lists, from a genealogical point of view, are those deriving from the nineteenth-century censuses. For Hampshire a variety of lists and indexes have been published. A brief general guide is provided by White's work cited under Voters Lists above. The works listed below are arranged by census date and place.

1841

Croker Hill

J., A. 'Crocker Hill, Fareham', *Fareham past and present* **2**(11), 1982, 5-9. Extracts from 1841 census.

NEWTON, P. 'Crocker Hill, Fareham', *H.F.H.* **9**(2), 1982, 58-9. Extracts from 1841 census.

1851

Index to 1851 census. 68 vols. Record series. Southampton: Hampshire Genealogical Society, 1980-90. In this many-volumed work, names for each parish are indexed separately. Essential. Supplemented by:

MERRITT, DAVID C. *Hampshire 1851 census: place listing.* [ ]: [Hampshire Genealogical Society], 1991. Parishes are also listed in *H.F.H.* **20**(1), 1993, 52-4.

HALL, BARRY. *Isle of Wight 1851 surname index.* Sandown: the author, 1992.
See also:

'Nonagenerians in Hampshire, 1851 census', *H.F.H.* **12**(3), 1985, 162-3. List.

ETHERIDGE, JOHN. 'Carisbrooke House of Industry, 1851', *H.F.H.* **14**(2), 1987, 66; **14**(3), 1987, 170; **14**(4), 1988, 229; **15**(1), 1988, 40; **15**(2), 1988, 91. 1851 census.

'Hampshire born inhabitants of Jersey', *H.F.H.* **12**(2), 1985, 92. From the 1851 census.

'Hampshire born residents in the 1851 census for Kinson, H0107/1855', *H.F.H.* **9**(4), 1983, 145-7. Kinson is in Dorset.

'Hampshire references in the 1851 Wiltshire census', *H.F.H.* **16**(3), 1989, 185-6.

'Strays', *I.O.W.F.H.S.* **17**, 1990, 8. Isle of Wight 'strays' found in Dorset in the 1851 census.

1861

'Ryde Hospital', *I.O.W.F.H.S.* **8**, 1988, 10. 1861 census, listing staff and patients.

CUMNOR, JANET. 'Patriotic girls - and those doing a stretch at Wandsworth', *H.F.H.* **12**(2), 1985, 117. Hampshire extracts from the 1871 census returns for Wandsworth Prison, and for the Patriotic Asylum for Girls, Wandsworth Common, Surrey.

LAST, C.F. 'Norfolk strays, 1871/1881 census', *Norfolk ancestor: journal of the Norfolk and Norwich Genealogical Society* **5**(4), 1989, 81. In Winchester.

1881

The Mormons are currently compiling a full index of the 1881 census. When this is complete, it will supersede most of the items listed below.

LAWES, EDWARD. '1881 census', *H.F.H.* **9**(1), 1982, 19-26. Lists reference numbers at the Public Record Office for Hampshire parishes.

'1881 census: parish of Eling, Hants', *Wiltshire Family History Society [journal]* **33**, 1989, 14. Lists Wiltshire strays.

HAUGHEY, BETTY. 'Looking after the ship', *H.F.H.* **13**(3), 1986, 232-4. 1881 census, listing crews of ships in Cowes harbour.

LAWES, W. 'In the Union Workhouse, Kingsclere, census night, 6 April 1881', *H.F.H.* **17**(3), 1990, 224. List of inmates.

COLE, ROSEMARY. 'Within the prison walls', *H.F.H.* **18**(2), 1991, 140-43. Names from the 1881 census of Parkhurst Prison.

OAKLEY, T. 'Hampshire folk in Devon', *H.F.H.* **17**(4), 1991, 307-8. Strays in the East Stonehouse census, 1881.

WILLMOTT, HARRY. 'They went to the Dogs', *H.F.H.* **18**(1), 1991, 45-7. Hampshire strays on the Isle of Dogs, Poplar, from the 1881 census.

See also 1871

1891

1891 census index, Isle of Wight. Sandown: John and Janet Few, 1993- . v.1 (2 pts): West Wight RG12 897.

Landowners Census

In 1873, a different type of census was taken. This provides a complete list of persons owning an acre or more of land:

'Southampton', in *Return of owners of land, 1873,* C1097. House of Commons Parliamentary papers, 1874, **LXXII**, 237-77. Covers the whole county.

11. DIRECTORIES AND MAPS *etc.*

Directories are an invaluable source for locating people in the past. For the nineteenth century, they are the equivalent of the modern phone book. Many directories for Hampshire were published; the list which follows is selective, especially for the twentieth century. In order to identify others, consult the works listed in *English genealogy: an introductory bibliography.* Arrangement here is by date and place.

The Hampshire directory... Winchester: J. Sadler, 1784.

The Hampshire pocket companion ... for ... 1790. Southampton: A. Cunningham, 1790.

Pigot and Co's national commercial directory, comprising a directory and classification of the merchants, bankers, professional gentlemen, manufacturers and traders in all the cities, towns, sea-ports and principal vilages in the following counties, viz, Berkshire, Buckinghamshire, Gloucestershire, Hampshire, Oxfordshire, with historical and topographical delineations ... J.Pigot & Co., 1830. Reprinted in facsimile, Kings Lynn: Michael Winton, 1994.

Post Office directory of Hampshire ... Kelly & Co., 1848-1939. Many issues; title varies. From 1880, *Kelly's directory of Hampshire with the Isle of Wight.* Also issued in one volume with directories for various other counties.

Hunt & Co's directory of Hampshire and Dorsetshire, comprising comprehensive lists of the commercial, professional and private residents in every town, village and hamlet throughout those counties, including the Isle of Wight, also in the city of Salisbury, together with a descriptive account of each town ... E. Hunt & Co., 1852.

Craven and Co's commercial directory of the County of Hampshire, containing an alphabetical list of the nobility, gentry, merchants, professions, trades, etc. ... Nottingham: Craven & Co., 1857.

WHITE, WILLIAM. *History, gazetteer and directory of Hampshire and the Isle of Wight, comprising general historical surveys of the County & Island, and of the Diocese of Winchester, and separate historical, statistical and topographical descriptions of* the town and county of the town of Southampton, the city of Winchester, the populous port, borough & suburbs of Portsmouth, and of all the towns, boroughs, ports, bathing places, unions, parishes, tithings, villages, hamlets, seats, &c. in this interesting county and beautiful channel isle, shewing their extent and population, their trade, commerce, manufacturers, markets, fairs, fisheries and agricultural and mineral productions, their churches, chapels, charities and public institutions, their eminent men, the patrons, incumbents and value of the benefices, the tithe commutations, the lords of the manors and principal owners of the soil, the civil and ecclesiastical jurisdictions, the addresses of the principal inhabitants, the Post Office regulations, seats of the nobility and gentry, the magistrates and public officers, and a great variety of other useful information. 2 issues. Sheffield: Wm. White, 1859-78.

J.G. Harrod and Co's postal and commercial directory of Hampshire with the Isle of Wight containing a brief descriptive account of the towns, parishes and villages, followed by a directory. Thomas Danks for J.G. Harrod & Co., 1865.

Smith & Co's Hampshire directory including the Isle of Wight, 1866-67. Smith & Co., 1866.

Mercer & Crocker's general topographical and historical directory for Hampshire, &c ... Leicester: Mercer & Crocker, 1871.

Deacon's South Hants court guide, gazetteer, and royal blue book: a fashionable register and general survey of the county ... C.W. Deacon & Co., 1879.

HOLBROOK, ARTHUR R. Hampshire (Holbrook's) county year book ... with official directory for Hampshire and Isle of Wight. Portsmouth: Holbrook & Son, 1896-1916(?). Much information on the nobility and gentry, magistrates, local councillors, M.P's etc. Not, however, a trade directory.

The Hants and Dorset court guide and county blue book: a fashionable register, professional register, and general survey of the counties. Charles William Deacon & Co., 1897. Includes lists of county seats, justices, councillors, local officials, M.P's, and various professionals, but not a topographical directory.

Bennetts business directory for Isle of Wight and Hampshire. Birmingham: Bennett & Co., 1907.

Hampshire directory. Walsall: Aubrey & Co., 1911-40. At least 8 issues.

Hampshire and Isle of Wight trades directory, including Bournemouth, Portsmouth and Southampton. Edinburgh: Town and County Directories, 1914-39. At least 6 issues.

Aldershot

Drew's Aldershot and Farnborough directory and almanack. Aldershot: J. Drew, 1893-1928. Many issues.

Alton

The Hampshire Herald directory and yearbook for Alton, Alresford, and 46 neighbouring villages. Alton: Hampshire Herald, 1905-8. 3 issues.

Andover

Kelly's directory of Andover and neighbourhood. Kelly's Directories, 1934-74. 19 issues.

Basingstoke

Kelly's directory of Basingstoke and neighbourhood. Kelly's Directories, 1929-74. Many issues.

Bournemouth

Directory of Bournemouth (East and West) and neighbourhood, including Boscombe, Christchurch, Poole, Parkstone, Southbourne-on-Sea, Westbourne, and all villages within six miles of Bournemouth (West), containing a street directory of Bournemouth ... George Stevens, 1888-94. 2 issues.

The annual trades and private residents directory of Bournemouth and vicinity ... Bournemouth: Wilson & Prady, 1884. Probably no more published.

W. Mate and Sons' business, professional and private residents directory for Bournemouth, Boscombe and Westbourne. Bournemouth: W. Mate & Sons, 1887-1905. 5 issues. Continued as: Sidney J. Mate's Bournemouth business directory and year book. Bournemouth: S.J. Mate, 1911-40. Almost annual; title varies.

Gosport

Kelly's directory of Gosport, Alverstoke, Fareham and district. Kelly's Directories, 1886-1943. Many issues.

Isle of Wight

HILL, J.W. *Historical and commercial directory of the Isle of Wight.* J.W. Hill, 1871-9. 2 issues.

Kelly's directory of the Isle of Wight. Kelly & Co., 1888-1924. 17 issues. Continued by *Kelly's directory of Newport, Cowes and neighbourhood.* Kelly & Co., 1933-51. 5 issues, by *Kelly's directory of Ryde and neighbourhood.* Kelly & Co., 1931-51. 5 issues, and by *Kelly's directory of Shanklin, Sandown, Ventnor and neighbourhood.* Kelly & Co., 1931-51. 5 issues.

Directory of the Isle of Wight, including a street directory of Newport, East and West Cowes, Ryde, Ventnor & Yarmouth, and all villages on the island, containing the private and commercial residents ... Geo. Stevens, 1883.

Lymington

Directory of Lymington, Ringwood, Christchurch, Fordingbridge, Brockenhurst, Lyndhurst, and the principal villages and places in the New Forest, containing a street directory of Lymington and Ringwood ... Stevens Postal Directories, 1891.

New Forest

JAMES, JUDE, ed. *Comyn's New Forest: 1817 directory of life in the parishes of Boldre & Brockenhurst.* Ringwood: C.J. Newsome & Associates/Lymington Historical Record Society, 1982. An unofficial, but very detailed, census.

Portsmouth

Simpson's Portsmouth directory and court guide, including Southsea, Landport and Kingston, Portsea and Gosport with list of churches and chapels, Post Office information, cab fares, etc., also the magistracy, aldermen, board of guardians, registrars and parochial officers. Tomkies and Son, 1863.

Butcher & Co's Borough of Portsmouth directory, including Gosport, Fareham, & Havant for 1874-5 ... Butcher & Co., 1874.

Chamberlain's Portsmouth, including Portsea, Southsea, Landport and District, with an account of the parish and government officials, public institutions, and borough members of Parliament, and magistrates, local charities, churches and chapels, local postal and telegraph services; also a list of streets, private residents, commercial and trade directory. Portsmouth: G. Chamberlain, 1879-87. 3 issues.

Directory of Portsmouth, Portsea, Southsea, Landport and Gosport ... G. Stevens, 1883-90. 3 issues.

Kelly's directory of Portsmouth, Portsea, Landport, Southsea, Gosport and suburbs. Kelly & Co., 1886-1948. Many issues; title varies.

Southampton

The directory for the town of Southampton ... Southampton: A. Cunningham, 1803.

The directory for the town of Southampton in 1811, to which are appended, the Southampton register, with the assessed taxes and other duties ... 2nd ed. Southampton: A. Cunningham, 1811.

The Southampton register for 1811. 4th ed. Southampton: A. Cunningham, 1811.

Fletcher's Southampton directory. Southampton: Fletcher & Son, 1834.

Fletcher's directory of the Borough of Southampton, including the neighbouring villages. Southampton: Fletcher and Son, 1836.

Directory of the Borough of Southampton, including the neighbouring villages. Southampton: Fletcher & Son, 1839.

COOPER, WILLIAM. *Post Office directory of the Borough of Southampton and the neighbourhood ...* Southampton: Fletcher Forbes & Fletcher, 1843-9. 4 issues. Continued by Williams (see below).

Rayner's directory of the town and neighbourhood of Southampton for 1849. Southampton: C. & J. Rayner, 1849.

WILLIAMS, E.D. *The Post Office directory of the Borough of Southampton and the neighbourhood ...* Southampton: Forbes & Knibb, 1851-65. 8 issues; publisher varies.

COX, W. *The Southampton directory of the Post Office district for the borough and the surrounding neighbourhood.* Southampton: Thomas G. Gutch, 1867-80. 5 issues. Publisher and title varies.

Tucker's Southampton directory for 1874. Southampton: Tucker & Son, 1874.

Foster & Roud's Southampton directory, 1883, for the borough and the surrounding neighbourhood. Southampton: Foster and Roud, 1882.

Directory of Southampton and neighbourhood, including Romsey, Netley (Hound), Netley (Totton), Bitterne, Sholing, Bishopstoke, Eastleigh, Woolston, Shirley, Freemantle, Millbrook, Redbridge, and all villages within seven miles of Southampton ... George Stevens, 1884-95. 4 issues; title varies.

Kelly's directory of Southampton and suburbs. Kelly & Co., 1886-1975. Many issues; title varies.

Southsea

Wallis and Ades annual directory for Southsea. 2 vols. Southsea: Wallis & Ades, 1887-8. Title varies.

Winchester

Gilmour's Winchester almanac and post-office directory. Winchester: G. & H. Gilmour, 1854. Described as '14th annual issue' - but no other issues found.

Masters City of Winchester directory for 1880. Winchester: F.W. Masters, 1880-81. 2 vols.

Warren's Winchester & District directory, including 160 neighbouring places. Warren & Son, 1877-1960/61. Almost annual.

Kelly's directory of Winchester and neighbourhood. Kelly's Directories, 1927-1973/4. Many issues.

Maps

In addition to directories, the genealogist also needs maps - and especially historic maps - to identify the places mentioned in his sources. No genealogist should be without the sheet map of Hampshire parishes issued by the Institute of Heraldic and Genealogical Studies. Also of particular value are the early Ordnance Survey maps. Facsimiles of these are available in two works:

HINTON, DAVID A., & INSOLE, A.N. *Hampshire and the Isle of Wight.* Ordnance Survey historical guides. George Philip & Son, 1988. Includes facsimiles of early Ordnance Survey maps.

The old series Ordnance Survey maps of England and Wales ... volume III: South-Central England ... Lympne Castle: Harry Margary, 1981. Covers all but the Surrey border area (for which see vol.I).

Reprinted sheet maps from the original 1" survey are also available from the publishers David and Charles.

See also:

HAMPSHIRE ARCHIVISTS GROUP. *Guide to location of large scale Ordnance Survey maps for Hampshire and the Isle of Wight.* The Group, 1988.

For a general introduction to printed Hampshire maps, see:

PENFOLD, ALASTAIR. *An introduction to the printed maps of Hampshire.* [ ]: Hampshire County Museum Service, [1989?]

On the Isle of Wight, see:

TURLEY, RAYMOND V. 'Printed county maps of the Isle of Wight, 1590-1870: a check-list and guide for students (and collectors)', *P.P.H.F.C.* **31,** 1974, 53-64.

A brief but useful guide to tithe, enclosure, and Valuation Office maps *etc.* is in:

BEECH, GERALDINE. 'Maps and the genealogist', *H.F.H.* **10**(2), 1983, 60-63.

An important collection of maps is listed in:

'Hampshire County Library: maps', *H.F.C.L.H.N.* **1**(5), 1982, 121-3. For a collection of facsimiles of historic Hampshire maps, see:

Two hundred and fifty years of map-making in the County of Hampshire: a collection of reproductions of printed maps published between the years 1575 and 1826. Lympne Castle: Harry Margary, 1976. In portfolio.

Portsmouth

HODSON, D. *Maps of Portsmouth before 1801: a catalogue.* Portsmouth Record Series **4**. City of Portsmouth, 1978.

Southampton

ROGERS, W.H., ed. *Maps and plans of old Southampton.* P.S.R.Soc., 1907. In portfolio; 13 historic maps - mainly facsimiles.

WELCH, EDWIN. *Southampton maps from Elizabethan times.* S.R.Ser., **9**. 1964. Not uniform with rest of series. Includes list of public Acts of Parliament relating to Southampton.

Place-names

If you want to locate an obscure placename, you may need to consult a place-name listing. Unfortunately the English Place Name Society has not yet published its volumes on Hampshire. References may, however, be made to:

COATES, RICHARD. *The place-names of Hampshire.* B.T. Batsford, 1989. Etymological dictionary.

KÖKERITZ, HELGE. *The place-names of the Isle of Wight.* Uppsala: Appelbergs Boktryckeriaktiebolag, 1940. Scholarly.

Petersfield place names. Petersfield papers 1. Petersfield Area Historical Society, 1976. Gazetteer with brief historical notes.

COATES, RICHARD. *A bibliography of place-names in Hampshire and the Isle of Wight.* Brighton: Youngsmere Press, 1988.

Dialect

Obscure local words may occur in historical documents - or, indeed, in the dialect of local people. There are a number of guides to Hampshire dialect which may assist interpretation:

COPE, SIR WILLIAM. *A glossary of Hampshire words and phrases.* Trübner & Co., for the English Dialect Society, 1883.

LONG, WILLIAM HENRY. *A dictionary of the Isle of Wight dialect ...* 2nd ed. Portsmouth: W.H. Barrell, 1931.

SMITH, HENRY, & SMITH, C. ROACH. 'Isle of Wight words', in SKEAT, W.W., ed. *Original glossaries.* Trübner & Co., for the English Dialect Society, 1881, 1-64.

12. ECCLESIASTICAL RECORDS

Ecclesiastical records are of the greatest importance to genealogists. This reflects the fact that ecclesiastical involvement in society was formerly much wider than it is today. Some ecclesiastical records, e.g. parish registers, probate records, churchwardens' accounts, estate records, are dealt with in other sections of this book. This section focuses on those records which are more directly concerned with ecclesiastical matters. For a general introduction to the history of the diocese see:

BENHAM, WILLIAM. *Winchester.* Diocesan histories. Society for Promoting Christian Knowledge, 1884.

Two books provide lives of the bishops of Winchester:

CASSAN, S.H. *The lives of the Bishops of Winchester, from Birinus, the first bishop of the West Saxons, to the present time.* 2 vols. C. & J. Rivington, 1827.

STEPHENS, W.R. WOOD, & CAPES, W.W. *The Bishops of Winchester.* Winchester: Warren and Son; London: Simpkin & Co., 1907. Medieval lives.

The study of church bells and plate may yield much information of genealogical interest, since they frequently carry inscriptions naming clergy, churchwardens, benefactors, founders, *etc.* See:

COLCHESTER, W.E. *Hampshire church bells: their founders and inscriptions.* Winchester: Warren and Son, 1920.

BRAITHWAITE, P.R.P. *The church plate of Hampshire.* Simpkin & Co., 1909. Gives many names of donors, *etc.,* but unfortunately no surname index.

A detailed introduction to the records of the Diocese of Winchester is:

LEWIN, SARAH. *Records of the Diocese of Winchester in the Hampshire Record Office.* [Winchester]: the Office, 1991.

See also:

DEEDES, CECIL. *Report on the muniments of the Bishopric of Winchester preserved in the Consistory Court in Winchester Cathedral, including a subject index to Bishop John de Pontissaro's register.* Winchester: Warren and Son, 1912.

A number of medieval bishops' registers *etc.,* have been published. These contain many names, especially of the clergy, but also of the laity. The list following is in chronological order:

FRANKLIN, M.J., ed. *English episcopal acta, VIII: Winchester, 1070-1204.* British Academy, 1993.

DEEDES, CECIL. *Registrum Johannis de Pontissara, episcopi Wyntoniensis AD MCCLXXXII-MCCCIV.* 2 vols. Canterbury and York Society **19 & 30.** 1916-24. Also issued by the Surrey Record Society.

OWEN, DOROTHY M., ed. *John Lydford's book.* Devon and Cornwall Record Society N.S., **20.** 1974. Also published as HISTORICAL MANUSCRIPTS COMMISSION *Joint Publication* **22.** Memorandum book of a 14th c. Winchester diocesan official.

GOODMAN, A.W. *Registrum Henrici Woodlock, diocesis Wintoniensis, A.D. 1305-1316.* 2 vols. Canterbury and York Society **43-44,** 1940-41.

BAIGENT, FRANCIS JOSEPH, ed. *The registers of John de Sandale and Rigaud de Asserio, Bishops of Winchester (A.D. 1316-1323), with an appendix of contemporaneous and other illustrative documents.* Hampshire Record Society. Simpkin and Co., 1897.

HOCKEY, S.F., ed. *The register of William Edington, Bishop of Winchester, 1346-1366.* 2 vols. H.R.S. **7-8,** 1986-7.

KIRBY, T.F., ed *Wykeham's register.* 2 vols. Hampshire Record Society. Simpkin & Co., 1896-9. Vol.1. Pt.1. Institutions. Pt.2. Ordinations. Vol.2. Pt.3. Official instruments. Pt.4. Crown writs and returns. Covers 1367-1404.

CHITTY, HERBERT, ed. *Registrum Thome Wolsey, Cardinalis ecclesie Wintoniensis administratoris.* Canterbury and York Society **32.** 1926. Covers 1529-30.

CHITTY, HERBERT, ed. *Registra Stephani Gardiner et Johannis Poynet, episcoporum Wintoniensium.* Canterbury and York Society, **37.** 1930. Covers 1531-55. Includes lists of institutions and collations, index to the first fruits composition books, 1536-57, the 1536 valor (i.e. valuation of benefices, identifying incumbents), list of stipendiary priests, 1541, *etc.*

MAYBERRY, TOM, & LEWIN, SARAH. 'The household account book of Stephen Gardiner,

Bishop of Winchester, 1547-1551', *Newsletter of the Hampshire Archives Trust,* Summer 1987, 39-43. Brief discussion.

Registrum Johannis Whyte, episcopi Wintoniensis, A.D. MDLVI-MDLIX. Canterbury and York Society **16.** 1914. Includes list of institutions and collations.

HAINES, ROY M. 'Adam Orleton and the Diocese of Winchester', *Journal of ecclesiastical history* **23,** 1972, 1-30. Discusses the administration of the Diocese. A variety of published sources throw light on the history of the Diocese during the Reformation and succeeding centuries; those listed here include much of genealogical value. 'Church goods in Hampshire A.D. 1552', *P.P.H.F.C.* **7**(3), 1916, 67-98; **8**(1), 1917, 1-39; **9,** 1920-24, 92-8. See also **8**(3), 1919, 336-49. Gives names of the clergy and churchwardens who signed inventories of church goods.

WILLIS, ARTHUR J., ed. *Winchester Consistory Court depositions, 1561-1602: selections.* Folkestone: the editor, 1960. 'Metropolitical visitation of the Archdeaconry of Winchester, 1607-1608: an abstract of court book no 75 in the Diocesan Registry, Winchester', in [WILLIS, ARTHUR J., ed.] *A Hampshire miscellany.* Lund Humphries, 1963-7, 1-79. Lists persons accused of offences before the ecclesiastical court.

GOODMAN, FLORENCE REMINGTON, ed. *The diary of John Young, dean of Winchester, STP; Dean of Winchester, 1616 to the Commonwealth.* S.P.C.K., 1928. Many notes on churchmen, family, *etc.,* includes folded pedigree of Young, 16-17th c.

WILLIS, ARTHUR J., ed. 'Exhibit books, terriers, and *episcopatus redivivus,* from records of the Diocesan Registry', in WILLIS, ARTHUR J., ed. *A Hampshire miscellany.* Arthur J. Willis, 1963-7, 201-84.

MADGE, F.T. *Hampshire inductions.* Winchester: Warren & Son, 1918. 17-19th c.

WILLIS, A.J., ed. *Winchester ordinations, 1660-1829.* 2 vols. Folkestone: A.J. Willis, 1964-5. v.1. Ordinands' papers, 1734-1827 (with a few earlier surviving); v.2. Bishops' registers; subscription books; exhibition of orders.

GATTY, ALFRED SCOTT. 'Institutions of clergymen in the Diocese of Winchester', *Genealogist* N.S. **6,** 1890, 34-43, 120-24, 187-8

& 236-9; **7,** 1891, 115-7 & 196-200; **8,** 1892, 223-6.

PINK, WILLIAM DUNCOMBE. 'Institutions to livings in the county of Southampton', *H.N.Q.* **2,** 1884, 113-23. See also 124-5 & **3,** 1887, 83.

'Laymen's licences of the Diocese of Winchester, 1675-1834 (and a few earlier records)', in [WILLIS, ARTHUR J., ed] *A Hampshire miscellany.* Lund Humphries, 1963-7, 83-108. Calendars licences for schoolmasters and lecturers, physicians and surgeons, midwives, parish clerks and sextons, *etc.*

VICKERS, JOHN A. *The religious census of Hampshire, 1851.* H.R.S. **12.** 1993. Gives names of the clergy, *etc.,* making the returns.

A number of works provide information on the personnel, *etc.,* of the church in particular places. They are listed here by parish.

Alverstoke

WILLIAMS, G.H. 'Rectors of Alverstoke', *G.R.* **10,** 1975, 22-6. List with biographical notes, 16-20th c.

Barton

HOCKEY, S.F. 'The cost of founding Barton Oratory, Isle of Wight', *Journal of ecclesiastical history* **13,** 1962, 55-60. Lists founders.

Basingstoke

LE FAYE, D.G. 'Selborne Priory and the vicarage of Basingstoke', *P.P.H.F.C.* **46,** 1990, 91-99. Includes list of Basingstoke vicars, 13-15th c.

Beaulieu

HOCKEY, FREDERICK. *Beaulieu, King John's Abbey: a history of Beaulieu Abbey, Hampshire, 1204-1538.* Old Woking: Pioneer Publications, 1976. Includes list of abbots, wills of Thomas Skevington, Bishop of Bangor, 1528, and Thomas Stephens, the last abbot, 1559, and a bibliography.

Elvetham

FORD, MICHAEL. '[List of persons confirmed in Elvetham, 1832-3, from the parish register]', *H.F.H.* **14**(2), 1987, 138.

Hamble

KIRBY, THOMAS F. 'The alien priory of St.Andrew, Hamble, and its transfer to Winchester College in 1391', *Archaeologia* **50**(2), 251-2. Includes list of 14th c. priors and deeds.

Hordle

'The old church, Hordle, Hants', *Milford-on-Sea Record Society: an occasional magazine* **3**(6), 1927, 5-24. Includes transcript of an appeal for a new church signed by many parishioners, c.1830; also list of vicars, 1339-1891.

Isle of Wight

COX, J. CHARLES. *Isle of Wight: its churches and religious houses.* Country churches series. George Allen & Sons, 1911. Little of direct genealogical interest.

Milford

Milford parish church. Milford-on-Sea Record Society: an occasional magazine 1(4), 1911. Includes list of clergy, *etc.*

Newport

HOCKEY, S.F. 'The Newport chantry', *P.P.H.F.C.* 23(3), 1968, 90-95. Includes names of some chantry priests.

Portsmouth

BARRETT, PHILIP. *The organs and organists of the Cathedral Church of St Thomas of Canterbury at Portsmouth.* Portsmouth papers **4.** 1968. Includes biographical notes.

LILLEY, HENRY T., & EVERITT, ALFRED T. *Portsmouth parish church.* Portsmouth: Charpentier & Co., 1921. Includes extensive biographical notes on clergy.

Quarr Abbey

HOCKEY, S.F. 'The recruitment of Quarr Abbey, 1132-1536', *Proceedings of the Isle of Wight Natural History and Archaeological Society* **5**(1), 1956, 36-9. Notes on the origin of the monks.

Rockbourne

WINSER, ANDREW. *Rockbourne clergy and churchwardens of the 17th century.* Rockbourne: the author, 1979. Includes biographical notes on clergy; also churchwardens rate, 1681, *etc.*

Romsey

LIVEING, HENRY G.D. *Records of Romsey Abbey: an account of the Benedictine house of nuns with notes on the parish church and town (A.D. 907-1558).* Winchester: Warren and Son, 1906. Includes folded pedigree of the De Romesay family, medieval; also many names of abbesses, nuns and others connected with the Priory. General history.

Royal Hampshire County Hospital

MOXLEY, CYRIL. *Cathedral, college and hospital: an account of the chaplaincy of the Royal Hampshire County Hospital, 1736-1986.* Winchester: Cyril Moxley, 1986. Includes list of chaplains, 1736-1986.

St.Swithin's Priory

BAIN, PRISCILLA. *St.Swithun's: a centenary history.* Chichester: Phillimore & Co., 1984. General account.

Selborne Priory

LE FAYE, DEIRDRE. 'Selborne Priory, 1233-1486', *P.P.H.F.C.* **30**, 1973, 47-71. Includes list of priors.

Titchfield

'Alphabetical list of names on seating plan of Titchfield church, 1713-1849', *H.F.H.* **6**(4), 1980, 135.

Weeke

BAIGENT, FRANCES JOSEPH. 'On the parish church of Wyke near Winchester', *Journal of the British Archaeological Association* **19**, 1863, 184-212. Includes list of rectors, with wills of William Atkinson, 1539, Nicholas Harpsfield, 1550, Agnes Complyn, 1553, and Stephen Complyn, 1543.

Winchester
Blackfriars

PALMER, C.F.R. 'The friar-preachers, or blackfriars, of Winchester', *Reliquary* N.S. **3**, 1889, 207-15. Includes notes on religious and benefactors.

Cathedral

BUSSBY, FREDERICK. 'Winchester Cathedral, 1079-1979. Southampton: Paul Cave Publications, 1979. Includes lists of bishops, priors and deans, prebendaries and canons, and organists; also many notes on persons associated with the Cathedral.

CROOK, JOHN, ed. *Winchester Cathedral: nine hundred years, 1093-1993.* Phillimore, 1993. Essay collection; little of direct genealogical interest.

GOODMAN, A.W. 'The Cathedral church and the Archdeaconry of Winchester in 1562', *P.P.H.F.C.* **14**, 1940, 63-85. List of incumbents of the Cathedral and Archdeaconry.

KITCHIN, G.W., & MADGE, F.T., eds. *Documents relating to the foundation of the Chapter of Winchester, A.D. 1541-1547.* Hampshire Record Society. Simpkin & Marshall, 1889. Includes 'book of portions', 1541, naming clergy; also list of stipends of the petty canons.

MATTHEWS, BETTY. *The organs and organists of Winchester Cathedral.* 2nd ed. Winchester: Friends of Winchester Cathedral, 1975. Includes biographical notes.

RANNIE, ALAN. 'Some early deans of Winchester', *Winchester Cathedral record* **26**, 1957, 22-5 & **27**, 1958, 14-18.

STEPHENS, W.R.W., & MADGE, F.T., eds. *Documents relating to the history of the Cathedral church of Winchester in the seventeenth century.* Hampshire Record Society. Simpkin & Co., 1897.

See also section 8 above for other works on the Cathedral.

Fromonds Chantry

C[HITTY], H. 'Chaplains of Fromond's Chantry at Winchester', *Notes and queries* 12th series **2**, 1916, 221-4. List, 1446-1546.

Winchester College

CHITTY, HERBERT. *Chaplains of Winchester College, 1417-1542.* Athaeum Press, [1914]. Reprinted with additions from *Notes and queries* 11th series **10**, 1914, 201-3 & 221-3. Lists 92 chaplains; includes will of Thomas Vole, 1558.

Nonconformist Records

'Dissenters' meeting house certificates in the Diocese of Winchester', in [WILLIS, ARTHUR J., ed.] *A Hampshire miscellany*. Lund Humphries, 1963-7, 109-200.
For nonconformist registers, see section 7C.

Congregationalists

STAINER, S. *History of the Above Bar Congregational church, Southampton, from 1662 to 1908*. Southampton: Southampton Times Co., 1909. Includes list of deacons, and much information on ministers.

Albion Chapel, Southampton: the church book for 1872 containing a list of members, and information respecting the services, societies and institutions connected with the church and congregation. Southampton: A. Randle, 1872. Continued annually until 1877 - and perhaps thereafter.

Huguenots

'Huguenot records: a postscript', *Archives* 11(52), 1974, 211-12. Summary of conference discussion, concerning records in Kent, Southampton, and Norfolk.

SCOULOUDI, I. 'The French Protestant Church, the Chapel of St.Julien or Godshouse, Southampton', *Proceedings of the Huguenot Society of London* 20(6), 679-80. Brief note on its archives.

WELCH, EDWIN. *The minute book of the French church at Southampton, 1702-1939*. S.R.Ser. 23. 1979.

Methodist

CANTELO, BARRY W. 'Were they Methodists?' *H.F.H.* 10(2), 1983, 71-4. Index to obituaries and death notices in the *Methodist magazine*, 1832.

COOPER, W. DONALD. *Methodism in Portsmouth, 1750-1932*. Portsmouth papers 18. 1973. General account.

Roman Catholic

SCANTLEBURY, ROBERT E. 'The Hampshire Clergy Fund notes and the Hampshire ledger', *Publications of the Catholic Record Society* 43, 1949, 1-86. Account book, late 18th c., with many names.

HANSOM, JOSEPH S., ed. 'The register book of professions, *etc.*, of the English Benedictine nuns at Brussels and Winchester, now at East Bergholt, 1598-1856', *Publications of the Catholic Record Society* 14, 1914, 174-203.

'Some aspects of local recusancy, 16th and 17th century', *Fareham past and present* 9, 1969, 13-16. Includes some names of Fareham recusants.

BOGAN, PETER PAUL. 'The archival heritage of Dr. Milner and Archbishop King of St.Peter's parish, Winchester', *Catholic archives* 10, 1990, 8-16. Includes summary list of the records of a Roman Catholic parish, 18-20th c.

PAUL, JOHN E. 'Hampshire recusants in the time of Elizabeth I, with special reference to Winchester', *P.P.H.F.C.* 21, 1958-60, 61-81. General discussion.

Jews

SLOGGETT, BRIAN. 'Finding a Jewish ancestor in Hampshire', *H.F.H.* 8(4), 1982, 125-7.

NEWMAN, EUGENE. 'Some new facts about the Portsmouth Jewish community', *The Jewish Historical Society of England transactions* 17, 1951-2, 251-68. Includes transcript of circumcision registers, 18th c.

WEINBERG, AUBREY. *Portsmouth Jewry*. Portsmouth papers 41, 1985. General account.

13. RECORDS OF NATIONAL AND COUNTY ADMINISTRATION

Official lists of names, such as tax lists and census returns, have already been mentioned. There are, however, many other records of national and local government which provide useful information. A number of publications provide information on Members of Parliament:

JONES, R. ARNOLD. *Members of Parliament for Andover, 1295-1885: a chronological list with an introduction.* Andover: Andover Local Archives Committee, 1972.

BLACK, SIR FREDERICK. *An outline sketch of the Parliamentary history of the Isle of Wight, with lists of M.P's and several portraits.* Newport: County Press, 1929.

SURRY, NIGEL. *Petersfield and Parliament: one hundred years of a pocket borough, 1685-1783.* Petersfield papers 7. Petersfield: Petersfield Area Historical Society, 1983. Includes list of M.P's and a poll book of 1715.

For sheriffs, see:

'High sheriffs of Hampshire connected with the Isle of Wight', in JAMES, E. BOUCHER. *Letters archaeological and historical relating to the Isle of Wight.* Henry Frowde, 1896, v.1, 212-3.

'Isle of Wight sheriffs of the County of Hants, A.D. 1236-1764', in JAMES, E. BOUCHER. *Letters archaeological and historical relating to the Isle of Wight.* Henry Frowde, 1896, v.1, 207-11.

County government was largely conducted by Quarter Sessions. A general introduction to its activities in the seventeenth century is provided by:

FURLEY, J.S. *Quarter sessions government in Hampshire in the seventeenth century.* Winchester: Warren and Son, [1937].

See also:

J[ACOB], W.H. 'A Winchester presentment', *H.N.Q.* 9, 1898, 23-4. Presentments made at quarter sessions, 1624.

The letters of a sheriff and justice of the peace are printed in:

HAMPSHIRE RECORD OFFICE. *Sir Henry Whithed's letter book, volume 1: 1601-1614.* H.R.S. 1. 1976. To be continued.

Jurors at Hampshire assizes in 1791 are listed in:

WEBB, N.R. 'Tried, convicted, sentenced: progress report', *H.F.H.* 14(3), 1987, 182-3.

For an important guide to the records generated by the Poor Law, see:

HAMPSHIRE ARCHIVISTS' GROUP. *Poor law in Hampshire through the centuries: a guide to the records.* Hampshire Archivists' Group publication 1. 1970.

In the nineteenth century, many inquiries were instituted into social questions, and many trees were chopped down in order to print reports of Commissioners. Amongst these reports were those of the Charity Commissioners, which give much information drawn from wills, deeds, accounts, *etc.* Their reports are voluminous; see, for example:

'County of Southampton', in *Abstracts of the returns of charitable donations for the benefit of poor persons, made by the ministers and churchwardens of the several parishes and townships in England and Wales, 1786-1788.* House of Commons Parliamentary papers, 1816, XVIB, 275-302. Summary list of benefactors.

CHARITY COMMISSIONERS. *The reports of the Commissioners appointed in pursuance of various acts of Parliament to enquire concerning charities in England and Wales, relating to the County of Hampshire, 1819-1837.* Henry Gray, [1839?]

In 1889, county councils took over many of the functions of quarter sessions. The history of Hampshire County Council is told in:

RUSHTON, GILLIAN A. *100 years of progress: Hampshire County Council, 1889-1989.* Winchester: Hampshire County Council, 1989. Includes list of chairmen, vice-chairmen, leaders and chief officers.

An important but under-used source, which lists all landowners c.1910, is discussed in:

BROOKS, E.M. 'Inland Revenue valuation records', *Section newsletters ... [Hampshire Field Club]* 3, 1985, 7-8.

14. RECORDS OF PAROCHIAL AND BOROUGH ADMINISTRATION

Churchwardens' accounts, settlement examinations, rate lists, freemen's rolls, *etc.*, - these are the documents left to us by government at its most basic level. For an introduction to churchwardens' accounts, see: WILLIAMS, JOHN FOSTER, ed. *The early churchwardens' account of Hampshire.* Winchester: Warren and Son, 1913. Transcript of pre-1600 accounts from Andover, Bramley, Stoke Charity, Crondall, Ellingham, Weyhill, Winchester (St.Johns and St.Peter Cheesehill) and Portsmouth.

Settlement examinations record the movement of migrants. Abstracts of those from Staines, Middlesex, relating to Hampshire men and women, are printed in:

LAMBERT, HOWARD. 'Strangers in Staines', *H.F.H.* 17(1), 1990, 10-11.

Alverstoke

BUGDEN, ERIC. 'Bound to cotton', *H.F.H.* 17(4), 1991, 255-6. Lists Alverstoke children apprenticed to a Manchester cotton factory, 1791.

WILLIAMS, G.H. 'Hampshire parishes no.10: Alverstoke', *H.F.H.* 4(4), 1978, 92-7. Includes notes on parish records.

Andover

ANSTRUTHER, IAN. *The scandal of the Andover Workhouse.* Geoffrey Bles, 1973. General account.

CLUTTERBUCK, R.H. *The archives of the Corporation of Andover.* [Andover]: Andover Advertiser, 1891. Reprinted from the *Andover advertiser.* Many abstracts from a wide variety of corporation documents - recognizances, indictments, wills, tything mens' returns, presentments, *etc.*

COLLIER, C., & CLUTTERBUCK, R.H., eds. *The archives of Andover.* 2 vols. Andover: J.C. Holmes, [188-?] Pt.1. Churchwardens' accounts, 1470. Pt.2. Charters and grants.

DARRAH, M.J., & SPAUL, J.E.H. *The corporation of Andover, 1599-1835.* [Andover]: Andover Local Archives Committee, 1970. Brief; includes extracts from minute books.

Register of the unreformed Corporation of Andover, 1599 until 1835. Andover records 7. [Andover]: Andover Local Archives Committee, 1971. Lists capital burgesses, approved men, and stewards.

Arreton

'Extracts from Arreton overseers of the poor accounts, 1758-1786 ... ', *I.O.W.F.H.S.* 30, 1993, 26.

Basingstoke

MILLARD, JAMES ELWIN, ed. *The book of accounts of the wardens of the Fraternity of the Holy Ghost in Basingstoke, A.D. 1557-A.D. 1654.* [Basingstoke]: J.E. Millard, 1882. Extensive, with many names - but no index.

Bishopstoke

SEAGRAVE, LINDA. 'Hampshire parishes, no.11: Bishopstoke', *H.F.H.* 5(1), 1978, 7-8. Includes list of parish records.

Broughton

'Broughton parish records', *H.N.Q.* 10, 1900, 29-31. General discussion.

Chalton

EDWARDS, F., & E. 'Hampshire parishes and their records, 2: Chalton & Idsworth', *H.F.H.* 2(4), 1975, 59-62. Includes list of parochial records of genealogical interest.

Dibden

WYATT, SIR STANLEY. 'Old rate books of a Hampshire parish', *Genealogist's magazine* 11(13), 1954, 442-7. Dibden; discusses overseer's poor rate book, 1818-48, and churchwardens' account book, 1772-1832.

Elson

'Elson landowners, 1859', *H.F.H.* 13(4), 1987, 317. List of ratepayers.

Fareham

MATTRAVERS, PHILIP. 'Why not look in the Workhouse?' *H.F.H.* 3(4), 1977, 63-5. Discusses records of Fareham Board of Guardians, 19th c.

'Association of the inhabitants of the town and parish of Fareham ...', *Fareham past and present* 4(2), 1992, 18-24. Lists members of the 'loyal' society founded in 1792.

Farlington

'The parish of Farlington', *H.F.H.* 2(3), 1975, 27-9. Includes list of documents from the parish chest of genealogical interest.

Fordingbridge

WEBB, N.R. 'Fordingbridge on fire', *H.F.H.* 15(2), 1988, 111-12. Includes petition from inhabitants of Fordingbridge to Quarter Sessions, 1702.

Idsworth

See Chalton

Isle of Wight

'Outdoor relief', *I.O.W.F.H.S.* 16, 1990, 26-9; 17, 1990, 16-18; 18, 1990, 16-18; 19, 1990, 19-21. See also 21, 1991, 11. Index to 1834 outdoor relief books from the Isle of Wight House of Industry.

[GRIFFIN, J.] 'Poor relief: more extracts from the Isle of Wight Guardians of the Poor weekly minutes and outdoor relief books', *I.O.W.F.H.S.* 16, 1990, 16-17; 17, 1990, 12-13; 18, 1990, 30-31; 20, 1991, 26-7; 21, 1991, 24-5. For 1787-92.

'The Isle of Wight House of Industry, 1770-1834', *I.O.W.F.H.S.* 18, 1990, 8-12. General discussion.

FEW, JANET. 'The people of the House of Industry under the old Poor Law', *I.O.W.F.H.S.* 19, 1990, 6-10. Includes some names, early 19th c.

GRIFFIN, J. 'Outdoor relief: Isle of Wight Guardians of the Poor weekly minutes and out relief book, 1833-1834', *I.O.W.F.H.S.* 14, 1989, 25-7; 15, 1989, 19-21.

Knights Enham

CLUTTERBUCK, R.H. 'Briefs', *H.N.Q.* 4, 1889, 105-9. Lists of charitable donors to various causes in Knights Enham, 1701.

Lymington

ST.BARBE, CHARLES. *Records of the Corporation of the Borough of New Lymington in the County of Southampton extracted from the muniments in the possession of the mayor and town council, and other authorities, in the year 1848.* Nichols & Son, [1860?]

Milford

HARRIS, V.D. 'The endowed charities of the parish of Milford, Hampshire', *Milford on Sea Record Society: an occasional magazine* 1(3), 1910, 11-28.

HARRIS, V.D. 'Poorhouses in England, with special reference to Milford Poorhouse and the relief of the poor in the parish', *Milford-on-Sea Record Society: an occasional magazine* 3(5), 1926, 3-31. Gives names of vestrymen, 1819-26.

SEARS, F.W. 'Milford churchwardens' accounts, 1713-1800', *Milford-on-Sea Record Society: an occasional magazine* 5(5), 1951, 14-41. Extracts only.

SYKES, W.S. 'The threatened invasion by the French in 1794-8', *Milford on Sea Record Society: an occasional magazine* 2(1), 1914, 44-8. Lists subscribers to a voluntary contribution, 1798, from Milford churchwardens' accounts.

New Forest

STAGG, D.J., ed. *A calendar of New Forest documents, 1244-1334.* H.R.S. 3. 1979. Includes list of officers of the Forest.

STAGG, D.J., ed. *A calendar of New Forest documents: the fifteenth to the seventeenth centuries.* H.R.S. 5. 1983. Includes list of forest officers.

STAGG, DAVID J., ed. *New Forest commoners, A.D. 1792.* [ ]: New Forest Association, 1983. Return of commoners, their holdings and their rights, made in connection with the New Forest Bill, 1792.

Abstract of claims preferred at a justice seat held for the New Forest, Hants., in ... A.D. 1670, with a return made by commissioners acting under the acts of the 39 & 40 Geo. 3 cap. 86 and 41 Geo. 3 cap. 108, as to incroachments, &c in the said Forest. W.H. Dalton, 1853. Includes *Schedule of lands in the several walks in the New Forest ... 1801* listing occupiers.

Newport

HOCKEY, S.F. 'Terrier book of Newport (I.W.), 1563', *P.P.H.F.C.* 19, 1955-7, 227-37. Lists tenants of town properties.

North Hayling

'Removal orders: North Hayling', *H.F.H.* 5(4), 1979, 129. List, 1772-1832.

Portchester

EDWARDS, E. 'Hampshire parishes no.14: Portchester', *H.F.H.* 5(3), 99-102. Includes list of parochial records.

Portsmouth

EAST, ROBERT. *Extracts from records in the possession of the municipal corporation of the Borough of Portsmouth, and from other documents relating thereto.* 2nd ed. Portsmouth: Henry Lewis, 1891. Extensive. Includes lists of mayors, aldermen, burgesses and other officers, rent rolls of 1469, 1693, 1702 and 1880, *etc., etc.* Reference should also be made to the 1st edition by Richard J. Murrell and Robert East, published 1884.

Catalogue of an exhibition of documents depicting eight centuries of Portsmouth history at the Cumberland House Museum, Portsmouth ... 1956. Historical Manuscripts Commission, 1956.

Roll of freemen of the Borough of Portsmouth, 1573-1924. Portsmouth: W.H. Barrell, [1926?]

WILLIS, ARTHUR J. *Borough sessions papers, 1653-1688.* ed. Margaret J. Hoad. Portsmouth Record Series 1. Phillimore, 1971. Includes list of J.P.'s.

ALBERT, WILLIAM, & HARVEY, P.D.A., eds. *Portsmouth and Sheet turnpike commissioners minute book, 1711-1754.* Portsmouth Record Series 2. City of Portsmouth, 1973.

SURRY, N.W., & THOMAS, J.H. *Book of original entries, 1731-1751.* Portsmouth Record Series 3. City of Portsmouth, 1976. Includes lists of mayors, J.P's and officers, with biographical notes on aldermen and burgesses.

EDWARDS, E. 'Portsmouth borough sessions', *H.F.H.* 2(1), 1975, 15-18; 2(3), 1975, 43-4; 2(4), 1975, 69-70; 3(2), 1976, 48-9; 4(4), 1978, 123. Calendar of sessions records, 1777-8.

WILLIS, A.J. 'Portsmouth settlement certificates', *F.H.J.S.E.H.G.S.* 1(2), 1974, 41-3. List, 1681-1768.

WILLIS, ARTHUR J. 'Register of persons examined concerning their settlement', *F.H.J.S.E.H.G.S.* 1(5), 1975, 97-9. 18th c., Portsmouth.

WILLIS, A.J. 'Register of persons who have provided certificates of settlement', *H.F.H.* 2(1), 1975, 10-14. Portsmouth; late 17th-18th c.

WILLIS, A.J. 'Removal orders from Portsmouth', *F.H.J.S.E.H.G.S.* 1(3), 1974, 59-62. List, 1698-1744. Includes facsimile of removal order of Barbara Trivett, to Titchfield, 1748/9.

WILLIS, A.J. 'Removal orders to Portsmouth', *F.H.J.S.E.H.G.S.* 1(4), 1974, 75-80. Lists, 1712-1802.

NEWNHAM, A.J. 'Staff and inmates of the St.Mary's Institution, Portsmouth, 1850', *Family history* 3(16), 1965, 117-32. List giving ages, birthplace, position and occupation.

St.Thomas

SAUNDERS, W.H. 'Churchwardens' accounts of St.Thomas, Portsmouth, A.D. 1566', *Journal of the British Archaeological Association* 44, 1888, 257-63.

THOMAS, E.G. 'The apprenticeship and settlement papers of the parish of St.Thomas, Portsmouth', *Portsmouth archives review* 4, 1979-80, 12-24. Discussion; few names.

Ringwood

JUDSON, T. 'Notes on Ringwood Workhouse master's remembrance book, 1826-1830', *H.F.C.L.H.N.* 1(6), 1982, 128-30.

Romsey

STAGG, STELLA. 'Names taken from Romsey Union poor law records at Kew R.O.1854 (MH12-10984/5)', *H.F.H.* 12(2), 1985, 96.

SUCKLING, MRS. 'The arms in the Town Hall at Romsey', *P.P.H.F.C.* 6, supplement, 1914, 19-31. Arms of the town's high stewards and recorders with notes on them, 17-19th c.

Ryde

'Hospital benefactors', *I.O.W.F.H.S.* 7, 1987, 12. Lists benefactors' surnames, 1847, of Ryde Hospital.

Southampton

A number of accounts of the borough's archives are available:

HEARNSHAW, F.J.C. *The records of Southampton: a brief account of some of the borough documents.* Southampton: Cox & Sharland, 1906.

Southampton *continued*

HISTORICAL MANUSCRIPTS COMMISSION. *The manuscripts of the corporations of Southampton and Kings Lynn.* 11th report, appendix, pt.3. Cd.5060-ii. H.M.S.O., 1887.

JEAFFRESON, JOHN CORDY. *Borough of Southampton: lists of charters, letters patent, and other muniments, of the Corporation of Southampton.* Southampton: Warren & Son, 1886.

VAUX, W.S.W. 'Some notices of records preserved amongst the Corporation archives at Southampton', *Archaeological journal* 3, 1846, 229-33.

For borough charters, see:

GIDDEN, H.W., ed. *The charters of the Borough of Southampton.* 2 vols. P.S.R.Soc. 7 & 9, 1909-10. v.1. 1199-1480. v.2. 1484-1836.

WELCH, EDWIN. *Southampton city charters.* Southampton papers 4. Southampton: City of Southampton, 1966.

Mayors and sheriffs are listed in:

The Southampton chronology of all the names of mayors and sheriffs with the number of years each served; from the first year of the incorporation granted by Hen. VI in 1446 until the present time, September 14, 1785. Southampton: A. Cunningham, 1785.

Many volumes of Southampton records have been edited and published; they include much information of genealogical interest. The following list is in rough chronological order. See also below under Winchester, and check the place-name index.

STUDER, P., ed. *The oak book of Southampton of c. A.D. 1300.* 2 vols. P.S.R.Soc. 10-11. 1910-11.

STUDER, P., *Supplement to the Oak Book of Southampton of c. A.D. 1300 ... containing notes on the Anglo-French dialect of Southampton (early fourteenth century) glossary and indexes.* P.S.R.Soc. 12. 1911.

CHAPMAN, A.B. WALLIS, ed. *The black book of Southampton.* 3 vols. P.S.R.Soc. 13, 14 & 17. 1912-15. v.1. 1388-1414. v.2. 1414-1503. v.3. c.1497-1620. Deeds, wills *etc.*

GIDDEN, HARRY W., ed. *The sign manuals and the letters patent of Southampton to 1422.* P.S.R.Soc. 18. 1916.

ANDERSON, R.C, ed. *Letters of the fifteenth and sixteenth centuries from the archives of Southampton.* 2 vols. P.S.R.Soc. 22. 1921-2.

GIDDEN, HARRY W., ed. *The letters patent of Southampton (1415 to 1612).* P.S.R.Soc. 20. 1919.

GIDDEN, H.W., ed. *The stewards' books of Southampton from 1428.* 2 vols. P.S.R.Soc. 35 & 39. 1935-9.

GIDDEN, H.W., ed. *The book of remembrance of Southampton.* 3 vols. P.S.R.Soc. 27, 28 & 30. 1927-30. v.1. 1440-1620, with pedigree of Fleming, 16-19th c., and list of town officers to 1620. v.2. 1303-1518. v.3. 1483-1563.

BURGESS, L.A., ed. *The Southampton terrier of 1454.* S.R.Ser. 15. 1976. Also published as HISTORICAL MANUSCRIPTS COMMISSION *Joint publication* 21. Identifies tenants of city properties.

ANDERSON, R.C., ed. *The assize of bread book 1477-1517.* P.S.R.Soc. 23. 1923. Record of fines and other small payments received by the Corporation - not just from bakers.

MERSON, A.L., ed. *The third book of remembrance of Southampton, 1514-1602.* S.R.Ser. 2-3, 8 & 22. 1952-79. Final vol. ed. T.B. James.

HEARNSHAW, F.J.C., & D.M., eds. *Southampton court leet records, vol.1.* 4 vols. P.S.R.Soc. 1, 2, 4 & 6. 1905-8. Pt.1. 1550-1577. Pt.2. 1578-1602. Pt.3. 1603-1624. The final part (unnumbered) is *Supplement to court leet records, vol.1. A.D. 1550-1624, containing glossary of select terms, notes on syntax and dialect, and indexes.*

HEARNSHAW, F.J.C., ed. *Leet jurisdiction in England, especially as illustrated by the records of the Court Leet of Southampton.* P.S.R.Soc. [5]. 1908. Includes list of free suitors.

THOMPSON, S.C. *The story of Southampton's court leet.* City of Southampton, 1987. Brief discussion.

WELCH, EDWIN, ed. *The admiralty court book of Southampton, 1566-1585.* S.R.Ser. 13. 1968.

HAMILTON, GERTRUDE H., ed. *Books of examinations and depositions, 1570-1594.* P.S.R.Soc. 16. 1914.

ANDERSON, R.C., ed. *The book of examinations, 1601-1602, with a list of ships belonging to Southampton in the year 1570-1603.* P.S.R.Soc. 26. 1926.

HORROCKS, J.W., ed. *The assembly books of Southampton.* 4 vols. S.R.Soc. 19, 21, 24 & 25. 1917-25. v.1. 1602-8. v.2. 1609-10. v.3. 1611-1614. v.4. 1615-16.

CONNOR, W.J., ed. *The Southampton mayors book of 1606-1608.* S.R.Ser. 21. 1978.

Southampton in 1620 and the "Mayflower": an exhibition of documents by the Southampton City Record Office to celebrate the 350th anniversary of the sailing of the Mayflower from Southampton in 1620 ... Southampton: Southampton City Record Office, 1970. Includes a 'directory of Southampton about 1620', based on many sources, which attempts to identify all residents.

ANDERSON, R.C., ed. *The book of examinations and depositions, 1622-1644.* 4 vols. P.S.R.Soc. **29, 31, 34 & 36.** 1929-36. v.1. 1622-1644. v.2. 1627-1634. v.3. 1634-1639. v.4. 1639-1644.

HAMPSON, GEOFFREY, ed. *Southampton notarial protest books, 1756-1810.* S.R.Ser. **16.** 1973.

STOVOLD, JAN., ed. *Minute book of the Pavement Commissioners for Southampton, 1770-1789.* S.R.Ser. **31.** 1990.

PATTERSON, A. TEMPLE, ed. *A selection from the Southampton corporation journals, 1815-35, and borough council minutes, 1835-47.* S.R.Ser. **10.** 1965.

CROCKER, RUTH HUTCHINSON. 'The Victorian poor law in crisis and change: Southampton, 1870-1895', *Albion* **19**, 1987, 19-44.

DENMAN, M.J. 'Sources for urban history, 12: documents and urban growth, Southampton, 1878-1914', *Local historian* **12**, 1977, 353-9. Discussion of the Corporation building registers, which give names of developers, etc.

DOUGHTY, MARTIN, ed. *Dilapidated housing and housing policy in Southampton, 1890-1914.* S.R. Ser. **29.** 1986. Reprints appendix to *Detailed report of dilapidated and unhealthy houses in the Borough of Southampton ...,* 1893, listing owners of properties mentioned.

Stoke Charity

EDWARDS, E., & F.H., & BROWN, MURIEL. 'Hampshire parishes, no.4: Stoke Charity', *H.F.H.* 3(2), 1976, 44-7. Brief note on parish records.

Tichborne

WILLIAMS, E.J. WATSON. *Odd tit-bits from Tichborne old church books.* Elliot Stock, 1909. Includes brief abstracts of accounts. No index.

Titchfield

SHAW, W.J. 'Some records from Titchfield church', *Fareham past and present* **3**, 1966, 8-10; **4**, 1966, 11-13; **5**, 1967, 15-16; **6**, 1967, 8-11; **7**, 1968, 14-15; **9**, 1969, 17-18; **10**, 1969, 11-12; **13**, 1971, 15. Abstracts from documents in the parish chest.

Westbourne

ELLACOTT, PETER. *The poor of the parish and the work of the Westbourne select vestries, 1819-1835.* Bygone Westbourne 3. [Westbourne]: Westbourne Local History Group, 1986. Includes lists of select vestrymen and ratepayers, plus many other names.

Winchester

RILEY, HENRY THOMAS. 'The Corporation of Winchester', in HISTORICAL MANUSCRIPTS COMMISSION *Sixth report ...* pt.1. C.1745. H.M.S.O., 1877, 595-606.

WRIGHT, THOMAS. 'Report on the municipal records of Winchester and Southampton', in *Transactions of the British Archaeological Association at its second annual congress, held at Winchester, August 1845 ...* Henry G. Bohn, 1846, 28-39. Brief discussion.

SHENTON, F.K.J. 'Winchester records', *Gentlemen's magazine* N.S. **8**, 1872, 163-84. General discussion.

BAILEY, CHARLES. *Transcripts from the municipal archives of Winchester, and other documents, elucidating the government, manners and customs of the same city, from the 13th century to the present period.* Winchester: Hugh Barclay, 1856. Includes rate of 1671.

City of Winchester: a catalogue of charters and other objects exhibited at St.John's Rooms, during the celebration of the 700th anniversary of the mayoralty ... 1884. Winchester: Warren & Son, 1884.

City of Winchester: calendar of charters. Winchester: Jacob and Johnson, 1915. Many names are recorded in the city charters.

Exhibition of books, charters and manuscripts: Winchester, 4-14 July 1951. Oxford: Oxford University Press, 1951. Lists some borough documents which could be of relevance.

BIDDLE, MARTIN, ed. *Winchester in the early middle ages: an edition and discussion of the Winton Domesday.* Oxford: Clarendon Press, 1976. The 'Winton Domesday' in fact includes two surveys of the city, dated c.1110 and 1148. This volume includes a detailed analysis of personal names.

BIRD, W.H.B., ed. *The black book of Winchester (British Museum Additional ms. 6036).* Winchester: Warren & Son, 1925. Record of the corporation acts and proceedings, 1423-1552.

COOPER, REGINALD H. 'The early mayors of Winchester', *H.F.C.L.H.N.* 1(5), 1982, 99-106. Includes list to 1304.

CHITTY, HERBERT. *Mayors and bailiffs of Winchester during the fourteenth century.* Winchester: Jacob & Johnson, 1930. Reprinted from the *Hampshire chronicle.*

JACOB, W.H. 'Mayor and M.P', *H.N.Q.* 4, 1889, 34-6. List of those who served in both capacities in Winchester.

SMIRKE, E. 'Winchester in the thirteenth century', *Archaeological journal* 7, 1850, 372-83. Inquest giving names of jurors, and making reference to a list of tenants.

FURLEY, JOHN S., *City government of Winchester from the records of the xiv and xv centuries.* Oxford: Clarendon Press, 1923. General history.

F[URLEY], J.S. *Town life in the XIV century as seen in the court rolls of Winchester City.* Winchester: Warren and Son, [1946]. Includes many abstracts, with names, but no index.

FURLEY, J.S. 'Merchants' courts at Winchester', *English historical review* 35, 1920, 98-103. Discussion of 15-16th c. records of a borough court.

WILLIS, ARTHUR J., ed. *Winchester settlement papers, 1667-1842, from records of several Winchester parishes.* Folkestone: the editor, 1967.

MOODY, HENRY. *A handbook to the Winchester charities ...* Winchester: H. Moody, 1843. Includes information on benefactors.

MOXLEY, CYRIL. *An introduction to the history of St.Paul's Hospital, Winchester, the New Winchester Union, 1835-1846.* Winchester: Winchester Health Authority, 1987. General study.

St.Cross

CAVE, PAUL. *The history of the hospital of St.Cross.* Ringwood: Paul Cave Publications, [197-?] Includes list of masters, 12-20th c., and brief note on muniments.

MOODY, HENRY. *History and description of the Hospital of St.Cross, near Winchester, with a list of the masters since its foundation to the present time.* Winchester: G. & H. Gilmour, [183-]? Almshouse.

St.John

COLLIER, I.C. 'The churchwardens' account of St.John the Baptist, Winchester', *Reliquary* 17, 1876-7, 81-5, 155-7 & 219-24. 16-17th c.

DEVERELL, JOHN. *St.John's Hospital and other charities in Winchester.* Davis & Son, 1879. Includes the Hospital's rental, 1878, and a list of inmates from the year 1835.

TURNER, BARBARA CARPENTER. *St.John's Winchester charity.* Chichester: Phillimore & Co., 1992. General account.

'A 16th century account book of the parish of St.John Baptist, Winchester', *H.N.Q.* 6, 1892, 107-21.

Yarmouth

'Town account of Yarmouth, 1646/47', *Proceedings of the Isle of Wight Natural History and Archaeological Society* 1(9), 1928, 580-81.

15. ESTATE RECORDS

A. *General*

The records of estate administration constitute a mine of information for the genealogist. Much is in print, but far more still lies untouched in the archives. Two collections of deed abstracts are in print:

'The value of old parchment deeds in genealogical and topographical research', *Topographical quarterly* 4(3), 1936, 261-78.

'Palaeography genealogy and topography', *Topographical quarterly* 6(4), 1938, 228-64.

Enclosure awards normally list all landowners with an interest in the land being enclosed. For Hampshire, awards are listed in:

TATE, W.E. 'Field systems and enclosures in Hampshire', *P.P.H.F.C.* 16, 1947, 257-75.

The salvage of a Romsey solicitor's archive is described in:

THICK, ANNE. 'An experience not to be missed: the salvage of an archive', *Journal of the Society of Archivists* 15(2), 1994, 173-9,

B. *Private Estates*

The larger proprietors in Hampshire had land in various parts of the county, and sometimes in other counties as well. Publications listing or abstracting their estate papers include:

Bolton

'Bolton mss', *Bulletin of the National Register of Archives* 10, 1959, 8-11. Includes brief list of the archives of the Marquesses of Winchester, who owned estates in Hampshire, Dorset, Wiltshire, Devon, etc.

Botreaux

HICKS, MICHAEL. 'Landlady sells up: businessman turns country gent: the sale of the Botreaux lands in Hampshire in the 1460s', *Section newsletters [Hampshire Field Club]* 5, 1986, 5-6. Identifies purchasers.

Jervoise

MACRAY, W.D. 'Manuscripts of F.H.T. Jervoise esqre., preserved at Herriard Park, Hampshire', in HISTORICAL MANUSCRIPTS COMMISSION *Report on manuscripts in various collections, vol.IV.* Cd.3218. H.M.S.O., 1907, 140-174. Deeds, *etc.,* medieval-17th c., relating to various places.

C. *Ecclesiastical Estates*

Ecclesiastical estates were of great importance, especially prior to the Reformation. Their records had a much greater chance of survival than the records of private families since they were 'perpetual' institutions. Their deeds were frequently collected together into chartularies, some of which have been published. These, together with other ecclesiastical estate records, are listed here.

For a list of manors and realty held by Hampshire's nunneries, see:

COLDICOTT, DIANA K. *Hampshire nunneries.* Chichester: Phillimore, 1989.

Beaulieu Abbey

FOWLER, SIR JAMES K. *A history of Beaulieu Abbey, A.D. 1204-1539.* Car Illustrated, 1911. Includes note on the medieval lay owners of the manor of Beaulieu.

DAVIS, G.R.C. 'A 13th c. account book of Beaulieu Abbey', *British Museum quarterly* 20, 1955-6, 81-3. Brief description only.

HOCKEY, S.F., ed. *The account-book of Beaulieu Abbey.* Camden 4th series 16. Royal Historical Society, 1975. Medieval accounts of Beaulieu Abbey and its manor of Faringdon.

HOCKEY, S.F., ed. *The Beaulieu chartulary.* S.R.Ser. 17. 1974.

TALBOT, C.H. 'A Cistercian account book', *The Listener* 54, 1955, 177-9. Of Beaulieu Abbey, 13th c., brief description.

Carisbrooke Priory

HOCKEY, S.F., ed. *The cartulary of Carisbrooke Priory.* Isle of Wight record series 2. [ ]: Isle of Wight Record Office, 1981. Includes list of priors.

HORWOOD, ALFRED J. 'The manuscripts of Mrs. Prescott, Oxford Square', in HISTORICAL MANUSCRIPTS COMMISSION *Second report ...* C.441. H.M.S.O., 1874, 97-8. Includes brief note on a survey of the estates of Carisbrooke Priory, 16th c.

Hyde Abbey

EDWARDS, EDWARD, ed. *Liber monasterii de Hyda, comprising a chronicle of the affairs of England ... and a chartulary of the Abbey of Hyde, in Hampshire, A.D. 455-1023.* Rolls series 45. Longmans, Green, Reader and Dyer, 1866.

Mottisfont Priory

GOLDING, B. 'The Mottisfont rental', *H.F.C.L.H.N.* 1(8), 1983, 166-7. Rental of Hampshire and Wiltshire properties of Mottisfont Priory.

Netley Abbey

MEEKINGS, C.A.F., & HUNNISETT, R.F. 'The early years of Netley Abbey', *Journal of ecclesiastical history* **30,** 1979, 1-37. Mainly concerned with estate history, 13th c.

Portsmouth

HOCKEY, FREDERICK. 'The first post-dissolution account of the Domus Dei of Portsmouth', *Portsmouth archives review* **4,** 1979-80, 2-11. Transcript; records rents in Broughton, Frodington, Kingston, Portsmouth and the Isle of Wight, 1540.

Quarr Abbey

HOCKEY, S.F. *Quarr Abbey and its lands, 1132-1631.* Leicester: Leicester University Press, 1970.

St.Denys Priory

BLAKE, E.O., ed. *The cartulary of the Priory of St.Denys, near Southampton.* S.R.Ser. **24-5.** 1981.

St.Swithins Priory

DREW, J.S. 'Manorial accounts of St.Swithins Priory, Winchester', *English historical review* **62,** 1947, 20-41. Reprinted in CARUS-WILSON, E.M., ed. *Essays in economic history* **2.** Edward Arnold, 1962, 12-30. General discussion.

GREATREX, JOAN, ed. *The register of the Common Seal of the Priory of St.Swithun, Winchester, 1345-1497.* H.R.S. **2.** 1978.

KITCHIN, G.W., ed. *Compotus rolls of the obedientiaries of St.Swithun's Priory, Winchester.* Hampshire Record Society. Simpkin & Co., 1892.

Selborne Priory

MACRAY, W. DUNN, ed. *Calendar of charters and documents relating to Selborne and its priory preserved in the muniment room of Magdalen College, Oxford.* 2 vols. Hampshire Record Society. Simpkin & Co., 1891-4.

BAINE, JAMES. 'Sir Adam Gurdun and Selbourne Priory', *Genealogist* N.S. **5,** 1888, 90-91. Deed abstracts, 13th c.

Southampton. Gods House

KAYE, J.M., ed. *The cartulary of God's House, Southampton.* S.R.Ser. **19-20.** 1976.

KAYE, J.M., ed. *A God's House miscellany, consisting of I: two early Southampton rolls. II: a calendar of correspondence relating to the Queen's College estate in Southampton.* S.R.Ser. **27.** 1984. The 'rolls' are terriers listing tenants, 13th c., the correspondence is 16-18th c.

RILEY, HENRY THOMAS. 'Queens College, Oxford: third report: God's House at Southampton, *temp.* Edward I - Edward III', in HISTORICAL MANUSCRIPTS COMMISSION. *Sixth report ...* C.1745. H.M.S.O., 1877, 551-69. Originally founded as an almshouse.

POSTLES, DAVID. 'Manorial accountancy of God's House, Southampton', *Archives* **18,** 1987, 36-41. Discussion of medieval accounts.

Southwick Priory

HANNA, KATHARINE A., ed. *The cartularies of Southwick Priory.* 2 vols. H.R.S. **9-10.** 1988-9.

HANNA, KATHARINE A. 'The Southwick cartularies: an editor's view', *Section newsletters ... [Hampshire Field Club]* **3,** 1985, 4-6.

Winchester Cathedral

GOODMAN, A.W., ed. *Chartulary of Winchester Cathedral.* Winchester: Warren & Son, 1927.

WATKINS, AELRED, ed. 'Fragment of a thirteenth-century receiver's roll from Winchester Cathedral Priory', *English historical review* **61,** 1946, 89-105.

Winchester College

HIMSWORTH, SHEILA, *et al. Winchester College muniments: a descriptive list.* 3 vols.

Chichester: Phillimore, 1976-84. Lists records of the College estates, principally in Hampshire, but also in many other southern counties. Also lists headmasters and other staff.

CUSTANCE, ROGER. 'The archives of Winchester College', *Section newsletters [Hampshire Field Club]* **6**, 1986, 9. Brief discussion.

HARVEY, JOHN H. 'The archives of Winchester College', *Bulletin of the National Register of Archives* **12**, 1963, 22-5. Brief description.

HARVEY, JOHN H. 'Winchester College muniments: an introduction with a summary index', *Archives* **5**(28), 1962, 201-16.

Winchester Diocese

Detailed lists of Diocesan records are to be found in the works of Lewin and Deedes, listed above, section 12. See also:

MAYBERRY, T.W. *Estate records of the Bishops of Winchester in the Hampshire Record Office.* Hampshire Record Office, 1988.

HALL, HUBERT. 'A list of the rent rolls of the Bishopric of Winchester (Ecclesiastical Commission) in the Public Record Office', *Economica* **4**, 1924. 52-61. 13-15th c. Lists an important series.

BLOOM, J.H. 'The account rolls of the manors of the Bishopric of Winchester: notes on some early rentals', *Genealogist's magazine* **7**, 1936, 337-43. Medieval; includes notes on the Honeywell family.

Two early account rolls have been published:

HALL, HUBERT, ed. *The pipe roll of the Bishopric of Winchester for the fourth year of the pontificate of Peter des Roches, 1208-1209 ...* P.S. King & Son for the London School of Economics, 1903. Diocesan manors.

HOLT, N.R., ed. *The pipe roll of the Bishopric of Winchester, 1210-1211 (PRO.Eccl.2-22-159270B).* Manchester University Press, 1964.

There have been many studies based on the medieval estate records of the Diocese. These include:

BEVERIDGE, SIR WILLIAM. 'The Winchester rolls and their dating', *Economic history review* **2**, 1929-30, 93-113.

BEVERIDGE, WILLIAM. 'Wages in the Winchester manors', *Economic history review* **7**, 1936, 22-43. Based on court rolls, 13-15th c.

FARMER, D.L. 'Grain yields on the Winchester manors in the later middle ages', *Economic*

history review 2nd series **30**, 1977, 555-66. Based on 14-15th c. court rolls.

MAY, ALFRED N. 'An index of thirteenth-century peasant impoverishment? Manor court fines', *Economic history review* 2nd series **26**, 1973, 389-402. See also **28**, 1975, 304-11. Based on the pipe rolls of the Diocese of Winchester.

POSTAN, M.M., & TITOW, J.Z. 'Heriots and prices on Winchester manors', *Economic history review* 2nd series **11**, 1958-9, 383-411. Based on manorial court rolls; heriots were payments made on the death of tenants.

Works dealing with the post-Reformation period include:

HEAL, F. 'Archbishop Laud revisited: leases and estate management at Canterbury and Winchester before the Civil War', in O'DAY, ROSEMARY, & HEAL, FELICITY, eds. *Princes and paupers in the English church, 1500-1800.* Leicester: Leicester University Press, 1981, 129-51.

BENHAM, W. 'Church lands in Hampshire in the 17th century', *H.N.Q.* **3**, 1887, 73-4. Gives names of purchasers of Winchester diocesan property during the Interregnum.

BURN, J.H. 'An accompte of the sale of the manors and church lands belonging to the See of Winton, to whom, and for what sums, sold during the time of the Civil War, and the reign of King Charles the First', *Transactions of the British Archaeological Association at its second annual congress held at Winchester, August 1845 ...* Henry G. Bohn, 1856, 45-8.

GOODMAN, FLORENCE REMINGTON. *Reverend landlords and their tenants: scenes and characters on Winchester manors after the Restoration.* Winchester: Warren and Son, 1930.

MOOR, JOYCE. 'Fines books', *H.F.H.* **11**(2), 1984, 116-8. Discusses entry fines paid by tenants of the Bishops of Winchester, using a case study of the Channell family of Bursledon, 17th c. Includes map of the Bishopric's Hampshire estates.

Windsor. St.George's Chapel

DALTON, JOHN NEALE, ed. *The manuscripts of St.George's Chapel, Windsor.* Windsor: the Dean & Canons, 1957. Relating to property in 17 Hampshire parishes, as well as to estates in many other counties.

D. Records of Individual Manors, etc.

Andover

SPAUL, J.E.H. *Andover documents no.3: inclosure award 1785.* [Andover]: Andover Local Archives Committee, [1969]

Appleshaw

GREEN, I.M. 'Sheep fair expense accounts', *H.F.H.* **10**(1), 1983, 389. Notes on accounts of Appleshaw fair, with names of Somerset and Dorset dealers and drovers, 1810.

Bishops Waltham

BARSTOW, HAROLD G., ed. *1332 and 1464 rentals of Bishops Waltham manors.* Chandlers Ford: H.G. Barstow, 1992.

BARSTOW, HAROLD G., ed. *1550 rentals of Bishops Waltham manors. Part 1.* Chandlers Ford: H.G. Barstow, 1993.

BARSTOW, HAROLD G.,ed. *1630 and 1693 rentals of Bishops Waltham manors, with 1550 Bursledon, 1550 Bitterne and Weston, 1573 Ashton. Parts 2 and 3.* Chandlers Ford: H.G. Barstow, 1994.

Bramshott

GILES, L.C., ed. *Bramshott manor court rolls.* Liphook: Bramshott and Liphook Preservation Society, 1990. 1274-1454 and 1605-1711.

Christchurch

STAGG, DAVID J., ed. *Christchurch court rolls in the time of Henry VIII.* New Milton: Red House Museum Archives Fund, 1983. Abstracts.

Crawley

GRAS, NORMAN B.S., & GRAS, ETHEL C. *The economic and social history of the English village (Crawley, Hampshire), A.D. 909-1928.* Harvard economic studies **34**. Cambridge: Harvard University Press, 1930. Includes transcripts of numerous manorial records; also some wills, extracts from registers and other parochial documents, census returns, 1841 and 1851, *etc., etc.*

Crondall

BAIGENT, FRANCIS JOSEPH, ed. *A collection of records and documents relating to the hundred and manor of Crondal, in the county of Southampton. Part 1: historical and manorial.* Hampshire Record Society. Simpkin & Co., 1891. Includes deeds, rentals, wills, accounts, *etc.* No more published.

Eastney

PEACOCK, SARAH. 'A 17th century survey of the manor of Eastney and Milton', *Portsmouth archives review* **2**, 1977, 16-25. 1632 survey.

Exton

ZELL, MICHAEL. 'Accounts of a sheep and corn farm, 1558-60', *Agricultural history review* **27**, 1979, 122-8. Exton.

Goodbegot

GOODMAN, A.W. *The manor of Goodbegot in the city of Winchester.* Winchester: Warren & Son, 1923. Includes court rolls, 1354-6, 1503, 1527 and 1535.

Hambledon

ROBERTS, C. BETTON. 'The Parliamentary survey of Hambledon, 1647', *P.P.H.F.C.* **15**, 1943, 297-303. Description of the survey, with some names of tenants.

Isle of Wight

SHERWIN, G.A. 'Some medieval documents of the Isle of Wight', *Proceedings of the Isle of Wight Natural History and Archaeological Society* **2**(6), 1935, 452-63. Discusses medieval deeds of the island.

Ludshott

GILES, L.C., ed. *Ludshott manor court rolls.* [ ]: Bramshott and Liphook Preservation Society, 1991. Medieval-19th c.

Manydown

KITCHIN, G.W., ed. *The manor of Manydown, Hampshire.* Hampshire Record Society. Simpkin & Co., 1895. Court rolls, *etc.*

Martin

See South Damerham

Meon Stoke

KIRBY, T.F. 'Charters of the manor of Meonstoke', *Archaeologia* **57**(2), 1901, 285-94.

Milford

'A list of the principal inhabitants of Milford, A.D. 1680-90, taken from the tithe account of the Rev. John Birket, vicar, to which have been added various details of their holdings traced in some cases down to A.D. 1800', *Milford on Sea Record Society: occasional magazine* 2(2), 1916, 35-75.

'Milford tithe award and map of 1840', *Milford-on-Sea Record Society: an occasional magazine* 3(1), 1923, 9-20. Includes names of 'the chief farmers and gentry of Milford parish' in 1840.

Milton

See Eastney

New Forest

LEWIS, PERCIVAL. *Historical enquiries concerning forests and forest law, with topographical remarks upon the ancient and modern state of the New Forest, in the County of Southampton.* T. Payne, 1811. Includes 'copy of proceedings of the Swainmote', 1662, listing tenants.

Over Wallop

PEARCE, D.H. 'The Over (Upper) Wallop enclosure award of 1787', *H.F.H.* 11(3), 1984, 168-9. Many names of landlords and tenants.

Portsmouth

HOCKEY, FREDERICK. 'The property and rents of Quarr Abbey in medieval Portsmouth', *Portsmouth archives review* 2, 1977, 9-15. Includes rental, 1257.

Quarley

COLDICOTT, DIANA K. 'The manor and court of Quarley, 1646-1741', *Lookback at Andover: journal of the Andover History and Archaeology Society* 2(1), 1991, 5-10. General discussion.

Ringwood. Cowpits

JUDSON, TOM. 'Cowpits or Couches Pits, Ringwood', *H.F.C.L.H.N.* 1(4), 1981, 63-6. Deed extracts *etc.,* 18-19th c.

Rockbourne

WINSER, ANDREW. *Rockbourne in the 17th century: a survey of the manors of Rockbourne and Rockstead in the 17th century.* [Fordingbridge: the author], 1984. Detailed study - but *not* a transcript.

Rockstead

See Rockbourne

Ropley

KIRBY, T.F. 'Charters of the manor of Ropley, Hants', *Archaeologia* 58, 1902, 227-36. medieval; includes pedigrees of Gerveys and Tyghale.

Shawford Mill

GALE, MAUREEN. 'An account of the seventeenth century construction of Shawford Mill and millhouse', *Section newsletters [Hampshire Field Club]* 12, 1989, 9-13. Accounts give names of various tradesmen and labourers, *etc.*

South Damerham

WATKIN, AELRED, ed. *The great chartulary of Glastonbury, vol.III.* Somerset Record Society 64, 1956. Includes deeds relating to the manors of South Damerham and Martin.

Southampton

RUTHERFORD, J., ed. *The miscellaneous papers of Captain Thomas Stockwell, 1590-1611.* 2 vols. P.S.R.Soc. 32-3, 1932-3. Stockwell was the bailiff of Sir Oliver Lambert's Southampton estate, to which most of these papers relate.

Southsea

RILEY, R.C. 'The use of rate books as a means of dating properties: T.E. Owen's houses in Southsea, Hampshire', *Southern history* 2, 1980, 93-100.

Sutton Scotney

See Wonston

Titchfield

WATTS, GEORGE. 'Titchfield rental, 1377-78', *H.F.H.* 13(3), 1986, 227. List of almost 90 tenants.

Ventnor

HERRIDGE, K. 'Ventnor estate accounts', *I.O.W.F.H.S.* 22, 1991, 269. Lists purchasers of plots of land and some lessees, early 19th c.

Winchester

MAY, D. 'The Somer rentals in the Winchester City Archives', *P.P.H.F.C.* **18**, 1954, 325-31. Discussion of rentals of Winchester property belonging to Henry Somer, 15th c., includes transcript of one, 1432-3.

Wonston

SMITH, W.C.G. 'Two travellers to Wonston', *H.F.H.* **4**(3), 1977, 8490. Tithe apportionment, 1838, for Wonston and Sutton Scotney.

Woodgarston

BIGG-WITHER, R.F. 'On the manor of Woodgarston and some documents relating thereto', *P.P.H.F.C.* **4**, 1898-1903, 241-52. Deeds, 14-15th c.

Wymering

BIGG-WITHER, REGINALD F., ed. 'Rental of Wymering', *P.P.H.F.C.* **7**(1), 1914, 1-19. Early 14th c.

E. *Manorial Descents, etc.*

The descent of many properties have been traced; a number of the older histories listed in section 1 include much information on manorial lords. Works tracing the descents of particular properties are listed here.

Alton. Amery House

BOWDEN, MARK, *et al.* 'The archaeology and history of Amery House, Alton', *P.P.H.F.C.* **44**, 1988, 49-65. Includes descent.

Alton. Johnsons Corner

MILLETT, MARTIN, *et al.* 'The history, architecture and archaeology of Johnson's Corner, Alton', *P.P.H.F.C.* **39**, 1983, 77-109. Includes descents of properties.

Appuldurcombe

BENSON, G.C. 'Appuldurcombe manor', *Proceedings of the Isle of Wight Natural History and Archaeological Society* **4**(5), 1950, 151-4. Manorial descent, medieval-19th c.

Bensted St.Clair

WILLIAMS, C.L. SINCLAIR. 'The manor of Bensted St.Clair', *P.P.H.F.C.* **42**, 1986, 109-23. Descent; especially in the medieval St.Clair family.

Bonchurch

WHITEHEAD, J. 'Bonchurch parish', *P.P.H.F.C.* **5**, 1904-6, 65-81. Primarily concerned with manorial descents; includes folded pedigree of De Insula (otherwise De Lisle), medieval; also pedigrees showing relationship of Lisle, Dennys and Popham, 16-17th c., and of Popham and Hill, 18-19th c., with list of rectors.

Brockenhurst

See Lymington

Chawton

LEIGH, WILLIAM AUSTEN, & KNIGHT, MONTAGU GEORGE. *Chawton manor and its owners: a family history.* Smith Elder & Co., 1911. Descent of the manor through Knight, Lewkenor, Martin, May, Brodnax and Austen. Includes list of clergy, monumental inscriptions, wills *etc.,* and pedigrees, medieval-19th c.

Cosham

DAVEY, C.R. 'The survival of tenement names at Cosham', *H.F.C.L.H.N.* **1**(3), 1981, 40-42. Discussion of place-names which mainly derive from surnames, with brief notes on the persons whose names were borrowed.

Earlstone

MONEY, WALTER. 'Earlstone Manor house, Burghclere', *P.P.H.F.C.* **4**, 1898-1903, 155-64. Descent; includes pedigree of Beconshaw, 16-17th c.

East Tytherley

SUCKLING, MRS. 'Some notes on the manor of East Tytherley', *P.P.H.F.C.* **9**, 1920, 1-22. Descent; includes pedigree of Columbars, 12-13th c., and of Camoys and Goring, 15-16th c.

Farley Chamberlayne

SUCKLING, MRS. 'Lords of the manor of Farley Chamberlayne', *P.P.H.F.C.* **7**(1), 1914, 86-100. Includes list of arms, medieval-19th c.

Farlington

DAVEY, C.R. 'Drayton and Beamonds in Farlington parish', *P.P.H.F.C.* **45**, 1989, 129-34. Descents.

Foxcott

RUSSEL, ANDREW D., *et al.* 'Foxcotte: the archaeology and history of a Hampshire hamlet', *P.P.H.F.C.* **41**, 1985, 149-224. Includes descent.

Great East Standen

See Merstone

Hydegate

COLDICOTT, DIANA K. *Hydegate & its people: four hundred years of a Tudor farmhouse.* Long Sutton: the author, 1970. Traces descent; includes pedigrees of Terry, 17-18th c., and Harris, 18-19th c.

Knighton

DAVIS, R.G. 'Historical notes on the manor of Knighton, in the Isle of Wight', *P.P.H.F.C.* **3**, 1894-7, 295-302. Descent.

WHITEHEAD, JOHN L. 'Notes on the manor of Knighton, I. of W., and the early manor lords, A.D. 1066-1343', *P.P.H.F.C.* **6** supplement, 1914, 7-18; 7(2), 1915, 64-8; 8(2), 1918, 213-9. Includes pedigree of Morville and Gorges. Not completed.

Lymington

COLES, ROBERT. *Lymington High Street then and now.* Ringwood: Brown & Son, 1984. Traces occupiers from 1840.

PINNELL, BLAKE. *Country house history around Lymington, Brockenhurst, and Milford on Sea.* Christchurch: Eon Graphics, 1987. Includes information on descents.

Merstone

DAVIS, R.G. 'Historical notes on the manors of Merstone and Great East Standen in the Isle of Wight', *P.P.H.F.C.* **3**, 1894-7, 59-98. Descents.

Milford

COLDICOTT, DIANA K. *Milford House: the manor house of Milford Baddesley in the parish of Milford-on-Sea, Hampshire.* Lymington: the author, 1979. Traces descent through Rickman, Reynolds, Whitby, Agar, *etc.,* 17-20th c. Includes pedigrees.

HEYGATE, A.C.G. 'Notes on the older houses of Milford and its neighbourhood', *Milford-on-Sea Record Society: an occasional magazine* 3(2), 1924, 5-42. Many names, with some descents.

'Place names of the ancient parish of Milford', *Milford on Sea Record Society: an occasional magazine* 2(6), 1921, 5-86. Gives many names of former owners and occupiers.

See also Lymington

Nether Wallop

HICKS, MICHAEL. 'Lessor v. lessee: Nether Wallop rectory, 1700-1870', *P.P.H.F.C.* **46**, 1990, 145-56. Traces lessees of the Vicars Choral of York Minster.

Osborne

GROVES, DR. 'Osborne, and the families who have held it', *P.P.H.F.C.* **2**, 1890-93, 317-30. Traces descent.

GROVES, DR. 'Osborne, Isle of Wight, and the families who have held it', *H.N.Q.* **7**, 1893, 139-47. Descent.

Peacock Hill

MEADOWS, J.E. 'Peacock Hill', *I.O.W.F.H.S.* **11**, 1988, 10-12. Traces descent, 16-19th c.

Petersfield

High Street, Petersfield. Petersfield monographs 2. Petersfield: Petersfield Area Historical Society, 1984. Documents descents; includes folded chart showing occupiers of properties, 1613-1981.

Portsmouth

WAIGHT, S.W.J. '[Descent of 27, Great Southsea Street, Portsmouth, 1816-1914]', *H.F.H.* **9**(4), 1983, 154-5.

Roche Court

SKINNER, MISS. 'Roche Court and its former owners', *P.P.H.F.C.* **7**(2), 1915, 70-79.

St.Mary Bourne

STEVENS, JOSEPH. *A parochial history of St.Mary Bourne, with an account of the manor of Hurstbourne Priors, Hants.* Whiting and Co., 1888. Includes descent of the manor; also lists of vicars and churchwardens, abstract of 1672 hearth tax, various subsidy rolls, *etc., etc.*

Southampton

JAMES, T.B. 'Administration and aspiration: some Southampton property owners, c.1400-1600', *P.P.H.F.C.* **37**, 1981, 55-62. Discusses descents of property; some names.

LE MAY, KEITH. 'Thornhill Park, Southampton', *H.F.H.* **6**(2), 1979, 91-5. Descent, 19-20th c., through Hoy, Dumbleton, Willan and Campbell.

Stanbridge Earls

SUCKLING, MRS. 'Some notes on the manor of Stanbridge Earls in the parish of Romsey Extra', *P.P.H.F.C.* **6**, 1907-10, 41-64. Descent; includes will of John Kirkeby, 1558.

Stansted Park

PIPER, A. CECIL. 'Stansted Park and its owners', *P.P.H.F.C.* **8**(3), 1919, 289-301.

Stockbridge

HILL, ROSALIND M.T. 'The manor of Stockbridge', *P.P.H.F.C.* **32**, 1975, 93-101. Descent, medieval-20th c.

Swarraton

EYRE, WILLIAM L.W. *A brief history of the parishes of Swarraton and Northington, with notices of the owners of the Grange, in the County of Southampton.* Simpkin & Co., 1890. Primarily an account of the manorial lords - Cobb, Henley, Drummond and Baring; also includes abstracts of tax records, and a transcript of the (very brief) parish register of Northington, 1579-1691.

Ventnor

ODELL, W.R. 'The old church, St.Lawrence, Ventnor, I.W.', *P.P.H.F.C.* **4**, 1898-1903, 61-74. Primarily a descent of the manor; includes folded pedigree showing relationship of Unton, Hyde, and Cottesmore, 16th c., also pedigree of De Aulay, medieval, and list of medieval clergy.

The Vyne

CHUTE, CHALONER W. *A history of The Vyne in Hampshire; being a short account of the building & antiquities of that house, situate in the parish of Sherborne St.John, Co.Hants., & of persons who have at some time lived there.* Winchester: Jacob & Johnson, 1888. Traces descent from the medieval period.

Wherwell Abbey

CLUTTERBUCK, R.H. 'The story of Wherwell Abbey part II', *H.N.Q.* **6**, 1892, 88-103. Descent from 16th c., includes pedigree of Kingsmill, 16/17th c. wills of West family, *etc.*

Whitchurch

WHITCHURCH LOCAL HISTORY SOCIETY. *The history of a parcel of land in the centre of Whitchurch.* [Whitchurch]: the Society, 1990. Descents from the 18th c., also includes list of preachers at the Independent Chapel, 1699-1920.

Winchester

CROOK, JOHN, ed. *The wainscot book: the houses of Winchester Cathedral Close and their interior decoration, 1660-1800.* H.R.S. **6**, 1984. Identifies occupants, and includes biographical notes on workmen, table of chapter clerks, *etc.*

KEENE, DEREK. *Survey of medieval Winchester.* 2 vols. Winchester studies **2**. Oxford: Clarendon Press, 1985. An astonishingly detailed attempt to trace the medieval descent of Winchester properties; includes an extensive biographical register. Important.

COOPER, PETER. 'Hunts the Chemists of Winchester', *H.F.H.* **20**(1), 1993, 41-3. Traces descent of a chemists shop through Earle, Gunner, Hunt and Chaston, 19-20th c.

16. EDUCATIONAL SOURCES

The records of schools can provide the genealogist with a great deal of information. An extensive listing of school records, together with a full listing of school histories, is provided in:

DAVEY, C.R., ed. *Education in Hampshire and the Isle of Wight: a guide to the records.* Publication 3. Winchester: Hampshire Archivists Group, 1977.

For a list of private 18th century schools, see:

OLDFIELD, J.R. 'Private schools and academies in eighteenth-century Hampshire', *P.P.H.F.C.* **45**, 1989, 147-56. Includes some names of headmasters, *etc.*

Many school histories *etc.* have been published. The list which follows is not comprehensive; it only includes those works containing information likely to be of genealogical value.

Andover

BENNETT, ARTHUR C., & PARSONS, EDMUND. *A history of the free school of Andover latterly called Andover Grammar School.* Andover: Edmund Parsons, 1920. Includes list of free scholars, 1904-20, and many other names.

LONGSTAFF, STELLA M. *Andover Grammar School, 1569-1951.* Andover: Holmes & Sons, 1953. Includes list of headmasters.

Appley

LOWE, J.B. 'Appley House School (Isle of Wight College, Appley, Ryde)', *I.O.W.F.H.S.* **15**, 1989, 26-7. Includes some names, especially of 'old Vectonians' killed 1914-18.

Arreton

'Class of '69', *I.O.W.F.H.S.* **18**, 1990, 23-5. Admission register, 1869, for Arreton school.

Basingstoke

JOHN, JANET R. *Fairfields School, Basingstoke (1888-1979): a foundation book.* [ ]: [ ], 1980. Includes lists of head-teachers, 1888-1979, prominent former pupils, and scholarship winners.

Bedales School

WAKE, ROY, & DENTON, PENNIE. *Bedales School: the first hundred years.* Haggerston Press, 1993. General history; includes list of chairmen and heads.

Bramshaw

MERSON, ELIZABETH.] *Once there was ... : the village school.* Southampton: Paul Cave Publications, 1978. Bramshaw School; includes list of staff and managers, 19-20th c.

Cowes

SAUNDERS, R. 'Did your ancestors go to Denmark?' *I.O.W.F.H.S.* **23**, 1991, 28-9. Lists scholarships won by pupils from Denmark Road School, Cowes, 1912-19.

Gosport

WHITE, L.F.W. 'Education in Gosport in the early 19th century', *G.R.* **1**, 1971, 20-23. Includes list of subscribers to the Gosport & Alverstoke Society for the Education of the Infant Poor, early 19th c.

Odiham

HOLMES, PETER J. *A history of Robert May's school at Odiham.* The author, 1991. Includes roll of headmasters, 1694-1987, list of trustees, 17-19th c., *etc.*

WILLSON, C.H.S., & HANSFORD, F.E. *The story of Odiham Grammar School, 1694-1930.* Winchester: Warren & Son, [1931]. Includes lists of foundation scholars, 1727-1873, trustees, 18-19th c., and headmasters.

Petersfield

SMITH, J.H. *Churchers College, Petersfield.* Manchester: Manchester University Press, 1936. Includes list of trustees, 1722-1876, and governors, 1876-1935, pedigree of Jolliffe, 18-19th c., list of headmasters, 1730-1927, *etc.*

The history of Churcher's College, Petersfield, Hants ... Joseph Butterworth and Son, 1823. Prepared for a case in Chancery; includes list of boys admitted, 1745-1819, with many other names.

Portsmouth

SUMMERS, A.H. *Portsmouth Grammar School roll of honour, November 1st, 1915.* Portsmouth: W.H. Barrell, 1915. Also see supplement, 1917.

Portsmouth *continued*

GATT, LAURENCE V. *The Portsmouth Beneficial School, 1755-1939*. Portsmouth papers **46**. 1986. Includes list of headmasters.

WASHINGTON, E.S., & MARSH, A.J. *Portsmouth Grammar School, 1732 to 1976*. Portsmouth: Eyre & Spottiswoode, [1976?]. Includes list of staff and rolls of honour for the Boer War and the two world wars.

WELCH, EDWIN, ed. *Records of University adult education, 1886-1939*. Portsmouth Record Series **5**. City of Portsmouth, 1985. Includes many names of students.

Romsey

SPINNEY, JESSICA, & GENGE, PAT. *Romsey schools, 900-1940*. [ ]: L.T.V.A.S., 1991. General survey.

St.Paul's, London

WILLMOTT, H.J. 'Hampshire names at St.Paul's School', *H.F.H.* **6**(4), 1980, 155-6. Brief biographies, 17-19th c.

Southampton

FREEMAN, F.L. *A short history of King Edward VI School, Southampton*. Southampton: the School, 1954. Includes lists of staff, *etc.*

RUSSELL, C.F. *A history of King Edward VI School, Southampton*. Cambridge: Privately printed, 1940. Includes list of headmasters, and chapters on prominent old boys.

SPOONER, H. *A history of Taunton's School, Southampton, 1760-1967*. Southampton: Camelot Press, 1968. Includes list of masters, 18-20th c.

GADD, E.W. *Victorian logs*. Studley: K.A.F. Brewing Books, 1979. Logbook of Northam Boys' and Girls' Schools, 1863-77. Many names of pupils, *etc.*

Twyford

WICKHAM, C.T. *The story of Twyford School from 1809 to 1909*. Winchester: Warren & Son, [1909]. Includes various lists of staff and pupils.

Winchester

CROOK, JOHN. *A history of the Pilgrims School and earlier Winchester choir schools*. Chichester: Phillimore & Co., 1981. General history.

FINLAY, E. *S. Swithun's School, Winchester, 1884-1934*. Winchester: Warren and Son, 1934. Includes register of staff and various lists of pupils.

Winchester College

There is a considerable literature on Winchester College, not all of it listed here. General histories include:

BISHOP, T.J.H. *Winchester and the public school elite: a statistical analysis*. Faber & Faber, 1957. Includes many bibliographical notes, and pedigrees showing relationships between pupils - Birley, Awdry, Portal, Nicholson, Waldegrave, Wyndham, Tennant, Asquith, Bonham-Carter, Randolph, *etc.,* 19-20th c.

CUSTANCE, ROGER, ed. *Winchester College: sixth-century essays*. Oxford: Oxford University Press, 1982. Scholarly history of general interest.

KIRBY, THOMAS F. *Annals of Winchester College from its foundation in the year 1382 to the present time ...* Henry Frowde, 1892. Includes list of headmasters, and an appendix of documents.

LEACH, ARTHUR F. *A history of Winchester College*. Duckworth & Co., 1899. General account; many names.

SABBEN-CLARE, JAMES. *Winchester College after 600 years, 1382-1982*. Southampton: Paul Cave Publications, 1981. General account.

WALCOTT, MACKENZIE E.C. *William of Wykeham and his colleges*. Winchester: David Nutt, 1852. Includes a 'roll of distinguished Wykehamists', giving biographical information.

A variety of lists of old boys have been published. They are arranged here in rough chronological order, beginning with two works covering long time-spans:

KIRBY, THOMAS FREDERICK. *Winchester scholars: a list of the wardens, fellows, and scholars of St.Mary College of Winchester, near Winchester, commonly called Winchester College*. Henry Frowde, 1888. 1397-1887; chronological listing with detailed index of names.

CHITTY, HERBERT. *An index of names of Winchester scholars in the 'Dictionary of national biography'*. Winchester: P. & G. Wells, [1902]. Reprinted from the *Wykehamist* **388**, 1901.

C[HITTY], H. *A College hall-book of 1401-2.*
Athenaeum Press, [1916]. Reprinted with
additions from *Notes and queries* 11th series
11, 1915, 393, 415 & 426. Gives many names of
fellows, guests, scholars, *etc.*

C[HITTY], H. 'College hall-book of 1401-2',
Notes and queries 11th series 11, 1915, 393-4,
415-6 & 426-7. Includes list of 19 boys
admitted during the book's currency.

C[HITTY], H. *The Winchester hall book of
1406-7.* Athenaeum Press, [1916]. Reprinted
with additions from *Notes and queries* 11th
series 12, 1915, 293 & 313.

C[HITTY], H. *The Winchester hall-book of
1414-5 and other records.* Athenaeum Press,
[1916]. Reprinted from *Notes and queries* 11th
series 12, 1915, 494-7. Lists 17 new boys.

HOLGATE, CLIFFORD WYNDHAM, ed.
Winchester long rolls, 1653-1721. Winchester:
P. & G. Wells, 1899. Includes names of
wardens, fellows, masters, scholars, choristers,
commoners and some servants.

HOLGATE, CLIFFORD WYNDHAM, ed.
Winchester long rolls, 1723-1812. Winchester:
P. & G. Wells for the Wykehamist Society,
1904. Includes, as an appendix, 'A college
register of appointments', by Herbert Chitty.

HOLGATE, CLIFFORD WYNDHAM. *Winchester
commoners, 1800-1835: an index of the
surnames of commoners given on the 'long
rolls' of Winchester College for the years
1800 to 1835 inclusive.* Salisbury: Brown &
Co., 1893.

WAINEWRIGHT, JOHN BANNERMAN. *Winchester
College, 1836-1906: a register.* Winchester: P.
& G. Wells, 1907. Supersedes Holgate's
edition of the register, 1836-1890.

HARDY, HENRY JOHN, ed. *Winchester College,
1867-1920: a register.* Winchester: P. & G.
Wells, 1923.

LEIGH, MAXWELL STUBBY. *Winchester College,
1884-1934: a register.* 3rd ed. Winchester: P.
& G. Wells, 1940.

WILSON, E.R., & JACKSON, H.A. *Winchester
College: a register for the years 1901 to 1946.*
Edward Arnold, 1956.

LAMB, L.H., ed. *Winchester College: a register
for the years 1915 to 1960.* Winchester: P. &
G. Wells, 1974.

HOLGATE, CLIFFORD WYNDHAM. *A roll of
names and addresses of old Wykehamists.*
Winchester: R. & G. Wells, 1900.

A roll of old Wykehamists. 18th ed.
Winchester: Wykehamist Association, 1956.
Addresses of surviving old boys. Other
editions may also be available.

The Wykehamist First World War record is
dealt with in two works:

BRAMSTONE, J. TRANT, ed. *Wykehamist war
service roll.* 6th ed. Winchester: P. & G.
Wells, 1919.

MACDONALD, ALEXANDER, & LEESON, SPENCER.
Wykehamists who died in the war, 1914-1918.
4 vols. Winchester: Warren & Son; P. & G.
Wells, 1921. Includes portraits.

Wykehamist cricketers are also listed in two
works:

LYON, W.R. *The elevens of three great schools,
being all recorded scores of cricket matches
played between Winchester, Eton & Harrow,
with memoirs and biographies of the players.*
Eton: Spottiswoode Ballantyne & Co., 1930.

NOEL, E.B. *Winchester College cricket.*
Williams and Norgate, 1926. Includes many
lists of players.

17. MIGRATION

A. *Emigration*

Many Hampshire men have migrated to other parts of the world. Not a great deal of substance has been published on their comings and goings; the only general work which has come to my notice briefly lists emigrants to North America, South Africa, Australia and New Zealand from the records of the 19th century Poor Law Commissioners:

LAWES, EDWARD. 'Assisted emigration', *H.F.H.* **10**(4), 1984, 195-9; **11**(1), 1984, 51-4; **11**(2), 1984, 113-5.

Australia

For a general discussion of transportation to Australia, which includes a brief, but useful, list of sources, see:

SPENCE, MARGARET. *Hampshire and Australia, 1783-1791: crime and transportation.* Hampshire papers 2. Winchester: Hampshire County Council, 1992. Few names.

See also:

PEARCE, D.H. 'Hampshire's contribution to the First Fleet to Australia', *H.F.H.* **14**(3), 1987, 156-61.

Barbados

THOMAS, JAMES H. 'Some Hampshire strays, 1640-1750', *H.F.H.* **8**(3), 1981, 112-3. Includes list of Hampshire men who sailed from Southampton to Barbados in 1640; also briefer list of Hampshire marriages at Grays Inn, London, 1700-1748.

New Zealand

SMITH, GRACE M. 'New Zealand - a new life: Hampshire emigrants to Canterbury, New Zealand', *H.F.H.* **16**(2), 1989, 109-10. List of emigrants who sailed from London, mid-19th c.

PEARCE, D.H. 'A new life in New Zealand: British flock house trainees', *H.F.H.* **16**(1), 1989, 41-3. Lists sponsored migrants, 1924-31, from Hampshire, the sons of 1st World War seamen.

North America

For emigrants to North America, in the 17th and 18th centuries, reference must be made to Coldham's major compilation listing transported convicts:

COLDHAM, PETER WILSON. *Bonded passengers to America, volume V: Western Circuit, 1664-1775, comprising the counties of Cornwall, Devon, Dorset, Hampshire, Somerset and Wiltshire with a list of the rebels of 1685.* Baltimore: Genealogical Publishing, 1983.

Other than this, there are only a few brief notes in the pages of the *Hampshire family historian:*

HAUGHEY, BETTY. 'Sailing for Georgia', *H.F.H.* **12**(4), 1986, 253. Marriages at Southampton, St.Mary Extra, in 1738, of couples waiting to sail to Georgia.

'The British in Canada: Hampshire strays in Manitoba', *H.F.H.* **13**(1), 1986, 37-8.

'Settlers in Canada', *H.F.H.* **13**(4), 1987, 316. From Sherborne St.John, 19th c.

South Africa

WILLIAMS, J. ROBERT. 'Hampshire settlers in South Africa, 1820', *H.F.H.* **10**(1), 1983, 22.

B. *Immigration*

Southampton, as an important port, has always attracted many immigrants. For information on them, see the works on Huguenots listed in sections 7C and 12. Many of the published editions of Southampton borough sources may also be relevant; see section 14. See also, more specifically:

RUDDOCK, ALWYN A. 'Alien hosting in Southampton in the fifteenth century', *Economic history review* **16**, 1946, 30-37. Discussion of alien hosting records, which provide six lists of alien merchants and their hosts, 1439-45.

RUDDOCK, ALWYN A. 'Alien merchants in Southampton in the later middle ages', *English historical review* **61**, 1946, 1-17. General discussion.

Family Name Index

Abraham 23
Achard 23
Adams 23
Agar 83
Annett 23
Annetts 23
Arnold 23
Aslett 57
Asquith 86
Assheton 24
Atkinson 24, 68
Austen 82
Awdry 86

Bacheler 57
Baker 37
Bannister 24, 33
Baring 24, 84
Barlow 55
Barrett 24
Barry 24
Baskett 34
Bassett 57
Batchelder 57
Batson 24
Battelle 24
Bayliffe 24
Beall 25
Beazley 24, 26
Beconshaw 82
Bee 16
Bennett 24, 39
Bent 24
Berkeley 24
Bettesworth 30
Bignell 24
Bilson 24
Birley 86
Bisley 26
Blaker 25
Blakiston 39
Bligh 25, 55
Blower 25
Blundell 25
Bolton 77
Bonham-Carter 25, 86
Botreaux 77

Brickwood 25
Bridger 25
Brigstocke 25
Bristow 25
Brocas 25
Brodnax 82
Brooke 25, 55
Brown 57
Browne 50
Brune 35
Budd 25
Bull 25
Bullaker 25
Burden 25
Burfitt 25
Burleigh 37
Byseley 26

Calvert 30
Camoys 82
Campbell 84
Carver 26
Cassford 26
Castro 38
Cave 26
Cawte 26
Chance 26
Channell 79
Chaston 84
Cheese 55
Chitty 26
Chiverton 26
Christian 26
Clarke 37
Clerk 55
Cobb 84
Cole 26, 55
Columbars 82
Complyn 56, 68
Compton 26
Cooke 26
Cottesmore 84
Cotton 26
Cox 26
Cragg 40
Creeth 26
Cromwell 55

Culm 44
Curwen 55

Dabridgecourt 26
Dagwell 26
De Aulay 84
De Cosne 26
De Estur 27
De Insula 27, 82
De Lisle 27, 82
De Romesay 68
De Say 28
Delmé 27
Delmés 29
Dennet 58
Dennys 82
Devenish 27
Dewar 27
Dick 58
Dillington 27, 55, 57
Dimes 27
Ditchburn 27
Dobson 27
Dowling 27
Drake 57
Drummond 84
Du Moulin-Browne 27
Dumbleton 84
Dummer 27
Dyer 27

Eardley 29
Earle 84
Edmeade 28
Edwards 28, 37
Elliott 28
Ellis 28
Elton 28
Emery 28
Englefield 28
Evelyn 28

Fane 28
Fearnley 39
Fell 27
Fettiplace 28
Fitzpiers 28
Fleming 74

Fletcher 28
Fortescue 28
Foster 28
Fox 28
Fromond 57
Fruen 28

Gadd 28
Gannaway 29
Garnier 29
Gaveston 55
Gerveys 81
Gifford 31
Gignoux 29
Glamorgan 29
Goldwyer 29
Goodall 40
Goodridge 32
Gorges 83
Goring 82
Gosden 29
Gosling 29
Gough 29
Grace 29
Gray 29
Greene 38
Grove 57
Gudge 30
Guidott 29
Gunner 29, 84
Gurdun 29, 78

Hales-Lisle 16
Hall 29
Halliday 29
Hamme 57
Hammond 58
Hampton 55
Hanbury 30, 37
Hanmer 30
Harfell 30
Harpsfield 68
Harris 30, 83
Hattatt 30
Havill 30
Hayward 30
Hazelgrove 30
Heighes 30
Helyar 55
Heneage 50
Henley 30, 84
Henslow 16
Henwood 30

Herbert 55
Hill 30, 82
Hillier 29
Hinton 30
Hobhouse 29
Hobson 30
Hollis 31
Holloway 30, 31
Honeywell 79
Hoo 27
Hopson 30
Hoy 31, 84
Hulbert 31
Hunt 31, 84
Huntingford 31
Huxford 31
Hyde 84

Ingham 39
Ingpen 31

Jacob 58
Jeans 39
Jervoise 31, 77
Jolliffe 85

Kemp 31
Kempe 31
Kent 31
Kingsley 38
Kingsmill 31, 84
Kirkeby 84
Kittoe 37
Kneller 31
Knight 82
Knollys 31

Lake 58
Lambert 81
Lane 58
Lanyon 30
Larcom 31
Lavington 32
Ledelmre 58
Legay 32
Legg 32
Legge 30
Leigh 32
Lewkenor 82
Limesi 32
Lindeseie 32
Linnington 34
Linter 32
Linzee 32

Lisle 27, 32, 55, 56, 82
Lisle-Taylor 32
Littlefield 58
Long 32
Lovibond 32
Lymerston 32

Mackrell 32
Main 32, 33
Maitland 58
Mallett 29
Manser 33
Martin 58, 82
Mason 33
Masterman 30
Maudit 33
May 33, 82
Mayo 33
McKinley 31
Meux 33
Mew 33
Mewes 33
Mews 33
Mewys 33
Mildmay 33, 55
Mill 31, 36
Millington 38
Minter 33
Mitchell 33
Montagu 58
Moore 27
Morris 33
Morville 83

Nedham 37
Nenge 33
Newbolt 33
Newman 58
Nicholls 34, 58
Nicholson 86
Norton 34
Noyes 34
Nutty 34

Oglander 10, 34
Ogle 34
Oke 34
Orleton 66
Orton 38
Owen 37

Pagett 31
Paice 34
Paisy 56

Parry 29
Paulet 55
Pawlet 31
Payne 34
Pecover 35
Pendilton 55
Penton 34
Pert 34
Phillimore 34
Philpot 34
Pidgley 34
Pierce 34
Pincke 35
Pink 30, 34
Pinke 35
Pinnell 35
Pither 35
Pitman 35
Poore 35
Popham 35, 82
Port 35
Portal 35, 56, 86
Poulett 31
Prain 33
Prideaux 35
Priscott 35
Proctor 35
Prophete 56
Puleston 35
Purkis 36
Putnam 36
Puttenham 36
Puttnam 36

Randolph 86
Ransom 36
Ratsey 38
Redvers 10
Reynolds 83
Rickman 83
Rigby 29
Roberts 36
Roby 58
Rogers 36
Rolf 36
Rolfe 36
Rooke 36
Ruffell 36
Rushworth 36
Russell 36

Sabin 58
St.Clair 16, 82
St.John 36
Samborne 36
Sanborn 36
Sanderson 39
Sandys 36
Searle 24, 36, 37
Sewell 37
Seymour 37
Shaddick 37
Shayer 37
Shotter 58
Shrimpton 37
Sinclair 37
Skevington 67
Smallbones 37
Smith 37
Somer 82
Soper 18
South 37
Speed 37
Sprake 37
Stanes 37
Stanwix 37
Staples 26
Steele 37
Stephens 37, 67
Stiff 37
Stockwell 81
Symonds 38

Tattershall 28
Taylor 16, 29
Tennant 86
Terry 83
Thesiger-Tinling 38
Thistlethwayte 38
Thorne 53
Tichborne 32, 38
Tickner 38
Tinling 38
Trattle 38
Trivett 73
Turton 38
Tyghale 81
Tyrrell 38

Underhill 30
Unton 84

Urry 38, 50
Uvedale 38

Vaughan 37
Vignoles 29
Vincent 40
Vining 39
Vole 68

Wadham 39, 56
Waight 39, 58
Wake 39
Wakefield 39
Walcot 39
Waldegrave 86
Waller 55
Wallop 39
Warneford 39
Wassell 39
Watts 39
Wavell 39
Webster 39
Weekes 33
Welles 27
Wellington 10
West 84
Whitaker 39
Whitby 83
White 39, 40, 56
Whithed 70
Whitlock 40
Whyte 39, 40
Widdrington 38
Willan 84
Williams 38, 40
Willoughby 40
Winchester 77
Windebank 40
Wither 40
Woodford 40
Worsley 40, 58
Wright 38
Wriothesley 56
Wyeth 40
Wylkyns 33
Wyndham 40, 55, 86

Yelf 40
Young 40, 66
Youngs 58

Zimmerman 40

Place Name Index

Berkshire 17, 18, 23, 25, 28, 31, 34, 36, 37, 41, 50, 61
Aston Thorold 35
Combermere 22
East Shefford 28
Newbury 29
North Denchworth 28
Thatcham 42
Windsor; Saint George's Chapel 79

Buckinghamshire 61
Eton 87
Penn 36

Channel Islands 50
Guernsey 10, 25, 50
Jersey 10, 50, 60
Origny 50
Sark 10, 50

Cheshire 48
Oxton 24, 26

Cornwall 10, 19, 25, 35, 51, 88

Derbyshire 24

Devon 10, 19, 26, 28, 32, 35, 40, 51, 61, 77, 88
East Stonehouse 61
Plymouth 21, 25

Dorset 9, 10, 18, 19, 27, 28, 31, 32, 35, 51, 60-62, 77, 80, 88
Hawkchurch 40
Kinson 60

Essex 24, 25, 38, 41
Hutton 40
Marks 33

Gloucestershire 23, 51, 61
Bristol 23
Coln St.Aldwyn 28

Hampshire
Abbots Ann 39. 55

Aldershot 19, 40, 42, 56, 62
Alresford 62
Alton 27, 29, 35, 59, 62
Alton; Amery House 82
Alton; Johnsons Corner 82
Alton; Normandy Street 57
Alverstoke 24, 26, 51, 55, 63, 67, 71, 85
Amport 42
Andover 11, 14, 22, 36, 42, 57, 59, 62, 70, 71, 80, 85
Andwell 35
Appleshaw 18, 80
Appley 85
Appuldercombe 58. 82
Arreton 31, 71, 85
Ashe 42, 51
Ashton 80
Barton Oratory 67
Barton Stacey 18
Basing 35, 36, 42, 52
Basing House 9
Basingstoke 16, 24, 33, 34, 40, 42, 51, 58, 59, 62, 67, 71, 85
Baughurst 42, 50
Beaulieu 77
Beaulieu Abbey 67, 77
Beaurepaire 25
Bedales School 85
Bedhampton 51
Bensted St.Clair 82
Bentley 42, 52
Bentworth 42
Bighton 35
Binstead 25, 30, 52
Bishops Waltham 52, 80
Bishopstoke 64, 71
Bisterne 24
Bitterne 42, 64, 80
Boldre 42, 63
Bonchurch 52, 82
Boscombe 62
Bosmere Hundred 10
Bossington Hall 37
Botley 42
Bournemouth 19, 62
Brading 42, 52, 55

Hampshire *continued*
Bradley 30, 35
Bramley 42, 71
Bramshaw 85
Bramshott 80
Breamore 58
Breredyng 58
Brightstone 46
Brockenhurst 63, 83
Brockhampton 50
Broughton 37, 71, 78
Brown Candover 35
Bullington 18, 43, 51
Burghclere 43, 53
Burghclere; Earlstone Manor 82
Burley 58
Bursledon 79, 80
Calbourne 43
Cams 27
Carisbrooke 43, 46, 56, 60
Carisbrooke Priory 77
Catherington 52
Chale Green 37
Chalton 54, 71
Chawton 82
Cheriton 52
Christchurch 28, 43, 62, 63, 80
Church Oakley 43
Chutlye Hundred 59
Clamerkins Bridge 29
Cliddesden 43, 52
Colemore 10, 43, 60
Combe 43
Cosham 82
Cowes 50, 61, 63, 85
Crawley 43, 80
Crondall 27, 43, 56, 71, 80
Crondall Hundred 52
Deane 43, 51
Dibden 71
Dogmersfield 43, 52
Doles 27
Dummer 27, 43
Earlstone 82
East Dean 51
East Meon 33, 43
East Tytherley 82
East Wellow 44
East Woodhay 44
East Worldham 44
Eastleigh 64
Eastney 80

Easton 55
Eastrop 44
Efford Mill 20
Eling 23, 39, 61
Ellingham 71
Elmfield 52
Elson 71
Elvetham 44, 52, 67
Evenger Hundred 59
Eversley 40, 44, 52
Ewhurst 44
Exton 80
Faccombe 44
Fareham 14, 31, 38, 63, 69, 71
Fareham; Cams Hall 27
Fareham; Crocker Hill 60
Faringdon 77
Farley 52
Farley Chamberlayne 82
Farlington 72, 82
Farlington; Beamonds 82
Farlington; Drayton 82
Farnborough 44, 62
Farnham 16, 24
Fawley 27, 59
Fleet 54
Flowerdown 17
Fordingbridge 24, 30, 57, 63, 72
Foxcott 83
Freefolk 56
Freemantle 64
Freshwater 33, 44
Frodington 78
Froxfield 36
Froyle 52
Fyfield 39, 52
Godshill 55
Gosport 11, 14, 44, 50, 52, 63, 85
Gosport; Clayhall Cemetery 52
Grange 30
Grayshott Hall 39
Great East Standen 83
Hainton 50
Hamble 20, 67
Hambledon 18, 80
Hannington 44
Hartley Mauditt 33, 44
Hartley Wespall 44
Hartley Wintney 44, 58
Havant 10, 21, 50, 53, 63
Hayling 10
Hayling Island 21

Hampshire *continued*

Hazelgrove 30
Headbourne Worthy 31
Heckfield 45
Herriard 31, 45
Herriard Park 77
Highclere 45, 53
Hordle 53, 67
Houghton 36, 45
Hound 64
Hunton 45, 55
Hursley 55
Hurstbourne Priors 45, 83
Hurstbourne Tarrant 45, 53
Hyde Abbey 54, 78
Hydegate 83
Idsworth 71
Isle of Wight 9-13, 16, 17, 19-23, 26-29, 31-34, 37-41, 45, 51, 53, 57, 59, 60-65, 67, 70, 72, 78, 80, 85
Itchen Abbas; Bignells Cottage 24
Kings Somborne 31, 45
Kings Worthy 45, 58
Kingsclere 59, 61
Kingsclere Hundred 59
Kingston 63, 78
Knighton 83
Knights Enham 45, 72
Laborne 57
Lageham 36
Landport 63
Laverstoke 35, 45
Linkenholt 45
Litchfield 45
Long Sutton 45, 57, 60
Longdown 25
Ludshott 80Lymington 12, 20, 24, 37, 50, 53, 58, 63, 72, 83
Lymington; Pylewell House 50
Lyndhurst 63
Manydown 80
Maplederwell 45
Martin 81
Medstead 53
Meon Stoke 80
Meon Valley 9
Merstone 83
Micheldever 25
Michelmersh 45
Milford 14, 46, 53, 67, 72, 81, 83
Milford; Milford House 83
Milford; Rook Cliff 50

Millbrook 64
Milton 80
Minstead 26
Monk Sherborne Priory 23
Monxton 46, 55
Mottisfont Priory 78
Nately Scures 46
Nether Wallop 83
Netley 64
Netley Abbey 78
New Alresford 46
New Forest 12, 20, 23, 59, 63, 72, 81
Newchurch 46, 55, 57
Newnham 46
Newport 19, 38-40, 46, 50, 53, 63, 67, 72
Newport; Hunnyhill 53
Newton Valence 35
Newtown 46
Niton 46
North Baddesley 53
North Hayling 51, 73
North Tidworth 35
North Waltham 35, 46
Northington 84
Nunwell 10, 34
Nursling; Grove Place 31
Odiham 9, 46, 52, 53, 85
Old Alresford 57
Old Basing 51
Osborne 83
Over Wallop 81
Overton 46
Overton Hundred 59
Parkhurst Prison 61
Parkstone 62
Pastroe Hundred 59
Peacock Hill 83
Penton Mewsey 46
Petersfield 14, 19, 46, 59, 65, 70, 83, 85
Petersfield; High Street 83
Poole 24, 62
Popham 47
Portchester 20, 73
Portsdown 59
Portsea 28, 37, 47, 50, 63
Portsmouth 10-14, 17-22, 25, 32, 39, 47, 50, 58, 62-64, 67, 69, 71, 73, 78, 81, 83, 85, 86
Portsmouth; Old Point 35
Portsmouth Dockyard 11
Preshaw 32
Preston Candover 47
Priors Dean 10, 43, 60

Hampshire *continued*

Privett 53
Pylewell Park 39
Quarley 26, 35, 55, 81
Quarr Abbey 67, 78, 81
Ramsdell 53
Redbridge 64
Ridworth 24
Ringwood 18, 19, 56, 63, 73
Ringwood; Cowpits 81
Roche Court 25, 83
Rockbourne 57, 67, 81
Rockstead 81
Romsey 19, 22, 28, 36, 47, 53, 58, 64, 73, 77, 86
Romsey Abbey 47, 53, 68
Romsey Union 73
Ropley 81
Rotherfield 34, 36
Rotherwick 47
Rowner 47
Royal Hampshire County Hospital 68
Russell Island 36
Ryde 19, 26, 60, 63, 73
Saint Denys Priory 78
Saint Mary Bourne 47, 83
Saint Swithins Priory 68, 78
Sandown 53, 63
Selborne 11, 29, 39, 57
Selborne; The Wakes 39
Selborne Priory 29, 67, 68, 78
Shanklin 63
Shawford 33
Shawford Mill 81
Sheat 50
Shedfield 34
Sheet 73
Sherborne St.John 47, 52, 84, 88
Sherborne St.John; The Vyne 84
Sherfield 36
Sherfield upon Loddon 33, 47
Shirley 64
Sholing 30, 64
Silchester 37
Solent 39
Somerford Grange 29
Sopley 21, 26, 50
South Damerham 81
South Hayling 54
South Stoneham 47
South Warnborough 40, 47, 52
Southampton 9-23, 25, 26, 29, 32, 34, 37, 39, 50, 54, 57, 59, 62-65, 69, 73-75, 81, 84, 86, 88

Southampton; Above Bar 69
Southampton; Bargate 16
Southampton; Gods House 78
Southampton; Thornhill Park 84
Southbourne on Sea 62
Southsea 30, 37, 54, 63, 64, 81
Southwells 31
Southwick 34, 38, 56
Southwick Priory 78
Sparsholt 57
Stakes Hill Lodge 31
Stanbridge Earls 84
Stansted Park 84
Steventon 48
Stockbridge 54, 84
Stoke Charity 48, 55, 71, 75
Stratfield Saye 26, 48
Stratfield Turgis 48
Stubbington House 28
Sutton Scotney 82
Swarraton 84
Swarraton. The Grange 84
Tadley 48
Tangley 48
Test Valley 15, 57
Thornhill Park 31
Thruxton 52, 55, 56
Tichborne 50, 58, 75
Titchfield 26, 56, 58, 68, 73, 75, 81
Titchfield Hundred 60
Totton 23, 64
Tufton 43, 48
Tunworth 51
Twyford 25, 48, 54, 55, 86
Up Nately 48
Ventnor 63, 81, 84
Vernhams Dean 48
Wallop 30, 52
Waltham 18
Warblington 10, 26
Warnford 20, 54, 58
Wayhill 24
Weeke 56, 68
Well 57
West 38
West Meon 36, 54
West Stratton 35
West Worldham 44
Westbourne 22, 62, 75
Weston 80
Weyhill 48, 55, 71
Wherwell Abbey 84

Hampshire *continued*
Whitchurch 25, 48, 55, 84
Whitwell 48
Wickham 38
Winchester 9, 11, 17-19, 26, 28, 29, 31, 33, 34,
    50, 56-59, 61, 62, 64, 65, 66, 68-70, 75, 76,
    78-80, 82, 84, 86, 87
Winchester; Goodbegot 80
Winchester; Saint Bartholomew 48
Winchester; Saint Cross 48
Winchester; Saint Faith 48
Winchester; Saint John 71
Winchester; Saint John's Hospital 76
Winchester; Saint Lawrence 49
Winchester; Saint Maurice 49, 54
Winchester; Saint Michael 49
Winchester; Saint Peter Cheesehill 49, 71
Winchester; Saint Swithin 49
Winchester; Saint Thomas 49
Winchester Archdeaconry 68
Winchester Cathedral 48, 51, 54, 55, 65, 68,
    78
Winchester Cathedral Priory 78
Winchester College 19, 49, 54, 56, 57, 67, 68,
    78, 86, 87
Winchester Diocese 9, 10, 41, 61, 65, 66, 79
Winchfield 49, 52
Winslade 49, 51
Winslade; Kempshott 35
Wodeton 32
Wolverton 49
Wonston 33, 49, 55, 82
Woodgarston 82
Woodmancott 49
Woolston 64
Wootton St.Lawrence 49
Worston 18
Worthy Park 34
Worting 49
Wymering 57, 82
Wyntney 58
Yarmouth 39, 63, 76
Yateley 40, 49, 57
Yaverland 50

Hampshire, North West 30

Hampshire, South 18

Hertfordshire
Furneaux Pelham 30
Hertford 35

Long Marston 36
Puttenham 36

Ireland 26, 27, 38
Tyrone 35

Kent 26, 69
Brenchley 50
Canterbury 79
Meopham 28
Sheerness 28
Strood 28

Lancashire 40, 48
Manchester 71

Leicestershire 28

Lincolnshire 26

London and Middlesex 25, 28-30, 32-35, 40,
    41, 60, 88
Fleet 41
Grays Inn 88
Harrow 87
Isle of Dogs 61
Saint Pauls 86
Staines 71
Walthamstow 29

London, South 28

Norfolk 31, 69
Great Yarmouth 23
Kings Lynn 74
Norwich 23
Norwich Diocese 9

Oxfordshire 61
Nettlebed 29
Newington 26
Oxford University; Queens College 78
Warborough 26

River Thames 29

Scotland 32, 35

Shropshire
Montford 30
Morton 30

Somerset 10, 18, 19, 28, 32, 35-37, 51, 55, 80, 88
  Glastonbury 81
  Hazel Grove 33
  Penne Domer 27

Staffordshire 30, 31
  Hanmer 30

Suffolk 24, 26, 31, 37
  Newmarket 29

Surrey 25, 26, 28, 41
  Farnham 40
  Farnham; Runwick 16
  Kenley 24
  Lambeth 29
  Titsey 38
  Wallington 24
  Wandsworth 61
  Willey 16

Sussex 24, 27, 34
  Beckley 57
  Chichester 25
  Easebourne 27

Westmorland 20

Wiltshire 9, 10, 17, 19, 23, 28, 32, 35-37, 44, 51, 55, 56, 60, 61, 77, 78, 88
  Britford 31
  Dinton 40
  Downton 36
  Norrington 40
  Plaitford 51
  Rood Ashton 32
  Salisbury 40, 41, 61
  Salisbury; The Close 29
  Semington 32

Yorkshire 25
  Hesley Hall 39
  York 83

Overseas

Australia 29, 88
  New South Wales 31
  South Australia 21

Belgium
  Brussels 69

Canada 88
  Manitoba 88
  Newfoundland; Fogo 28
  Ontario 51

India 40

Italy
  Palermo 39

New Zealand 88
  Canterbury 88

South Africa 88

Spain
  Minorca 38

Turkey
  Gallipoli 22

United States 36, 88
  Georgia 88
  Maryland 25
  New England; Charlestown 40
  New England; Sudbury 24

West Indies
  Barbados 88

Author Index

A., M. 55
Abraham, A.G. 23
Adams, R.H. 12
Albert, W. 73
Albery, E.M. 34
Allan, G.K. 25
Allen, A. 13
Allen, M.D. 40
Altham, H.S. 18
Anderson, R.C. 74, 75
Andrews, S. 42-50
Annette, F.H. 23
Anstruther, I. 71
Armstrong, J.H. 30
Arnold, C.J. 20
Asher, R. 57
Ashley-Cooper, F.S. 18
Aslett, B. 57
Aspinall-Oglander, C. 34
Atkinson, C.T. 22
Atkinson, T. 11
Attwood, J.S. 51, 59
Ayling, K.G. 19

Baigent, F.J. 32, 66, 68, 80
Baigent, R.C. 50
Bailey, C. 75
Bain, J. 29
Bain, P. 68
Baine, J. 78
Balch, T.W. 25
Baldwin, M.R. 18
Bamford, E. 10
Barber, N. 34
Barber, N.D. 60
Barrett, J. 24
Barrett, P. 67
Barron, O. 38
Barstow, H.G. 60, 80
Barton, M. 34
Batchelder, C.E. 57
Batson, P. 24
Battelle, L.C. 24
Bayley, A.R. 29
Bayliffe, B.G. 24
Beaumont, E. 56

Beazley, F.C. 24, 26, 33, 48
Beech, G. 64
Benham, W. 65, 79
Bennett, A.C. 42, 85
Bennett, J. 24
Benson, G.C. 82
Beresford, M. 9
Berry, W. 16
Beveridge, W. 79
Biddick, K. 9
Biddle, M. 76
Bigg-Wither, R.F. 40, 82
Bijlveld, C.J.H. 9
Bingley, W. 10
Bird, W.H.B. 76
Bishop, T.J.H. 86
Bisset-Thom, A. 24
Black, F., Sir 70
Blake, E.O. 78
Bloom, J.H. 79
Blore, G.H. 30, 54
Blundell, L.S. 25
Boddington, R.S. 58
Bogan, P.P. 69
Bolton, C. 17
Bostock, C. 53
Bowden, M. 82
Bowditch, J. 33
Boyce, E.J. 45
Braithwaite, P.R.P. 65
Bramstone, P.T. 87
Brayshay, M. 20
Brickell, G. 35
Brooks, E.M. 48, 70
Broom, C. 33
Brown, A.W.W. 46
Brown, M. 75
Brownbill, J. 32
Brownen, G. 24
Brune, E.S.P. 47
Bugden, E. 24, 44, 47, 71
Bull, W. 39
Bunyard, B.D.M. 20
Burch, L.L.R. 17
Burfitt, S. 25
Burgess, L.A. 74

Burn, J.H. 79
Burrowes, L.R. 32
Burrows, M. 25, 31
Bussby, F. 68
Butler, E.L. 25

C., H.D. 55
C., I.M. 27
Campbell, B.M.S. 9
Campion, P. 9
Cantelo, B.W. 69
Capes, W.W. 65
Carew, J. 28
Carson, E.A. 21
Carus-Wilson, E.M. 78
Cassan, S.H. 65
Cave, P. 76
Cave, T.S. 22
Cawser, J.R. 26
Cawte, E.C. 26
Cayley, R.A. 55
Cazalet, W.G. 42
Chalk, G. 19
Challen, W.H. 24
Chambers, J. 18
Chapman, A.B.W. 74
Charity Commissioners 70
Chester, J.L. 27
Chinneck, A. 38
Chitty, E. 26
Chitty, H. 19, 31, 43, 48, 49,
    66, 68, 76, 86, 87
Chorley, J. 33
Christie, P. 17, 58
Chute, C.W. 84
Chute, D.W. 47
Citizen 57
Clarendon, Earl of 54
Clark, Miss 49
Clark, P. 11
Clarke, M. 47, 51, 52
Clarke, M.K. 33
Clasby, V. 33, 43
Clennell, A. 11
Clifford, C.A. 59
Clissold, P. 21

Clutterbuck, R.H. 20, 39, 45, 46, 71, 72, 84
Coates, R. 65
Cobb, H.S. 20
Colchester, W.E. 48, 49, 65
Coldham, P.W. 88
Coldicott, D.K. 57, 77, 81, 83
Cole, H.D. 16
Cole, R. 61
Coleby, A.M. 9
Coleman, O. 20
Coles, E.T. 45
Coles, R. 20, 83
Collier, C. 71
Collier, I.C. 76
Collins, F.B. 51, 60
Collins, J. 12
Colpus, A.C. 51-55
Coltart, A.H. 47
Connor, W.J. 75
Cooper, M.K. 42
Cooper, P. 84
Cooper, R.H. 76
Cooper, W. 63
Cooper, W.D. 69
Cope, Mrs 35
Cope, W. 27
Cope, W., Sir 65
Courtney, S.T. 43, 48
Cox, J.C. 67
Cox, W. 64
Cramer, J. 20
Creeth, L. 26
Crocker, R.H. 75
Crook, J. 68, 84, 86
Cumnor, J. 61
Curtis, H.J. 40
Cust, L., Sir 25
Custance, R. 79, 86
Cutten, M. 37

Dagwell, D.N. 26
Dalton, J.N. 79
Daniell, D.S. 22
Darrah, M.J. 71
Davey, C.R. 59, 82, 85
Davidson, F.A.G. 50
Davies, J.S. 11
Davis, G.R.C. 77
Davis, R.G. 83
Davis, T. 25

De Grave, J.W. 50
Deacon, A.D. 20
Dean, J. 35
Deedes, C. 65, 66
Denman, M.J. 75
Denton, C. 35
Denton, P. 85
Devenish, B. 27
Devenish, R.J. 27
Deverell, J. 76
Devonshire, K. 24
Dewar, M.W. 27
Dickinson, C.R. 46
Dickinson, N. 55
Dodderidge, S.E. 37
Douch, R. 54
Doughty, M. 75
Drew, J.S. 78
Druitt, S. 58
Dunhill, R.C. 56
Durden, Mrs 53
Duthy, J. 10
Dyer, D. 27

Earl, E.G. 13
East, R. 73
Ebsworth, J. 30
Edwards, E. 12, 14, 71, 73, 75, 78
Edwards, F. 49, 71
Edwards, F.E. 11
Edwards, F.H. 12, 75
Edwin-Cole, J. 26
Eley, P. 18, 25
Ellacott, P. 22, 75
Elliott, A.G. 28
Ellis, W.S. 28
Elvin, C.R. 60
Epsom, C.W. 44
Etheridge, J. 36, 60
Evans, C. 39
Evans, D.M.H. 32
Everitt, A.T. 26, 47, 67
Everson, V. 30
Eyre, W.L.W. 84

Faish, A.N. 40
Farmer, D.L. 79
Faulkner, H.C. 22
Fearon, W.A.E. 41
Felton, E.C. 24
Ferguson, V. 44

Few, J. 15, 41, 72
Finlay, E. 86
Fletcher, J.S. 28, 29
Flower, N. 12
Ford, M. 44, 67
Forrest, G. 12, 16
Foster, B. 20
Foster, J. 30
Foster, R. 10, 20
Fowler, J.K., Sir 77
Franklin, M.J. 66
Freeman, F.L. 86
Freeman, M.J. 18
French, E. 36, 58
Fritze, R.H. 9, 31
Furley, J.S. 70, 76
Fussell, G.E. 9

G., G.N. 45
Gadd, E.W. 86
Gale, M. 57, 81
Gale, S. 54
Gard, J. 43
Gardiner, L. 39
Garnier, A.E. 29
Gates, W.G. 22
Gatt, L.V. 86
Gatty, A.S. 66
Genge, P. 86
George, B. 37
Gibson, J.S. 51
Gibson, W. 26
Gidden, H.W. 74
Gilbert, H.M. 11
Gilbert, M. 38
Giles, L.C. 80
Gill, W. 44
Godfray, H.M. 50
Godwin, G.N. 9, 11
Golding, B. 78
Goodman, A.W. 66, 68, 78, 80
Goodman, F.R. 66, 79
Goodman, W.L. 23
Gordon, J. 52
Gosden, H. 29
Gough, H. 58
Gower, G.L. 38
Graham, N.H. 36
Gras, E.C. 80
Gras, N.B.S. 80
Greatrex, J. 78

Green, I.M. 18, 80
Green, S. 33
Greenfield, B.W. 16, 31, 37, 55, 56
Greenwood, D. 51
Greenwood, I.J. 40
Greenwood, L. 14
Griffin, J. 72
Griffiths, J. 26
Groves, Dr 83
Gruggen, G.S. 42
Gubbins, E. 51
Gunner, W.H. 35, 57

H., J.J. 37
Haddon, G. 25
Haines, R.M. 66
Hall, B. 60
Hall, D. 34
Hall, H. 79
Halliday, C.A.T. 29
Hamilton, G. 74
Hamilton-Edwards, G. 28
Hampshire Archives Trust 12
Hampshire Archivists Group 12, 13, 41, 64, 70
Hampshire Field Club 14
Hampshire Genealogical Society 11, 15
Hampshire Record Office 70
Hampson, G. 75
Hancock, P. 22
Handley-Taylor, G. 17
Hanmer, C. 30
Hanna, K.A. 78
Hansford, F.E. 85
Hansom, J.S. 50, 69
Hapgood, E. 53
Harding. F.H. 44
Harding, J.C. 40
Hardy, H.J. 87
Hare, A. 22
Harries, J. 56
Harris, V.D. 72
Harrison, J.P. 24
Harvey, J.H. 79
Harvey, P.D.A. 73
Haughey, B. 61, 88
Hawker, A. 58
Hayes, D. 18

Hayward, K. 11
Heal, F. 79
Hearn, J.R. 21
Hearnshaw, D.M. 74
Hearnshaw, F.J.C. 73, 74
Herridge, K. 81
Hervey, T. 10, 43
Heygate, A.C.G. 83
Hicks, M. 77, 83
Hill, J.W. 63
Hill, R.M.T. 84
Himsworth, S. 78
Hinton, D.A. 64
Historical Manuscripts Commission 43, 66, 74, 75, 77, 78
Hitchin-Kemp, F. 31
Hoad, J.P.M. 18
Hoad, M.J. 12, 73
Hockey, S.F. 11, 12, 32, 66, 67, 72, 77, 78, 81
Hodgson, R.A. 29
Hodson, D. 64
Hogg, M. 28
Holbrook, A.R. 62
Holgate, C.W. 87
Holley, D. 19
Hollingsbee, K. 36
Holloway, R. 30
Holmes, P.J. 85
Holt, J.M. 42
Holt, N.R. 79
Homewood, H.R. 19
Honan, R.F. 29
Hooker, R.E. 28
Hope, J.F.R. 19
Hopkins, E.L. 46
Horrocks, J.W. 74
Horwood, A.J. 77
Houlbrooke, R.A. 9
Hughes, E. 13, 59
Hughes, G. 38
Hughes, M.H. 54
Hunnisett, R.F. 78
Hunt, J.M.F. 21
Hunt, L.W. 28
Hurst, N.H.G. 32, 33
Huxford, R.C. 31

Iceton, D. 30
Imperial War Graves Commission 22

Ingpen, A.R. 31
Insole, A.N. 64
Isaac, P. 17
Isaacs, V. 18

J., A. 60
Jackson, G.H.M. 31
Jackson, H.A. 87
Jacob, W.H. 16, 21, 33, 70, 76
James, E.B. 10, 26, 29, 30, 33, 37, 40, 46, 56, 70
James, J. 63
James, T.B. 12, 20, 74, 84
Jeaffreson, J.C. 74
Jervoise, F.H.T. 31
Jessel, H.M., Sir 22
Jewers, A.J. 53
John, J.R. 85
Jones, B.C. 20
Jones, J. 10
Jones, J.D. 9
Jones, K.R. 26
Jones, R.A. 70
Joyce, G.H. 27
Joye, G. 24
Judson, T. 73, 81

Kaye, J.M. 78
Keene, D. 84
Kent, D. 53
Kent, M. 53
Kent, T.A. 22
Kidd, R.A. 41
King, J.H. 50
Kirby, T.F. 66, 67, 80, 81, 86
Kitchen, F. 16
Kitchin, G.W. 68, 78, 80
Kitson, H., Sir 11
Knight, F.H.G. 43
Knight, M.G. 82
Knight, R.J.B. 18
Knott, D. 41
Kökeritz, H. 65

L., A.S. 38
L., C. 54
L., C.E. 26, 52, 53
Lake, P. 31
Lamb, L.H. 87
Lambert, H. 71

Lang, W.D.F. 43
Langdon, P.G. 54, 56
Last, C.F. 61
Lawes, E. 21, 61, 88
Lawes, W. 49, 61
Le Faye, D. 67, 68
Le May, K. 47, 84
Le Mesurier, J. 49
Leach, A.F. 86
Lee, A.J. 14
Leeson, S. 87
Leigh, M.S. 87
Leigh, W.A. 82
Levett, A.E. 9
Lewandowska, L. 54
Lewin, S. 65, 66
Lewis, P. 81
Lewis, R.W.M. 53
Lilley, H.T. 67
Linter, G. 32
Linzee, J.W. 32
Little, R.H. 21
Littledale, W.A. 53
Liveing, H.G.D. 68
Lloyd, A. 12, 21
Lloyd-Verney, Colonel 21
Lock, C. 46, 48
Lockhart, C. 10
Long, W.H. 10, 34, 65
Longstaff, S.M. 85
Loton, J. 21
Lowe, D. 28
Lowe, J. 17, 19, 22, 41
Lowe, J.B. 85
Lower Test Valley
  Archaeological Study
  Group 19
Luce, R., Sir 47
Lyon, W.R. 87

MacDonald, A. 87
Mackarill, D.R. 34
MacLean, J., Sir 35
MaCray, W.D. 77, 78
Madge, F.F. 45
Madge, F.T. 43, 45, 48, 49,
  66, 68
Main, M. 33
Mann, J.E. 16
Marsh, A.J. 86
Marshall, R.T. 45
Matthews, B. 68

Mattravers, P. 71
Maugham, Lord 38
May, A.N. 79
May, D. 82
Mayberry, T. 66, 79
Mayo, C.H. 58
McCann, T.J. 25
McCulloch, L. 31
McDougall, E. 39
McGowan, A. 41
McKechnie, A. 23
McLaughlin, C.H. 27
McNulty, P.M. 22
Meadows, J.E. 83
Meekings, C.A.F. 78
Merritt, D.C. 60
Merson, A.L. 17, 74
Merson, E. 85
Mettam, H.A. 19
Millard, J.E.
Millett, M. 82
Milner, J. 54
Minns, G.W. 27
Moberly, A.C. 49
Moens, W.J.C. 41, 44
Moloney, J.L. 24
Money, W. 59, 82
Monkhouse, F.J. 9
Monro, H.G. 48
Moody, H. 76
Moor, J. 79
Moore, C.A. 34
Moore, P. 9, 34
Morgan, J.B. 11
Moxley, C. 68, 76
Mukerji, J.A. 16
Munby, J. 59
Mundy, M. 46
Murrell, R.J. 73

Naish, S. 34
Nevill, E. 41
Newman, E. 69
Newman, N.F. 56
Newnham, A.J. 73
Newton, M. 31
Newton, P. 60
Nicholson, G.H. 22
Nineham, A.W. 27
Noel, E.B. 87
Norden, J. 16
Norgate, M. 18, 19

Nowell, F. 32

Oakley, T. 61
O'Day, R. 79
Odell, W.R. 84
Oglander, J., Sir 10, 12
Oglander, J.H. 42-44, 46,
  48, 50
Oldfield, J. 17, 85
Oliver, J. 60
O'Neill, S. 37
Overton, M. 9
Owen, D.M. 66
Owen, M.C. 37

Page-Phillips, J.C. 56
Palmer, C.F.R. 68
Palmer, R. 50
Parker, A.G. 12
Parker, G. 51
Parker, K. 57
Parsons, E. 85
Pasmore, A. 23
Patterson, A.T. 11, 12, 75
Paul, J.E. 69
Payne, S.K. 34
Peacock, S. 9, 80
Pearce, D.H. 81, 88
Pearce, J. 24
Peberdy, P. 11
Pedgley, D.E. 34
Pelham, R.A. 20
Penfold, A. 64
Pepper, F.W.C. 14
Perkin, M. 17
Perkins, W.F. 12
Petersfield Area Historical
  Society 14
Phillimore, W.P.W. 37,
  42-50, 53
Pike, W.T. 16
Pine, L.G. 39
Pinhorn, M. 19, 31, 47
Pink, W.D. 34, 35, 67
Pinnell, B. 83
Piper, A.C. 18, 84
Pither, J.S. 35
Pitman, H.A. 35
Platt, C. 11
Pledge, F.W. 43
Popham, F.W. 35
Popham, R.M. 12

101

Portal, W.W., Sir 35
Portsmouth and South East Hampshire Local Studies Centre 12
Postan, M.M. 79
Postles, D. 78
Powell, H.L. 22
Press, C.M. 16
Proctor, F.J. 35
Prowthing, J. 25
Pulman, J. 32

Quinn, D.B. 20

R. 55
R., J.S. 55
Ranger, P. 17
Rannie, A. 68
Raper, A.C. 22
Ravenhill, W.W. 9
Ray, F. 33
Raymond, P. 13
Reeks, L.S. 36
Reeves, J.A. 25, 30, 53
Reid, J.D. 57
Riley, D.F. 37
Riley, H.T. 75, 78
Riley, R.C. 81
Roberts, C. 17, 58
Roberts, C.B. 80
Roberts, E. 57
Roberts, H.B. 36
Robertson, A.J. 44
Rogers, J.C. 36
Rogers, P. 18
Rogers, W.H. 32, 64
Rooke, H.W. 36
Rose, S. 18
Rosen, A. 11
Rosser, W.H. 55
Round, J.H. 33, 35
Ruddock, A.A. 19, 88
Ruffell, L.E. 36
Rushton, G.A. 70
Russel, A.D. 83
Russell, C.F. 86
Russell, P.D.D. 59
Rutherford, J. 81

Sabben-Clare, J. 86
Sadler, A.G. 51
Sage, E.J. 33

Saint Barbe, C. 72
Sale, D.M. 19
Salter, S.J.A. 55
Sanborn, V.C. 33, 36
Saunders, R. 85
Saunders, W.H. 73
Scantlebury, R.E. 50, 69
Scouloudi, I. 69
Seagrave, L. 71
Sears, F.W. 46, 72
Seiles, K. 28
Seiles, M. 23, 26, 29, 45
Shaw, W.J. 75
Shenton, F.K.J. 75
Sherwin, G.A. 80
Sherwood, A. 27
Shirley, E.P. 58
Shorter, A.H. 20
Shotter, G. 58
Shrimpton, V. 37
Sinclair, C.L.S. 16
Skeat, W.W. 65
Skinner, Miss 83
Slade, J.J. 33, 55, 56
Slagle, A.R. 28
Slight, H. 38
Sloggett, B. 33, 41, 42, 69
Smallbone, K. 42
Smirke, E. 76
Smith, C.E. 36
Smith, C.R. 65
Smith, G.M. 88
Smith, H. 65
Smith, J.C. 28
Smith, J.H. 85
Smith, V. 41
Smith, V.F. 56, 57
Smith, W.C.G. 82
Spaul, J.E.H. 57, 71, 80
Spence, C. 53
Spence, M. 88
Spinney, J. 86
Spooner, H. 86
Squibb, G.D. 15
Stagg, D.J. 17, 72, 80
Stagg, S. 73
Stainer, S. 69
Stapleton, B. 9, 11
Stark, S. 36
Steele-Smith, H.F. 37
Stephens, W.R.W. 65, 68
Stevens, J. 83

Stevens, K.F. 20
Stewart, B. 37
Stooks, C.D. 42-44, 46, 47, 49
Stovold, J. 75
Strain, R.N.C. 19
Stringer, K.H. 23
Studer, P. 20, 74
Suckling, F.H. 29-31, 36
Suckling, Mrs 73, 82, 84
Summers, A.H. 85
Summers, P. 51
Surry, N. 20, 60, 70
Surry, N.W. 73
Sykes, W.S. 72

Talbot, C.H. 77
Talbot, M. 52
Talbot, M.J. 52
Tate, W.E. 77
Taylor, J. 9
Templeton, J. 34
Thick, A. 77
Thomas, E.G. 73
Thomas, J.H. 11, 17, 20, 58, 73, 88
Thompson, S.C. 74
Thorn, P. 18
Thorp, J.D. 25
Thoyts, F.W. 42
Thurston, E.J. 19
Tickner, V. 36, 37
Tilmouth, J.E. 24
Titow, J.Z. 9, 79
Tomlinson, J. 24
Trappes-Lomax, T.B. 28
Tremlett, M.R. 52
Trickett, F. 30
Tunnicliffe, W. 10
Turley, R.V. 11, 17, 64
Turnbull, B. 45
Turner, B.C. 9, 26, 30, 76
Tyrrell, J.H. 38

Urry, R.R. 38

Varilone, B. 40
Vaugham, J. 54
Vaux, W.S.W. 74
Vick, D. 43, 59
Vickers, J.A. 67
Vinson, A.J. 10

Virgoe, J.M. 31

W., H. 55
W., W.S. 55
Wade, E.F. 32
Waight, S. 39
Waight, S.W.J. 83
Wainewright, J.B. 87
Wake, R. 85
Walcot, M. 47
Walcot, N.J. 39
Walcott, M.E.C. 86
Walker, J. 46, 53
Waller, J.G. 55
Wallin, P.O.E. 38
Ward, C.S. 49
Warneford, F.E. 39
Warner, R. 10
Washington, E.S. 86
Watkin, A. 81
Watkin, J. 30
Watkins, A. 78
Watney, V.J. 39
Watson, D.M. 19
Watson, G.W. 28
Watts, G. 81
Webb, J. 9, 22
Webb, N.R. 18, 31, 70, 72
Webster, M. 39

Webster, M.C. 39
Weinberg, A. 69
Welch, E. 13, 65, 69, 74, 86
Wells, R. 15
Wetton, J.L. 23
Whitaker, R.S. 39
Whitchurch Local History
  Society 84
White, D.H.L. 52
White, G. 11
White, H.T. 9
White, L.F.W. 85
White, P. 59, 60
White, W. 61
Whitehead, Dr 52
Whitehead, J. 27, 82, 83
Whitting, C.J. 19
Wickham, C.T. 86
Wilcox, L.G.M. 36
Wilkinson, C.H. 17
Wilks, T.C. 10
Williams, C.L.S. 37, 39, 60,
  82
Williams, E.D. 63
Williams, E.J.W. 75
Williams, G.H. 28, 34, 38,
  40, 51, 55, 67, 71
Williams, I.L. 57
Williams, J.F. 41-49, 71

Williams, J.R. 21, 88
Williams, L. 21
Williams, M.E. 36
Williams, S. 45
Willis, A.J. 17, 41, 56, 66,
  67, 69, 73, 76
Willmott, H. 61
Willmott, H.J. 86
Willson, C.H.S. 85
Wilson, E.R. 87
Windebank, R. 40
Windle, W.H. 46
Winser, A. 57, 67, 81
Winter, C.W.R. 10
Wood, E. 34
Woodd, A.B. 20
Woodruff, J.D. 38
Woodward, B.B. 10
Worsley, R., Sir 10
Wright, T. 75
Wyatt, S., Sir 71

Yates, E.M. 59
Yates, N. 9
Yates, W.M. 13
Young, S. 40

Zell, M. 80